Great Parliamentary Scandals
Four Centuries of Calumny, Smear and Innuendo

Matthew Parris

Assistant Editors
David Prosser and Andrew Pierce

With a foreword by the
Rt Hon. David Mellor QC MP

 Robson Books

To Eileen Wright, helper, friend – and for
fifty years a Commons secretary of the
unscandalous sort

First published in Great Britain in 1995 by Robson Books Ltd,
Bolsover House, 5-6 Clipstone Street, London W1P 8LE

British Library Cataloguing in Publication Data
A catalogue record for this title is available from the
British Library

ISBN 0 86051 957 0

Typeset in Plantin by The Harrington Consultancy
Printed and bound in Great Britain by
Butler & Tanner Ltd, London and Frome

CONTENTS

FOREWORD

By the Rt Hon. David Mellor QC MP

This is of course a book Matthew Parris was destined to write. As a parliamentarian of seven years' experience, he writes of political events, the pressures of parliamentary life, and the occasional frailties revealed by the relentless scrutiny to which MPs are subjected, with sympathy and understanding. In that sense he is one of us, but never so much so that his instinctive compassion for his subjects ever tips over into special pleading. He has too many of the qualities of the best journalists for that. He brings to his task a sophisticated pen, finely honed by years of writing some of the most exquisitely crafted parliamentary pieces it has ever been my privilege to read, as well, of course, as a host of other miniatures about travel and the ways of the world, full of colour and sharp-eyed, enchantingly quirky observation.

It was a privilege at last year's British Press Awards to present Matthew with the coveted accolade, 'Columnist of the Year', and to convey to him, as a representative of his old profession, the esteem and affection in which he is held by his peers in his new one.

But Matthew doesn't buy his popularity through sycophancy either to his former colleagues or his present ones. He observes Parliament with a beady eye. He is slow to reach an adverse judgement – unlike, alas, many others of his ilk – but when he does it can be devastating. By the same token he refuses to pay lip-service to those of his confrères who moralize emptily about others while paying no more than lip-service to virtue in their own lives. He knows the gaping holes there would be in British journalism were the same price to be extracted for sexual peccadilloes from them as is now routinely demanded from politicians. He also knows the damage all this does to the profession of politics, to public perceptions of Parliament, and to the overall health of our democracy, as the sin of prurience is raised to a state of high art with each passing Sunday.

Matthew knows the job of the parliamentarian needs to be done, and believes it would be best if it were done well. The real threat to Parliament is not that it will be borne away by a tidal wave of sleaze – most of what he writes about here is almost pathetically trivial – but that the ranks of the best and the brightest, already pretty meagre in Parliament, will thin out even further. 'Who needs it?' they will say. It was William Deedes who recently observed that all the talented young people he meets these days are going into the media and not politics. And why not? The media conveys an air of glamour which the public finds deeply appealing, and who can doubt that opining on, or writing 1,000 words about, a problem is so much easier than trying to do something constructive about it. The copious quantities of fame and wealth on offer to leading media personalities must be infinitely more attractive to the young than the cup of bile from which top politicians are daily and publicly forced to drink. Some facts, however unpalatable, have got to be faced. In today's world, media celebrity conveys power without responsibility; Cabinet office, on the other hand, involves responsibility with little more than the outward trappings of power.

In a sense Matthew Parris's own career illustrates how difficult it is for people of real talent to stay in politics. An experienced political journalist said to me more than a decade ago – and things had far from reached their present pass then – that such was the intensity of the spotlight focused on politicians, that even the smallest flaw is cruelly exposed. How foolish I was, with hindsight, to ignore these sage words. Matthew was wiser. He has never regarded his homosexuality, about which he has always been admirably open, as a flaw, and nor of course is it. But he must have been aware when he decided to move from Parliament to *Weekend World* that the glittering prizes of politics, however great his talent, would have been that much further out of reach because of it, and his chances of advancement, whatever people might say to his face, seriously dented as a result. This is not how the world should be, but manifestly, it is how the world is – or at least how the political world is conditioned, as it has to be, by the realities of present-day media coverage.

So he opted out, a wonderful thing for his many readers, and no doubt deeply satisfying to him personally, but beyond question a bad thing for British politics. Hearing him make a rare political speech the other day, so graceful and so eloquent, renewed my awareness of just how much we have lost by his passing from our profession. And there have been others, and there will be more of like talent, who have drifted away from politics to find success elsewhere. Echoing down the centuries come the words of Francis Bacon in 1621, as persecution hounded him (see p.7): 'If this is to be a Chancellor, I think, if the Great Seal lay upon Hounslow Heath, nobody would take it up.' Parliament is too important to be left to the time-servers, to those for whom the diminished pleasures and unattractive terms and conditions offered today to a Member of Parliament retain appeal, compared to the other avenues down which their limited talents might take them.

Matthew also describes the great British joy in *Schadenfreude*, the pleasure we all take in the humiliation of our 'betters'. Indeed so British a characteristic is it, that it's astonishing we have to look to the Germans for a term to describe it. However, as Matthew is also aware, the British public's attitude to petty scandals, whether politicians in the wrong beds in London, or film actors in the wrong company on Sunset Boulevard, is intriguingly ambivalent. On the one hand we love to read all this stuff, and buy the newspapers that peddle it in millions every week, but equally, when given half a chance to make a massive award against them in the libel courts, we seize it with alacrity. It is as if we know, even while enjoying the secrets of the bedroom laid bare, how much of a rot it spreads through society, turning us all into a nation of peeping Toms. Anyone who doubts the damage it does should talk to a candid friend abroad. There they see it all as a sign of a peculiarly British immaturity confusing private and public acts. This confusion is everywhere apparent in this book, never more so than Matthew's account of all the silliness of recent years. Of course nobody should take cash for questions, and those who did were rightly condemned. But as for the rest of it, it's a pretty sad indictment of the way we live now, not only that these absurd little errors are made, but having been made, that some of their perpetrators are made to feel, by the time the alternative criminal justice system run by the press has had its way, that they would have suffered less had they been convicted by a proper court of mugging, rape or pillage.

In that sense, the cure is worse than the disease. There is no disease of systematic corruption in British politics, and journalists who claim that there is do themselves and the nation no service. By investing petty peccadilloes with the substance of graver, weightier scandals, the whole of our democracy is damaged; and if Parliament has come badly out of this, how much more eloquently could the same thing be said about the damage done by recent events to the royal family. Many decades ago, George Bernard Shaw wrote that Britain has produced thousands of blameless greengrocers, but never a blameless monarch. The trashing in so many ways of the Prince of Wales – in his concern for the public good and his awareness of the great issues of the day a more substantial figure than any of his predecessors – undermines not just him, but the whole institution of the monarchy. We are entitled to ask, what earthly good will come of that?

So there it is. Matthew is not judgemental. He presents the evidence, and makes his own measured comments about it. It's pretty clear what he thinks of it all, but in the end, dear reader, he leaves it up to you. But if you finish this book heartily sick of storms in teacups, and to change the metaphor, with a sinking feeling that British politics is going to hell in a handcart for reasons quite different from those offered to you in tabloid editorials, he will not, I think, in the end, feel his efforts were all in vain.

INTRODUCTION

'Feasting with Panthers'

The death in February 1994 of a backbench MP in what the BBC called 'unusual sexual circumstances' was not a great parliamentary scandal. It was not really a scandal at all. But it was bizarre, it was shocking and it involved an MP – and that is enough for British newspapers. My own, *The Times*, asked me to write about the pressure MPs face and the temptations to which they are exposed. Why do they get into trouble so often when theirs, above most others, is a career to which scandal can be fatal?

Under the title 'Feasting with Panthers' my subject was not Stephen Milligan but scandal itself: the fascination scandal holds not for those who read about it, but for those who make it. I wrote:

I hardly knew Stephen Milligan. What is said of his death may not be true, or there may be special circumstances which explain it. It is dangerous to proceed from the particular to the general and so I would like to make it clear that in a case like this the particular may not be an example of the general. But it has aroused interest in the famous general question: 'Why so they do it? Why do MPs, and JPs, and DPPs and VIPs of every type . . . why do public figures of all people take such risks?'

When Oscar Wilde called it 'feasting with panthers' he meant seeking sex with working-class youths. But it's an apt expression for many sorts of adventure. It means hazard. It means foolish, reckless excitement. It means danger, secrecy and shame.

How we find it depends on us. Some will run up crazy gambling debts; some will philander, kerb-crawl, drink and drive; some turn to drugs; some will pursue boys, some girls. Some will pursue dodgy money in crazy schemes. Each to his own, but we all have this in common: that if we are found out, the world will say *'why?'* He had everything going for him. He must have known he risked ruin. And he seemed such a steady chap. *'Why?'*

But the world misunderstands. The secrecy and danger are not a regrettable side-effect of the folly: they are the reason for the folly. They are the spice, the drug. That the visible part of a man's life looks respectable and safe should be no cause for surprise that in the shadows between the real and the imagined he has sought for himself a perilous other-life. Crushed by decency, he embraces hazard as a means of escape. To regret that he could not find something safer is like suggesting to those who crave furtive love-making behind the shelves of busy supermarkets that they buy a containerload of cornflakes and recreate the Tesco backdrop in their own bedrooms. It misses the point.

So what is the point? I shall talk about men, because the problem is mostly with men. I am clear from the start that I include myself in these observations.

The public has the impression that MPs take more personal risks than other citizens and I suspect the public is right. Of course, disproportionate publicity follows an MP's exposure and inflates the impression of the Commons as an exotic hot-house of sin, but I doubt whether this is the whole explanation. If the proportion of my ex-colleagues who philandered is true to the national average, then this is a philandering nation. If, proportionately, as many citizens are gay as MPs are, then homosexuality in Britain outruns even the wildest calculations of Outrage. I suspect MPs do take unusual risks in unusual numbers and the suspicion is reinforced whenever another is found out. He is almost never one of those I knew about.

And another misconception needs to be corrected. Miscreant MPs do not 'always get found out in the end'. I never was, and nor were any of my gay Tory friends. The calculation is not between safety and certain ruin, but between safety and risk.

But why does a career in public life in the Commons and in the constituency dispose an MP towards such risk? First, we must ask whether the risk-takers are self-selected. Are men with a weakness for surprising private behaviour especially drawn towards a political career? Secondly, we must ask whether the job itself, once secured, turns previously cautious men into secret risk-takers. The answer to both questions is Yes.

Nobody without a gambling streak, a taste for uncertainty and a belief in his own luck would embark upon a Commons career. Statistically, most must 'fail' within their own terms, which are (usually these days) the achievement of high ministerial office. The hours and conditions are arduous and the salary no more than what most MPs could have hoped to attract in a career outside. For many it is less. You may sacrifice a career in the hope of securing a seat which you may at any time subsequently lose, without compensation. However a candidate may present himself to his electors, no unadventurous family man in search of security is likely to want a career in politics.

And there is something, too, which I believe attracts men with a streak of exhibitionism, buccaneering or bravado. MPs are a miscellaneous bunch, but united by this: a craving for applause. They are attention seekers. The job rarely offers real power or influence. But regularly it offers publicity. You may do little, but you *are* somebody. It is remarkable how few MPs' biographies reveal boys who were the 'rounded' type at school: popular enough, clever enough, good enough at sport. The balanced all-rounder beloved of school reports does not, typically, seek election to Parliament. You will find that many MPs were unhappy, lonely or unpopular.

Men often go into politics to prove something which they feared might be in doubt. 'One day I'll be popular. I'll be Prime Minister, and be driven around in a big car, and everybody will cheer.'

In short, the parliamentary selection process attracts adventurers with more bravado than self-confidence, more *chutzpah* than emotional security. Then it lands them in what is, for long stretches, a spectacularly boring job. What follows, follows.

But, if the trait is not already there, the job itself creates deep dissatisfactions. Let me try tactfully to explain why, and I hope I shall not lose any of my MP friends in doing so. Being an MP feeds your vanity and starves your self-respect.

You are a little prince in your own constituency. In the House you may be a smaller fish, but still feel you belong to a most important – *the* most important – club. Your head swells.

But your heart troubles you because you know it's not true. You know you are only there because your party association chose you. Few ever voted for you as an individual, or ever will. You know, too, that your power at Westminster is almost zero – the whips humiliate you privately – and your influence in the constituency consists mainly in using your headed notepaper to help a pushy handful jump the queues in which more patient constituents quietly wait. You know you are a fraud and your position is a fraud.

It breeds an awful internal cynicism and an imperceptibly opening gap between your public life and your private, internal life. The latter becomes a world of its own in which you increasingly choose to dwell, all the while developing the skills you need to keep up appearances in the external world. The gap between these two worlds becomes, for some, almost unbridgeable. It generates terrible fears and anxieties.

I offer two examples. While I was an MP I found myself, once, in a gay pub called *The Two Brewers* in Clapham. A man came up to me and asked if I was Matthew Parris MP. I recognised him as a lobby correspondent at the House of Commons. I was immediately struck by complete terror and the absolute conviction that he had come there to find and expose me. Of course, he was gay himself and that is why he was there. But I shall never forget my immediate and irrational reaction.

The second example took place not long before I resigned. A mill was moving out of my constituency and I had invited a delegation of workers (all women) to come down and see the minister with me to try to stop it. The (Labour) leader of the county council had, like me, muscled in on this, and decided to accompany the women. He and I walked along with them from the little mini-bus that had brought them, towards the minister's office. Each of us was resentful of the presence of the other. Each of us was trying to impress the women with our own mastery of the situation. Both of us knew that nothing we could do would make the least difference.

One of the women turned to me and asked how I thought she should address the minister if he spoke to her. I looked at her and realised how completely genuine and how very nervous and how timidly hopeful she was. She believed in me. I suddenly felt a complete heel. Tears filled my eyes but as it was dark in the street nobody saw this.

It is not surprising that MPs learn to despise, if not themselves then the thing they are pretending to be. It is not surprising that they sometimes try to escape this, sometimes in a manner which to the rest of us looks desperate.

Re-reading that, it is not surprising that writing this book proved less of a giggle than perhaps I hoped.

Not that much within these pages isn't richly comic. Toe-sucking and Chelsea strips (both stories, incidentally, disputed) amused rather than horrified 1990s Britain. The corpulent figure of Horatio Bottomley, sewing mail bags in gaol after swindling the poor of millions as an MP in the 1920s ('Sewing, Horatio?' asked a visitor. 'No, reaping,' he replied) is a fit subject for amusement now, though Robert Maxwell isn't yet.

The thought of William Ewart Gladstone bringing prostitutes back to 10 Downing Street in the 1880s, to read them the Bible, raises a smile. The duel with pistols on Putney Heath in 1809 between two members of the same Cabinet now looks more hilarious than shocking. One can chuckle at the eighteenth-century John Wilkes's remark that, ugly as he was, lechery was easy and it only took 'half an hour to explain away his face', or his reply when a French visitor asked how far liberty of the press extended in England: 'that is what I am trying to find out'.

The seventeenth-century Commons Speaker Sir John Trevor, so cross-eyed that confusion reigned as two members caught his eye at the same time, and so corrupt that on being found out by the Commons he simply stayed at home and sent in a series of sicknotes until they sacked him, seems with the benefit of 300 years' distance, more ludicrous than wicked. And the Elizabethan and Jacobean Sir Francis Bacon was so great an essayist that his literary legacy has outlived his reputation for enjoying bribes, and boys, as Lord Chancellor.

Yes, there is enough to smile about. But after a year's work on this book, and re-reading what I have written, I cannot brush aside a pervading sadness. Most of the stories related here were a complete catastrophe for somebody. Almost every tale over which we now smile or tut-tut was for somebody a drawing back of the curtains one morning to realize, with hollow stomach, that everything was lost. As often as not it was not just a career which was wrecked, but a life.

Some deserved it. Sometimes there were other victims too – the women scorned or husbands cuckolded, the citizens robbed by a corrupt politician's wickedness – but more often than not the principal victim was the politician himself. On occasions he had nobody but himself to blame, but still I read these chapters with a growing feeling that the British press (and arguably the British readers whose appetites we serve) emerges too often as more than bystander, more than reporter; more, even than investigator: we emerge as aggressor. The problem is not diminishing.

Some who people these pages were badly wronged by reports, others destroyed by untruth or mere rumour. Many were hounded into ignominy by a press or public which had got its teeth into *something* which was culpable, got it all out of proportion, and simply would not let go. Some of the cruellest injustices you will find here arose not from media lies but from media half-truths: not from invention, but from too narrow a view of the facts. Readers will make their own judgement.

This vague but insistent unease has been renewed in recent weeks as I discussed my draft manuscript with many of those, still living, whom it fingers. I tried to send to most of those surviving parliamentarians and ex-parliamentarians who appear here (many of whom I know) my proposed words about them. It seemed a common courtesy and a good way of ironing out the many errors which creep in as journalists base stories on cuttings written by other journalists; but I committed my drafts to the post or fax with gritted teeth and bated breath, waiting for the explosion, the bellow of 'How dare you venture here!'

It almost never came. A few did not reply (and a few I never tracked down) and the reader must certainly not suppose that every modern politician here has vouchsafed the accuracy of my report; but I was overwhelmed by the helpful, matter-of-fact way most responded to what must have seemed an unwanted raking over of coals by which they were once badly burned.

As a result I have spent days discussing my text with some of the principal actors in these stories, and received reams of sensible corrections. Interestingly, very few have asked me to alter opinions, judgements or even gibes: wrong facts vex them more. Time and again the person concerned would ask me not to withdraw what had been alleged, but to add what was never printed at the time. Surrounding circumstances can greatly alter the light in which we see an otherwise isolated incident, complicating the moral perspective and fudging simplicity. That is why popular journalists so often ignore them.

Of these exchanges and conversations I would mention just this: that to interview a man who has been felled or crippled by scandal is like talking, long after the event, to the survivor of a road accident or natural disaster. He becomes gripped by a kind of post-traumatic horror, very intense, sometimes staring at the desk as though he were alone in the room, or talking to a psychiatrist.

Many of my interviewees said this had forced them to think again about a chapter they had buried from recollection. Some, amazingly, said this was the first time they had revisited those memories. Most found that painful, but a number also said that it had been interesting: they were surprised to realize that they had never mentally reviewed the episode before now, or written about it, or asked anyone else to do so.

I have tried to. There is therefore much in the later chapters of this book which, though not a 'revelation' (in the *News of the World* sense), has hardly been mentioned before. Do not read this book for revelations: there is only one, and its subject is a rather minor character.

What to include and what to leave out? Not every political scandal is a personal scandal, and this book concentrates on allegations which imply (sometimes unfairly) private disgrace as well as political error. Some readers may be disappointed not to find every peccadillo of the last decade, but many are notorious only for being recent. In terms of enduring disgrace, the late-twentieth-century harvest looks rather disappointing.

A number of ex-colleagues and still (I hope) friends have asked me rather sadly why I chose to add to the number of words already squandered in a distasteful realm of modern journalism. Let me avoid the pious excuse-making of modern newspaper editors and reply that I write for money, and for fun. People want to read about parliamentary scandal; I know something about it; and so I will write for them. I hardly expect to improve the world. But this does not relieve me of a duty (and the wish) to be fair. Perhaps by retailing stories honestly, so far as we can, and in proper context, we can add something to readers' own grasp of history and sense of proportion.

Readers might like to glance at my remarks concluding the chapter on Disraeli. Disgrace is too easily assumed to be disabling to a man's political career and personal development alike. But a certain knocked-about quality in a statesman can add proportion, compassion and a redeeming cynicism to his judgement. I include, at the close of this book, a poem by D. H. Lawrence. Readers may care, too, to review what the *New Statesman* of 3 June 1922 wrote of that unequalled rogue, Horatio Bottomley MP:

> He had elevated roguery to an art. He possessed the sort of genius that repeatedly drew our eyes from his victims, and even the moralist could on occasion suspend his moral sense in order to admire a brilliant display of effrontery.

Seventy years later, a press which succeeds in being both dirty and pious, has lost the generosity which once could admit an impish delight in the wickedness of the wicked. There is a sort of drabness in late twentieth-century disapproval, a meanness.

I expect this book will be read for amusement – and I hope so. But I hope also that it might be read with understanding, and sometimes sympathy. And that, most of all, it might be read for *perspective* too.

ACKNOWLEDGEMENTS

Mark Mason, Simon Christmas, Christopher Hope and David Prosser carried out much of the preliminary research, wrote up early drafts of many of these pages, and spent months in libraries and newspaper archives assembling evidence and anecdote for me. I have been amazed at what they could find. I am grateful.

David Prosser, resourceful and clever as always, has steered the whole project toward publication. Andrew Pierce has shown what you can do with a notebook, a confiding telephone manner, an eye for the nub of the affair, a breathless vocabulary and a certain cheerful cynicism. I wish to thank them both.

Edward Pearce offered to cast an eye over the manuscript, and ended up suggesting many new lines of thought, rescuing me from several vast historical blunders, countless stylistic infelicities, and at least one major libel action. A handful of the best lines in this book are his.

My thanks to the following for allowing me to use relevant extracts and illustrations from their publications: the *Daily Express*, the *Daily Mail*, the Mirror Group, the *News of the World*, *Private Eye*, the *Star*, the *Sun*, the *Sunday Times* and *The Times*. The extract from 'Shadows' by D. H. Lawrence, on page 334, is reproduced by permission of Laurence Pollinger Ltd and the Estate of Frieda Lawrence Ravagli.

It will be apparent from some of the modern chapters that a number of those concerned have spoken quite freely to us. Many of the trickier chapters I have been able to show to central figures in these tales for comment and correction. I am especially grateful to those who would have preferred not to be in these pages at all, but who have helped me get things right. But readers should note that grown-up politicians sometimes prefer to leave unchallenged what they very well could challenge. Silence does not imply authentication.

Jeremy Robson and Louise Dixon have been unbelievably patient publishers, trying through 1994 and 1995 to judge, with me, whether to wait for one last scandal to unfold and then another – and another – or when to say 'enough'. We had hoped that by winter 1994 MPs would offer us a pause in which to publish; then we moved our deadline forward to spring 1995. It is now autumn and still the stories come. But . . . enough!

Matthew Parris
Derbyshire
September 1995

FRANCIS BACON – 1621

'I am guilty of corruption and do renounce all defence'

Four centuries of sleaze catches in its web both the noble and the ignoble. Whatever his sins, Francis Bacon was among the noble. His vast abilities have rescued his name from clouds which would have cast lesser reputations into shadow. This brilliant lawyer, judge, philosopher, homosexual philanderer, adviser to Queen Elizabeth I and Lord Chancellor to James I – a man who in his spare time wrote some of the most thoughtful essays of his age – deserves (and usually receives) a broader assessment than the simple assertion that his was one of the most corrupt Lord Chancellorships in English history.

But it was. Part of the problem was carelessness. The King's most senior minister was accused of taking bribes, and the evidence was overwhelming, but how many of these bribes he actively sought, and how many he was too disorganized to return, is less clear.

Modern politicians would do well to learn from Bacon's mistakes. With his head in the philosophical clouds and his lackadaisical approach to office administration, the Lord Chancellor became an easy target for his opponents. He did receive gifts, probably far more than were alleged at his trial, probably far more than he knew about. Most were arranged and then pocketed by his beloved servants. Bacon cared little for worldly possessions, even less for professional niceties, and trusted too much. But neither carelessness nor gullibility is any defence for a minister of the crown, alas.

Yet Bacon's background should not suggest naivety. He was born in 1561 amid the grandeur of York House off the Strand. His father was Lord Keeper to Queen Elizabeth I, in effect deputy Lord Chancellor. By safeguarding the Great Seal of England, the Lord Keeper held huge executive sway.

Together with his elder brother Anthony, three years his senior, Francis went up to Trinity College, Cambridge. They were devoted companions, although over-influenced by their mother, whom the historian A. L. Rowse describes as 'very religious in the most tedious Protestant fashion'. Brilliant but both physically frail, they shared one other characteristic: homosexuality.

After Cambridge, Francis was sent to Paris with the English ambassador, Sir Amyas Paulet, but was recalled abruptly when his father died in 1579. Within three years he became a barrister and moved into Gray's Inn. Although he was one of the best jurists of his day, the law did not satisfy his political and philosophical ambitions, and in 1584 he was elected MP for Melcombe Regis on Weymouth Bay. He then sought a job in the government of Elizabeth I.

Anthony, on the other hand, left Cambridge to travel on the continent and fell in with the Protestant King, Henri of Navarre – the future Henri IV of France. Anthony lived happily in Montauban, near Toulouse, with a succession of obliging page-boys. He sent the English Queen regular intelligence reports.

That was until Anthony's own brush with scandal. His alliance with Henri made him an attractive match, but the thirty-four-year-old bachelor showed little interest in women. When he refused to marry a young noblewoman, he encountered her mother's wrath. The affronted mama had him charged with sodomy. The accusation was serious: a priest at nearby Cahors had recently been burned alive for the same offence. It was not difficult for the authorities to frighten a number of boys into

Francis Bacon, Viscount St Alban, by an unknown artist
(courtesy of the National Portrait Gallery)

testifying. Anthony was found guilty, but was saved when his royal friend stepped in to champion his appeal.

Nevertheless Anthony, by now suffering from gout in both hands and legs, returned to England in 1592. He moved into Francis's chambers in Gray's Inn. Much to their religious mother's horror, the two brilliant brothers also shared lovers and attendants.

The following year, Francis temporarily wrecked his hopes of political advancement when he took a principled stand in Parliament against the government. The Queen was demanding more subsidies to meet the huge cost of the war with Spain. Elizabeth was furious at Bacon's disloyalty. He refused to apologize. She left him to wander in the political wilderness.

In 1597, with one eye on regaining the Queen's favour, Francis dedicated his *Essays* to his invalid brother. In a Europe only recently emerged from a dark age, the work was one of the more significant contributions to human thought since the Greeks. He dedicated it to

> our love, in the depth whereof I sometimes wish your infirmities translated upon myself, that Her Majesty might have the service of so active and able a mind, and I might be with excuse confined to these contemplations and studies for which I am fittest.

The Queen did not take the hint. Francis had one other motivation for trying to gain office: he was chronically in debt. His father had left less money than he had hoped for. In 1598 Bacon, the future Lord Chancellor, was arrested for debt, but kept himself afloat by borrowing.

Anthony died in 1601 and was bitterly mourned by his brother. Two years later the Virgin Queen followed suit and James of Scotland was crowned English King. Now widely regarded as the best mind in England, Bacon could gain the official recognition he so richly deserved. For a time, though, his cousin and deadly rival, the Earl of Salisbury, kept him in lowly jobs. His star was not set to rise until Salisbury's death in 1612 when Bacon was already fifty-one.

Meanwhile, partly to ease financial worries, in 1606 Bacon married Alice Barnham, an heiress and a London alderman's daughter. They had no children. Historians express surprise that there is almost no evidence of their spending time together and it is likely that Bacon saw very little of Alice.

In 1607 Bacon became Solicitor-General, and after Salisbury's death Attorney-General, in 1613. It was a job the greatest lawyer in the land should have held twenty years earlier. His rise was now steep. James I fully recognized his skills. In 1617 Bacon followed his father's footsteps, becoming Lord Keeper; and the following year he finally achieved his ambition when he was appointed Lord Chancellor. He moved back to the royal residence of York House where he had been born and in 1620 took the title Viscount St Alban.

Bacon was the 'justest judge' England had seen but he was too detached, too relaxed and too philosophical to take notice of the bribes flowing in to his servants. His head in the clouds, he was absorbed in grander matters. Part of Bacon's problem was that he could never decide between the active and contemplative life. He had 'musique in the next room where he meditated', sweet herbs or flowers were always before him as he dined, and he was notoriously easygoing with his servants. In the words of one parliamentary diarist of the time, he had a habit of 'making his servants his bedfellows . . . [he keeps] still one Goderick, a very effeminate youth, to be his catamite and bedfellow'. The Lord Chancellor saw to it that all his servants wore boots made from Spanish leather – less a kink than an affectation: the smell of common English oxhide offended him.

His young charges did much as they pleased. It was partly thanks to Bacon that the Churchills are a wealthy family today. The first of their clan to drag themselves from the Dorset mire was John Churchill, who ran a very lucrative little bribe-collecting business as Bacon's Registrar in Chancery. There was no National Lottery fund to assist the Churchills at this time. Presents to Bacon himself were accepted graciously but (studying the Lord Chancellor's court judgements) probably without favour.

Bacon had an international reputation. In January 1621 he was at the height of his philosophical career with the publication of his great work on logic, *Novum Organum*. But he had enemies. Chief among these was the Catholic-baiter, Sir Edward Coke, the Lord Chief Justice, who had made his name prosecuting Sir Walter

Raleigh; and the Gunpowder Plotters. The Civil War was little more than twenty years away and already the battle-lines were being drawn. On the one side were ranged the parliamentarians: dry and puritanical, personified by Coke. On the other, those like Bacon defended the inconsistencies of the Royal Prerogative against the follies of Parliament.

Parliament had been looking for some time for an excuse to attack the excesses of the court. There were plenty to choose from. The King was homosexual. Once he had produced an heir from his wife, Anne of Denmark, a suitable match from a Protestant kingdom, he could barely abide seeing her. He outraged Puritan sentiment with his choice of favourites and lavished gifts of land and titles on a beautiful twenty-two-year-old boy, George Villiers.

Aware of the King's proclivities, the youth's mother had presented her son to the court in 1614. Villiers, described as 'the best male specimen in the land' and the last of the King's favourites, rose from being a threadbare hanger-on at court to become the second richest nobleman in England. We know him today as the Earl, later Duke, of Buckingham, but to the King he was 'Steenie' because of his resemblance to a stained glass depiction of St Stephen in the royal chapel. The fact that Steenie's tastes were at least partly heterosexual only seemed to inflame the King's desire. James once told his Council of Ministers: 'I love the Earl of Buckingham more than anyone else . . . Christ had his John, and I have my Steenie'.

When Buckingham's brother, Sir John Villiers, wanted to marry the daughter of Bacon's hated rival, Sir Edward Coke, Bacon unwisely tried to block the match. But the King could refuse his favourite nothing and the ceremony went ahead in 1617 with the King, rather than the father, giving the girl away. Coke was readmitted to the Council. Bacon was forced to grovel but he soon made it up to the King's favourite, for whom he had a genuine affection. Steenie's younger brother Christopher was made a Gentleman of the Bedchamber, then Master of the Robes, each job attracting a considerable pension. And there were other jobs for the favourite's half-brothers, and for other relatives too.

It seems that the court had few problems with homosexuality, but this is not to suggest the Puritans in Parliament and the country approved. When Steenie finally married, the King wrote to the newlyweds: 'The Lord of Heaven send you a sweet and blithe awakening, all kind of comfort in your sanctified bed, and bless the fruits thereof, that I may have sweet Bedchamber boys to play with me (and this is my daily prayer)'.

The former Bedchamber boy should have kept out of politics. Buckingham's political dalliances spelt danger for the King, but more immediately for the Lord Chancellor.

Bacon was essentially a moderate man, whose idea was to bring King and Parliament together. He served both tirelessly, but by the likes of Coke was seen as too closely allied to Buckingham and the excesses of the court. Coke, who had the ear of the Commons, attacked the monopolies the courtiers enjoyed. His real target was Buckingham and his brothers. Coke's complaints were justified and received widespread support. The court needed a scapegoat. Bacon was expendable. He was accused of accepting bribes to affect cases in the Court of Chancery. One concerned a man named Aubrey. He had heard that he would win his case if he gave 100 guineas to the Lord Chancellor. When he lost, his anger was turned upon Bacon. Another man, Egerton, told a similar story, although the price in his case was 400 guineas.

Facing the charges, Bacon felt he could rely on the King's support. He wrote of being in

purgatory . . . but my mind is calm . . . I know I have clean hands and a clean heart, and I hope a clean house for friends or servants. But Job himself, or whoever was the justest judge, by such hunting for matters against him as hath been used against me, may for a time seem foul.

He tried to make a pre-emptive speech in his defence during a parliamentary debate, but was rebuked and forced to apologize.

By mid-March 1621, Bacon was becoming anxious about the increasing level of public disapproval. New charges seemed to be laid daily. The Lord Chancellor hurried home from the Lords, pretended to be ill, and waited for the King to step in. 'If this is to be a Chancellor,' he wailed, 'I think, if the Great Seal lay upon Hounslow Heath, nobody would take it up.'

James did try to help. He suggested a special tribunal – a delaying tactic fashionable right through to our own time – but

Parliament refused. Asserting its new sense of authority, it insisted on pronouncing the items of impeachment. Bacon pleaded for time, writing from his 'sick bed' that he would not 'trick up an innocency by cavillations, but plainly and ingenuously (as your Lordships know my manner is) declare what I know or remember.'

The King did his best. He adjourned Parliament early to let the dust settle, an old trick. This proved counter-productive. Away from London, MPs measured the atmosphere in the country. Resentment against the King's courtiers was strong. When Parliament returned on 17 April, MPs were determined to bring the Lord Chancellor to justice. There were by now no fewer than twenty-three charges.

Hoping to throw enough meat to the wolves, Bacon wrote to the Lords giving a qualified admission of guilt: but in such general terms that he could not be said to have admitted any particular allegation. The House was having none of it, resolving that

> the Lord Chancellor's submission gave not satisfaction to their lordships; that he should be charged particularly with the briberies and corruptions alleged against him, and that he should make a particular answer thereunto with all convenient expedition.

At this point Bacon suddenly caved in. 'I do plainly and ingenuously confess that I am guilty of corruption, and do renounce all defence.'

The country was stunned. An incredulous House of Lords sent a delegation to inquire whether Bacon's confession was genuine. 'My Lords, it is my act, my hand, my heart.' He begged them: 'Be merciful to a broken reed.'

Bacon's sudden capitulation has never been satisfactorily explained. It is possible he hoped to be saved by procedure. While he retained the Great Seal of Office as Lord Chancellor, he would be required to pass sentence *on himself*. The historian A. L. Rowse suggests there was another reason. He was being blackmailed. A charge of sodomy was about to be brought against the sixty-year-old Lord Chancellor. Such was the atmosphere of the time, the King could not possibly allow that can of worms to be opened. Bacon had to surrender, and surrender completely.

With the King's support gone, four senior Lords were sent to retrieve the Great Seal. Bacon, in bed, handed it over with one hand while covering his face with the other. Bacon wrote to the King, rather pathetically offering to write a 'good History of England, and a better Digest of your laws' if he intervened. But it was too late. On 3 May, Bacon received his sentence: a massive £40,000 fine, imprisonment in the Tower at His Majesty's pleasure, and banishment from court, Parliament or any public office.

Only now could James be of service. The King saw to it that the prisoner was taken to the Tower by Thames barge to avoid the shame of having to proceed through the streets. Once there, he was given a comfortable apartment. James then released him after only two days, and annulled his fine. Although Bacon never regained any real degree of honour at court, he was given an annual pension of £1,200, and went on to write several more distinguished academic works.

By the end of his first year of disgrace he had finished his *History of Henry VII*. It was a model for future historians: compact and interpretative, unlike the heavy chronicles of the past. Then came the Latin translation of his *Advancement of Learning*. However, he was not for two years admitted to kiss the King's hand, and the full pardon that would have cleared his name never came.

The end of Bacon's life was absurd yet strangely typical. He was a keen amateur natural scientist. Travelling in Highgate one winter's day, he saw a dead chicken by the roadside. Wondering whether freezing would delay the onset of putrefaction, he jumped from his cab and stuffed the chicken with snow. It was one of the world's earliest experiments in refrigeration. But in the process he caught a chill, the chill led to pneumonia, and shortly afterwards, on 9 April 1626, he died aged sixty-five.

It was a great loss. Bacon pre-empted the Enlightenment. He believed in the progress of man. He strove all his life to resolve the political and religious disputes which dogged the age. Within a generation after his death, but only after the idiocy of the Civil War, the Royal Society was founded to advance his programme of scientific exploration and discovery.

In his essays, Francis Bacon wrote that 'all rising to a great place is by a winding stair' . . .

The rising into place is laborious, and by pains men come to greater pains; and it is sometimes base, and by indignities men come to dignities. The standing is slippery, and the regress is either downfall, or at least an eclipse.

Bacon had a difficult life. He might well have found in his own death confirmation of the epigraph in one of his essays: 'The sweetest canticle is *nunc dimittis*'. His epitaph, sad and perhaps a little bitter, read: 'For my name and memory, I leave it to men's charitable speeches and to foreign nations and the next ages.' The next ages have judged him well.

TITUS OATES – 1678–85

'A damnable and hellish plot'

Plots, true or false, are necessary things,
To raise up commonwealths, and ruin kings . . .
            Dryden, *Absalom and Achitophel*

In a wave of national paranoia best captured by the playwright Arthur Miller's portrait in *The Crucible* of witch-hunts in New England, and which pre-dated by centuries the McCarthyite anti-Communist hysteria which it so uncannily resembles, seventeenth-century England proved that our own country is as capable of insane collective fear and hatred as were the Spanish Inquisitors, or the Nazi Jew-baiters three centuries later.

The disgracing of Parliament in this affair arose not from the scandalous behaviour of any individual MP, but from a sort of corruption that tabloid newspapers never acknowledge: populism – a yielding without thought or principle to the opinions of the many. Democracy itself can amount to a kind of scandal.

Parliament's brutal repression of innocent Catholics following false allegations of a 'Popish Plot' to overthrow the government in 1678 is one of the most disreputable episodes in English history. The plot itself was an elaborate pack of lies dreamt up by a disgraced former Anglican cleric, Titus Oates. Although not an MP himself, he led MPs, and MPs led public opinion. His dire warnings of a Catholic-inspired uprising were seized upon by unscrupulous politicians. His allegations generated mass hysteria. At least thirty-five innocent people were executed.

How was the nation stirred to this? Before we look at Oates's role, it is worth pointing out that Catholic bigotry on the Continent, embodied by Louis XIV, was brutally repressive. Hundreds of thousands of Protestants had fled to Holland, north Germany and England. Most English Catholics enjoyed more practical toleration than did Protestants in south Germany or France and Oates was therefore able to exploit genuine fears, and appeal to a real sense of injustice.

Titus Oates, a child of the Civil War, was born in 1649, seven months after the execution of Charles I, at Oakham in Rutland. The son of an Anabaptist preacher, Oates soon established the tone of his life when he was expelled from Merchant Taylors' School in London. Yet he managed to enter Cambridge and took Holy Orders in the Anglican church. In an age of rumour and suspicion, his habit of making wild allegations against his clerical colleagues lost him a series of parishes. In 1674 he was actually imprisoned for a short time for perjury while serving as a curate in Hastings; but he escaped, or bribed his way out of prison, and joined the navy as a chaplain. From this too he was dismissed.

Soon after, in 1677, Oates met the Rev. Dr Israel Tonge, a half-mad rector who shared his hatred of Catholicism. He learned fast from his new acquaintance. Hired as chaplain to the Protestants in the Catholic Duke of Norfolk's household, Oates began passing to a government keen for information the names of his master the Duke's friends, some of them suspected of treason. But Oates was dissatisfied with the small cash rewards he received for his treachery. Together with his rector friend, Oates began further to cultivate his forte: religious espionage. The twenty-eight-year-old cleric feigned conversion to the Roman faith, and entered Jesuit colleges in Holland and Spain.

He returned in 1678 armed with enough inside knowledge to compose his plot. With England nervously watching the growing strength of Louis XIV's Catholic France across the Channel, he tapped into a rich vein of anti-Catholic phobia in the country. Oates knew he could also rely on the support of the nascent Whig Party in Parliament.

The King and Queen were childless. The heir to the throne was the King's brother, James, Duke of York, whose conversion to Catholicism ten years earlier had resulted in the formation of the Whig Party in Parliament: dissenters, low-church Anglicans and opponents of the Royal Prerogative who wanted the Duke of York excluded from the throne. Against them were ranged the King's high church and Catholic supporters: the Tory Party.

In the summer of 1678 Oates informed the Privy Council of a vast Jesuit conspiracy. They were planning, he said, a gruesome massacre of English Protestants. London, still recovering from the Great Fire in 1666 (widely believed at the time to have been a Roman Catholic conspiracy), would once again be thrown into turmoil. The conspirators' aim, said Oates, was to assassinate the King and place the Duke of York, his Roman Catholic brother, on the throne. After making a sworn statement to this effect before a popular London magistrate, Sir Edmund Godfrey, Oates repeated his allegations to Parliament. For the Whigs, led by the Earl of Shaftesbury, a former member of Cromwell's Council of State, Oates's allegations were manna from heaven.

Keen to associate the Duke of York with the conspiracy, Oates named the Duchess's private secretary, Edward Coleman, as being behind the plot. Coleman was arrested and letters he had received from a Jesuit priest in France were found. The priest was close to Louis XIV, hearing the French King's confession each week. Coleman was charged with treason.

Before Parliament had a chance to make a formal response to the plot allegations, events were taken out of its hands. Godfrey, the London magistrate who had first heard Oates's allegations and ordered the arrest of Coleman, was murdered. On 27 October, his mutilated body was discovered in a ditch below Primrose Hill. Proof! Oates was right, there was a murderous conspiracy against decent Protestants everywhere. London erupted in a wave of anti-Catholic frenzy. Others came forward to support Oates's story and the convicted perjurer was hailed as a hero.

Though some say the Protestant magistrate was murdered by

Oates's supporters, a young Catholic, Miles Prance, was dragged from the silversmith's where he worked, tortured, and forced to confess to the crime. On his evidence three innocent men were hanged.

Four days later Parliament gave its formal response to Oates's allegations. This declared that:

> there is and hath been a damnable and hellish plot contrived and carried on by Popish recusants for assassinating and murdering the King, for subverting the Government, and rooting out and destroying the Protestant religion.

The Whigs took the opportunity to pass a law, which Charles II was unable to resist, excluding Catholics from both Houses of Parliament. It remained on the statute books until 1829. Shaftesbury also introduced a bill excluding the Duke of York from the throne in favour of Charles's Protestant, though illegitimate, son, the Duke of Monmouth. This was one step too far for the King. He dissolved Parliament.

However, Charles was dependent on Parliament for his income, so he contacted the King of France and invoked a secret clause of the Treaty of Dover, negotiated eight years earlier. The clause allowed for a substantial private subsidy from French coffers if Charles II agreed to convert to Catholicism before his death. So by now there nearly *was* a Catholic plot. Nor should we miss the treachery implicit in such a clause. Had the secret clause, and Charles's sympathetic interest for continental Catholicism, been known, it would have appeared treasonable to the calmest minds. Oates's lies would have been superfluous.

Over the next two years, in what became known as the Exclusion Crisis, the King dissolved Parliament three times as Shaftesbury tried to introduce his bill to prevent the Duke of York taking over. Neighbour betrayed neighbour. On 21 November 1678, the Lord Chief Justice condemned a banker to death for 'treasonable words'; before the end of the year he had sent the Duchess of York's secretary, Edward Coleman, and three others the same way.

The hero, Oates, was awarded a weekly salary from public funds. On top of this he submitted a massive £678 12s 6d bill for his 'expenses' in uncovering the plot. It was paid instantly. While

Oates enjoyed the good life in London, all Popish recusants (Catholics who refused to attend Church of England services) were ordered to depart ten miles from the city.

Emboldened by his new-found status, the unassailable Oates went so far as to accuse the King's Catholic wife, Catherine, of being behind the plot. On 28 November 1678, he made this outrageous suggestion before the bar of the House of Lords. The King, though as famous for his adultery as for his religious tolerance, stood behind his beleaguered wife. She was one of the few who escaped from Oates's forked tongue. Others were less fortunate. The Roman Catholic Archbishop of Armagh, Oliver Plunkett, head of the Church in Ireland, was sentenced to death. He had gone into the dock facing the ridiculous charge of conspiring to bring a French army to Ireland. Thirty-five people were to lose their lives before the anti-Catholic frenzy subsided.

Nearly three centuries later, Plunkett was beatified by Rome. I worked on the Foreign Office desk dealing with the Vatican at the time and even then, three hundred years later, there were Protestant sensitivities in Britain – particularly in Northern Ireland – to be addressed.

In March 1681, Charles dissolved Parliament for the last time during his reign. The intractable Exclusion Crisis had gone on for more than two years. The fear generated by the Popish Plot was receding. Memories of the Civil War were still fresh in MPs' minds. They held as strong a horror of Republican anarchy as of a Catholic king. Slowly the country came to its senses.

One of the historian's most intractable tasks is to 'explain' changing public moods. Such changes may be of huge importance and clear and pressing to those alive when they occur, yet they are unaccompanied by much of what history and its students call evidence. There can be no doubt that anti-Catholic hysteria went off the boil in England after 1681. Precisely why, or how, is lost to us. The poet laureate, John Dryden, caught the new mood. His epic satire on the Exclusion Crisis, *Absalom and Achitophel*, appeared in November 1681.

> Nor is the people's judgement always true;
> The most may err as grossly as the few

Oates began to sink. He was thrown out of his lodgings at court and barred from the council chamber. In 1684 he was fined £100,000 for calling the Duke of York a traitor, a sum he could not pay. He was thrown into the King's Bench prison where he lay in irons.

Charles II died in 1685. He fulfilled his pledge to the French King and converted to Catholicism on his deathbed. With the Duke of York finally installed as James II, Oates was convicted of two of his perjuries. He was unfrocked, heavily fined, imprisoned for life, flogged repeatedly and annually exhibited in the pillory. The flogging was severe and expected to kill him, but he survived. He eventually served only three and a half years, securing his release after James II himself fled the invasion force of the Protestant William and Mary.

Oates lived the rest of his life in typical fashion, marrying a wealthy widow and being expelled from the Baptist church following a financial scandal. He died in relative obscurity in 1705.

Titus Oates, annually pilloried for his crimes

SIR JOHN TREVOR – 1694

An Unusual Sicknote

Possibly the ugliest Commons Speaker ever to occupy the chair, Sir John Trevor was probably also the most corrupt. 'He created a most unfavourable impression on all who saw him,' say Philip Smith and Arnold Wright in *Parliament Past and Present* as 'an ungainly figure, and with a lowering countenance which was made more repellent by a villainous squint'. Trevor's speakership was famous for the confusion caused whenever he chose a member to speak. He would appear to be looking at a different MP from the one he intended to call, and two or more would rise, each under the impression that Sir John was looking at him.

Trevor found it difficult in more ways than one to look Honourable Members in the eye. After a few years in the chair, his reputation for taking bribes to secure desired outcomes in Parliament began to grow. The East India Company was rumoured to have bribed him, successfully, for his influence over legislation touching its interests. He was also said to have accepted a large payment from the City of London Corporation to secure the passage of a measure compensating them for debts its members incurred through their responsibility for orphans.

The House appointed a committee (in the way that, as you turn these pages, you may note the House always does) to investigate, chaired by a Mr Foley MP. The committee uncovered a written record of the City's instructions: '. . . that Mr Chamberlain do pay to the Hon. Sir John Trevor, Knight, the sum of 1,000 guineas so soon as a bill be passed into an Act of Parliament for satisfying the debts of the orphans . . .' There was even a written endorsement of these instructions, confirming that the Act had passed and the money had been paid.

MPs drew up a resolution, effectively convicting their own Speaker of a 'high crime and misdemeanour'. It fell to Sir John himself, as Speaker, to put the motion to the House. 'Shame would have overwhelmed a less sensitive man,' say Smith and Wright, 'but Trevor was not constituted that way, though it was with blanched cheek and quivering lip that he put the fatal question'. The Ayes had it, by overwhelming acclamation. Sir John slunk out. He never returned. To put the motion for his own expulsion was more than he could bear. The next day an expectant House was delivered a note:

GENTLEMEN – I did intend to have waited on you this morning; but, after I was up, I was taken suddenly ill with a violent cholic. I hope to be in a condition of attending you to-morrow morning. In the meantime, I desire you will be pleased to excuse my attendance. I am, with all duty, Your most obedient humble servant,

J. Trevor. SPEAKER

The House adjourned. The following day another sicknote was brought.

The House expelled its Speaker and elected another one, William III raising no objection. No more was heard of Sir John.

JOHN WILKES – 1763

The Cross-eyed Ladies' Man

I have always suspected that having something wrong with you is a necessary, if not sufficient, condition for becoming a Member of Parliament. I am convinced that boys who were bullied in the playground, teased by teachers or mocked on the playing fields, have, since the earliest times, resolved to have the last laugh on a persecuting world by raising themselves above it through political office.

John Wilkes, a member of the Hellfire Club whose members devoted themselves to depravity as a creed, was a scoundrel, a gambler, a vulgarian, a womanizer, and one of the ugliest men in England. He was convicted and imprisoned for libel and expelled from Parliament repeatedly – though for his politics rather than his morals. He was also one of the wittiest men to grace the Commons. When Lord Sandwich told him he would 'die either on the gallows, or of the pox', Wilkes replied, 'That must depend on whether I embrace your lordship's principles or your mistress.'

He was an idealist whose fight against privilege earned him the epitaph he penned: John Wilkes, 'a friend of liberty'. He has many modern admirers, not least the Labour MP Tony Banks.

The son of a wealthy distiller, Wilkes studied at Leyden, and then gained further financial security in 1747 by marrying an heiress. He was twenty-one. Such was the vigour with which he pursued his debauchery and gambling that he was soon in debt. He joined a secret society, set up by the MP Sir Francis Dashwood, whose members became known as the 'Mad Monks of Medmenham' because of their obscene cavortings in the ruins of Medmenham Abbey in Buckinghamshire. Even without the mad monks' help, Wilkes overcame his chronic ugliness and severe squint to indulge in serial womanizing. It was Wilkes's boast that he only needed 'half an hour to talk away my face'.

He was famous for his barbed put-downs. When an elector told him, 'I'd rather vote for the devil,' Wilkes replied, 'Naturally, but if your friend is not standing, may I hope for your support?'

Wilkes made his first attempt to enter Parliament in 1754, standing in Berwick-on-Tweed. Part of his election strategy had been to bribe the captain of a ship bringing opposition voters from London. A generous inducement persuaded the captain to encounter navigational problems during the journey and the ship docked in Norway rather than Berwick. By the time it reached Berwick it was too late for the passengers to cast their votes. But Wilkes still lost the election.

His wife left him in 1757, fed up with his lechery. Wilkes redoubled efforts to deal with his mounting debts: his plan was to get elected to Parliament, where as an MP he would be free from arrest for debt. At a cost of £7,000, largely spent on bribes to the voters of Aylesbury, he was returned as an MP later that year.

He became a deadly enemy of the hated Tory, Lord Bute, the champion in Parliament of the Prince of Wales (later George III). Bute, forty-nine, ousted the popular William Pitt from his

John Wilkes, by William Hogarth

administration when he became Prime Minister in May 1762. The same year Wilkes started his own newspaper, the *North Briton*, to launch his attacks on Bute's government and, the following year, the government of George Grenville. In edition number 45 in April 1763, he finally went too far. He alleged that the speech from the throne was the result of ministers putting lies into the King's mouth. A general warrant was issued for the arrest of everyone connected with the *North Briton*, and Wilkes was thrown into the Tower of London.

Within a week, however, he was released. Lord Chief Justice Pratt decreed that Wilkes was immune from arrest for libel on the grounds of parliamentary privilege. The irrepressible Wilkes not only carried on precisely as before, but sought and won damages against the government for arresting him in the first place. Asked by a French acquaintance how far liberty of the press extended in Britain, Wilkes replied: 'That is what I am trying to find out.' His actions in fact secured a significant advance in civil liberties by establishing the illegality of general warrants: those which did not name a specific person.

To rid itself of the troublesome Wilkes, the government tried to remove his immunity from arrest by getting him thrown out of the Commons. The errant MP gave them every assistance. As well as reprinting the offending *North Briton* article (he had to do it on his own press as no other printer would touch it), he published a poem: Thomas Potter's *Essay on Women* which parodied Alexander Pope's *Essay on Man*. Both are reprinted below.

> O blindness to the future! kindly given,
> That each may fill the circle marked by Heaven:
> Who sees with equal eye, as God of all,
> A hero perish, or a sparrow fall;
> Atoms or systems into ruin hurled,
> And now a bubble burst, and now a world . . .
>
> Alexander Pope, *Essay on Man*

> O blindness to the future! kindly given,
> That each may enjoy what fucks are marked in Heaven:
> Who sees with equal eye, as God of all,
> The man just mounting, and the virgin's fall;
> Prick, cunt, and ballocks [sic] in convulsions hurled,

> And now a hymen burst, and now a world.
>
> Thomas Potter, *Essay on Women*

Potter was the son of the Archbishop of Canterbury.

At the start of the November session of 1763, both Wilkes's reprinting of the allegations about the King's lies and the pornographic poem were voted breaches of privilege. In the Christmas recess Wilkes decided to go and stay in Paris. He knew what was coming. In January 1764 the motion for his expulsion from the Commons was carried, and in February he was found guilty in his absence of publishing a seditious libel (about the King) and an obscene and impious libel (the poem). Sentence was deferred until his return.

This was not to be for some time. Wilkes was now living in Paris in the manner to which he had become accustomed in England. His friends included Madame de Pompadour. His wit never failed him. Declining the offer of a game of cards, he told a fellow gambler he was these days unable to 'tell a king from a knave'. Wilkes was no respecter of monarchs. Dining once in company which included the Prince of Wales he unexpectedly raised his glass and proposed a toast to the King's health – something he had never been known to do. The Prince asked him how long he had felt such concern for his father's health. 'Since I had the pleasure of your Royal Highness's acquaintance,' replied Wilkes.

He waited in France for a more sympathetic government in Britain but after four years there was still no sign of it. By then Wilkes had run up so many debts in Paris that to stay there any longer might have seriously damaged his health, so in early 1768 he returned to England. By March he had succeeded in becoming MP for Middlesex. Parliament continued to expel him. Anti-government feeling was running high. Wilkes, encouraged by the public support he was getting, tried a high-risk strategy. He voluntarily submitted himself to arrest. He was sentenced to twenty-two months in prison and a £1,000 fine for the outstanding charges against him.

His gamble paid off. There were riots outside the prison in St George's Fields where he was held. Troops were called and one man was killed. This profligate, womanizing, bankrupt, rich man's son had become a national hero for the poor and dispossessed and at the same time the moral leader of the middle-class campaign to assert popular control over Parliament. So when the Commons expelled him again in February 1769, the voters of Middlesex immediately re-elected their imprisoned candidate. A constitutional tug of war followed, in which Wilkes was again and again returned to the Commons, where he was denied his seat. At the fourth election, the Commons insisted on declaring Colonel Luttrell, the runner-up to Wilkes, as the winner, leading to widespread public anger.

A Society for the Defence of the Bill of Rights was formed in February 1769, primarily to fight his case, and even raised and donated £16,000 to pay off his debts. But his off-hand treatment of the Society alienated supporters.

In 1771 the Commons, wearying of the fight, decided not to prosecute three newspapers which had defied the ban on reporting parliamentary proceedings – one of Wilkes's chief demands. For the first time the right of the press to scrutinize and report Britain's elected representatives was accepted. The same year Wilkes, released from prison, was elected sheriff of Middlesex. Three years later he became Lord Mayor of London.

In 1774 the Commons allowed Wilkes to be elected without fuss for Middlesex. He had won all his major battles and remained the county's MP until 1790. He died on Boxing Day 1797 at the age of seventy-two.

With much scandal, a politician starts as a good chap, until unmasked as a sex beast. Wilkes reversed the process. He began as a man famous for his sexual activities but was finally discovered, constitutionally and politically, to be a splendid chap.

SPEAKERS NORTON and CORNWALL – 1770–89

Contrasting Pitfalls for a Commons Speaker

The late 1700s was a time when the parliamentary spotlight often moved from the benches and turned – to his embarrassment – on the Speaker himself.

Charles Wolfran Cornwall had difficulty keeping his own house in order – as well as his House to order. When his immediate predecessor, Sir Fletcher Norton, once cheerfully announced that he would treat the resolutions of the House 'as those of so many drunken porters' (a reference to *Macbeth*), he cannot have anticipated a successor who came to be seen in just this role. Cornwall sat – or slouched – in the Speaker's chair from 1780 until his death in 1789. He slurred his words and relieved his boredom with regular swigs of porter. A porter on porter.

> There Cornwall sits, and ah! compelled by fate,
> Must sit forever, through the long debate.
>
> Like sad Prometheus fastened to the rock,
> In vain he looks for pity to the clock,
> In vain th' effects of strengthening porter tries,
> And nods to Bellamy for fresh supplies.

Thus did the author Sir Nathaniel Wraxall commemorate Mr Speaker Cornwall. His overall summing-up was less poetic: 'Never was any man in public situation less regretted or sooner forgotten.'

Philip Ziegler, author of *Addington*, describes Cornwall as a 'lazy non-entity who diverted the House by keeping a supply of porter underneath his chair and noisily sipping at it during debates'.

He was also a Tory political defector, who changed sides to the

23

Whigs for a short time, following a fall-out with his brother-in-law, Charles Jenkinson, Secretary-at-War. Staggering from party to party, he lurched from constituency to constituency, too, representing Grampound in the Parliament of 1768, Winchelsea in those of 1774 and 1780, and Rye in the 1784 session, before dying in office in 1789.

He could not have presented a more ludicrous contrast with his predecessor in the chair, Sir Fletcher Norton. Cornwall cared little. Norton cared far too much, and ended up being burned in effigy outside the Tower of London.

A far more interesting and vital character, Norton did not mix, or slur, his words. Vehemently anti-government, he was drawn towards controversy, drawing back before things became impossibly uncomfortable. But his intensity and courage earned him friends.

Sir Fletcher Norton, already a controversial lawyer, was elected Speaker on 22 January 1770, with a huge majority over the Whig candidate, Thomas Townsend the younger. He created a sensation while presenting a bill voting funds for the King's expenses on 7 May 1777. He memorably barked that the Commons 'have not only granted to your majesty a large present supply, but also a very great additional revenue – great beyond example, great beyond your wants'. MPs and courtiers cringed. Norton was accused of having substituted the word 'wants' for 'expense'. Friends swiftly organized a damage-limitation exercise, and a resolution was carried that the Speaker had expressed 'with a just and proper energy the zeal of this House for the support of the honour and dignity of the Crown in circumstances of great public charge'. And for having declared 'in manly terms the real state of the nation to his majesty on the throne'.

Norton's candour brought him popularity with many, and he was awarded the freedom of the City. Undaunted by the fuss he had caused, he turned the Civil List into something of a hobby-horse.

This incident had occurred when Norton's popularity was already secure. He had been unanimously re-elected Speaker in 1774, even after a colossal furore in 1771, when Norton signed the warrant imprisoning Brass Crosby, the much-loved Lord Mayor of London and MP, in the Tower. Norton was a clever survivor and his battles helped advance privilege: the right of newspapers to report parliamentary proceedings with no fear of libel proceedings.

With neither the porter beneath her chair to console her, nor the perils of being burned in effigy to unnerve her, Madam Speaker in the 1990s has a more arduous, if less colourful, role than her predecessors 200 years ago.

CASTLEREAGH and CANNING – 1809

Pistols at Putney: a Duel Between Two Cabinet Ministers

These days, neither honour nor ambition would induce a politician to risk his life. Not so two centuries ago, when a summer of bitter feuding between two Tory Cabinet ministers led to pistols at dawn. Two days after Viscount Castlereagh resigned as War Secretary he challenged to a duel his scheming arch rival George Canning, who had just stood down as Foreign Secretary.

On a misty autumn morning in September 1809 the two men met at Putney Heath to take pot shots at each other. Canning missed. Castlereagh was more successful. His thirty-nine-year-old opponent was carried from the field with blood pouring from his left thigh. The press called it a 'disgusting exhibition'. George III, suffering increasingly frequent bouts of insanity soon to incapacitate him, privately hoped his entire Tory Cabinet would be carried off the field in wooden boxes. But both men lived to fight another day.

Historians describe the duel as epitomizing the struggle of interests in Britain during the Napoleonic Wars. The great landed aristocracies, which were represented by the forty-year-old Castlereagh, had been losing power to the new bourgeoisie: the thrusting mercantile class represented by Canning, aged thirty-nine. The military threat from Napoleon had given the old reactionary élite a breathing space and, under the cloak of national security, they resisted demands for greater political participation from the new breed.

The cool, Cambridge-educated aristocrat Castlereagh was looking for a chance to thwart the ambitions of George Canning. Canning, considered the sharpest mind in Parliament, never hid his desire to become Prime Minister. His biting wit made him popular in the country, but hated in Parliament where, despite being an Etonian, he lacked 'tone'. Was he entirely a gentleman? His background was a disadvantage. Canning's father had died in 1771, leaving his wife and year-old-son, George, destitute. Mrs Canning took up with an unemployed actor, to whom she bore five children. Her marriage in 1783 to another actor, by whom she had another five children, did nothing to rescue her from poverty and shame.

The young George was plucked from all this by a wealthy uncle, Stratford Canning, who sent him to Eton and Oxford. He proved a clever student, but eighteenth-century snobbery meant Canning was considered rather an *arriviste*. After graduation he decided on a political career and came under the protective wing of the Prime Minister, William Pitt, who, impressed by Canning's wit and intelligence, found him a safe seat. His ascent up the political ladder was rapid. By the spring of 1809, when Britain seemed to be losing against Napoleon, he was Foreign Secretary.

Canning took the credit for planning the brilliant seizure of the Danish fleet, allied to Napoleon: the cause of the biggest outpouring of patriotic joy since the Battle of Trafalgar in 1805. But the Foreign Secretary was quick to dissociate himself from military setbacks. In the disaster at Corunna – the Napoleonic equivalent of the retreat at Dunkirk – he made sure the blame was laid at the door of Castlereagh, the War Secretary. On 2 April he wrote to the Prime Minister, the Duke of Portland, threatening to resign as Foreign Secretary unless Castlereagh was sacked.

The ailing seventy-one-year-old Prime Minister was not the master of his own destiny. At a dangerous time in the country's history, the King had charged Portland with the delicate task of keeping Britain's two most able politicians in the government. Neither the King nor the Prime Minister held Castlereagh responsible for Napoleon's string of stunning victories, and Portland, who delegated most decisions to his ministers, could not afford to lose either man. He tried to placate Canning. But the Foreign Secretary would not compromise. The Prime Minister delayed. It was to prove a disastrous and near-fatal delay for both rivals.

Portland discussed Canning's ultimatum with three other members of the government including Castlereagh's uncle, Lord Cambden, the Lord President of the Council. Castlereagh himself was kept in the dark over Canning's demand. Besides, with Napoleon an imminent threat, he was busy planning an ambitious invasion force to capture the French naval base at Antwerp. While the King tried, and failed, to arrange a compromise solution under which War Office duties would be divided between Castlereagh and Canning, a huge British invasion force of 39,000 men – the Walcheren expedition – was dispatched to do battle with Napoleon. It proved to be England's most spectacular disaster in the Napoleonic era.

In Castlereagh's association with this disaster, Canning saw his chance. He repeated his demand that Castlereagh be sacked. For the Prime Minister it was too much, and Portland tendered his resignation to the King on 6 September.

The following day Canning offered himself as Prime Minister on condition that Castlereagh was made the public scapegoat for the Walcheren humiliation. The demand was refused. Believing that no creditable government could be formed without his involvement, Canning resigned as Foreign Secretary. Britain, in the middle of a long and debilitating war with the French, had gone from a weak and divided government to no government at all. An extraordinary twelve days elapsed before a new Prime Minister was chosen.

Puzzled about the sudden resignation of Canning, Castlereagh quizzed his uncle, Lord Cambden. Cambden came clean and told his nephew the full story of that summer's plotting. Remarkably, Castlereagh seemed to be the only member of the government who had not known. 'It is impossible for me to disguise,' he said, 'the extent to which my confidence in my colleagues has been shaken by what has passed.' He resigned too.

Canning waited for his summons from the Palace. It never

DUEL

BETWEEN LORD CASTLEREAGH AND MR. CANNING.

We regret to state, that a Duel took place early yesterday morning, between Lord CASTLEREAGH and Mr. CANNING, in which the latter received a wound in the left thigh, but happily, it is not dangerous, being merely a flesh wound. The meeting took place at Putney Heath. Lord YARMOUTH seconded Lord CASTLEREAGH, and Mr. R. ELLIS accompanied Mr. CANNING. We understand they fired by signal, at the disstance of ten yards. The first missed, and no explanation taking place, they fired a second time, when Mr. CANNING was wounded in the left thigh on the outer side of the bone; and thus the affair terminated. The wound, as we have already stated, is not dangerous. He was put into a coach, and conveyed to Gloucester Lodge, his newly purchased seat at Brompton; and Lord CASTLEREAGH returned to his house in St. James's-square, where he was shortly afterwards visited by Lord LIVERPOOL.—This very unpleasant affair was yesterday reported to have originated in the failure of the ulterior objects of the Expedition to the Scheldt, respecting which Mr. CANNING had expressed himself very pointedly; but this we are assured is not the fact. Lord CASTLEREAGH resigned the Seals of his office as Secretary of State last week; and Mr. CANNING having also tendered his resignation, remains in office only till a successor is appointed. Some misunderstanding has since arisen between them, the nature of which has not yet been publicly stated, but we understand it bore more of a private and personal, than of an official or public character. Indeed, as we have already stated, Lord CASTLEREAGH had ceased to be in office upwards of a week before the dispute took place. The challenge was given by his Lordship. Beyond this, we deem it prudent, at present, not to venture any statement. It is a delicate subject, and we are desirous of avoiding any statement, of the accuracy of which we are not perfectly assured.—In comtemplating the event, we derive considerable consolation from the consideration that the cause of combat was more of a private than of a public nature, and Lord CASTLEREAGH being no longer a Minister, that it was not between Members of the Administration. Were the case otherwise, it would, indeed, be most lamentable; for if our Statesmen were to vindicate their public measures by the sword or the pistol, what would become of the dignity, the controul, and the authority of Parliament?

The Morning Post, 22 September 1809

came. On 18 September George III called upon Spencer Perceval, the Chancellor of the Exchequer, to form an administration. (Perceval was later shot by John Bellingham, forebear to the present MP for South-West Norfolk, Henry Bellingham.)

The following day, with Britain's two most able ministers out of government, Castlereagh challenged Canning to a private duel to restore honour. Canning had never fired a gun in his life, but to refuse would have meant public shame. The same evening he made his will, signing off with a message to his wife: 'I hope I have made you a happy mother and a proud widow. I am content. Adieu. Adieu.'

The duellists met at six o'clock the next morning on Putney Heath after their aides failed to broker a last-minute compromise. Castlereagh, rumoured to have successfully duelled in Ireland, was calm and hummed songs by his favourite opera singer, Catalini, in the cab on the way to the showdown. Canning's aide, Ellis, was a bag of nerves. He gave his master the pistol, saying: 'I must cock it for him. I cannot trust him to do it himself.'

A distance of twelve paces was set between the duellists. They both fired and missed. Castlereagh's aide vainly pleaded with him to leave the field. He refused. They took aim a second time. Shots rang out. Canning missed. A piercing cry rent the air. Castlereagh's bullet had passed through Canning's left thigh. The wounded man exclaimed: 'But perhaps I ought to remain. Are you sure we are done?' before he was dragged from the field. The wound was not serious. Within a few hours Canning was propped up on a sofa at home writing letters to family and friends declaring all was well.

The affair was considered a monstrous scandal. There was an incredulous public reaction to the fact that two distinguished former ministers of the Crown had resorted to a duel: an ancient custom introduced by William the Conqueror, common in nineteenth-century French politics but, by 1809, astonishing between senior British politicians. The *Morning Chronicle* wrote: 'To suppose it possible, after the disgusting exhibition they have made, to form out of their dispersed and disordered ranks a government that could stand, is the height of absurdity.'

Publicly the King let his displeasure be known, but privately he was fascinated. After an audience at the Palace, Canning wrote that he had to 'show the situation of the wound which he made me point out to him on his own royal thigh'.

Castlereagh was blamed for demanding the duel and insisting on a second shot, but his career quickly recovered. He was back in his old job within two and a half years. Historians credit him with much success, but he never enjoyed public affection.

> Why is a pump like Viscount Castlereagh?
> Because it is a slender thing of wood,
> That up and down its awkward arm doth sway,
> And coolly spout and spout and spout away,
> In one weak, washy, everlasting flood.

wrote Sir Thomas More.

In 1821 the great Tory aristocrat began to show signs of paranoia. After a supposedly happy twenty-eight years of childless marriage, he was, or thought he was, being blackmailed for homosexual acts.

It was said that he had picked up a soldier whom he afterwards claimed had appeared to be a woman. He committed suicide in 1822. When his corpse was carried into Westminster Abbey, the solemn proceedings were disrupted by boos.

After the duel, Canning remained out of office until 1816. He did not return to the Foreign Office until after Castlereagh's suicide. Then, in 1827, after thirty-three years in Parliament, Canning finally achieved his dream and became Prime Minister. Half the Cabinet refused to serve under him. His tenure at Downing Street was short-lived. He died four months later, his health broken by the strain and his own sanity questioned. Duelling was outlawed in 1819.

BENJAMIN DISRAELI – 1826

'Youth is a blunder'

It was Disraeli who called politics a greasy pole, and the remark is usually applied to the snakes-and-ladders quality of high office. But for the young Disraeli, a low-born immigrant's grandson facing the nineteenth-century triple-whammy of debt, sexual scandal and Jewish ancestry, the pole was nowhere greasier than at its base. Disraeli got off to the most awful start. Just how awful is suggested in a new book by the historian Jane Ridley: *The Young Disraeli, 1804–1846*. Ridley goes further than previous studies in indicating the mess Disraeli got himself into as a young man, and from which he struggled to free himself as a politician. His career was a triumph over adversity. It points the lesson that when scandal looms, all is not necessarily lost.

Unable to afford a proper public school or university, Benjamin Disraeli's father, Isaac, had him trained as a solicitor. Benjamin had little love for his law textbooks. He plundered the literary classics and took a growing interest in Tory politics. A dandy at the age of eighteen, he followed the Byronesque craze of dressing almost entirely in black. Ridley describes him shocking the wives of solicitors by appearing at their dinners in a black velvet suit with ruffles and black stockings with red clocks (ornamental designs) on their sides. This was a youth with ideas and dreams way above his means or station.

At the age of twenty, with less than fifty guineas to his name, he saw an opportunity to make money. Canning had just recognized the newly independent republics of South America. London was awash with rumours of the untold riches that would accompany those who invested in the joint-stock companies springing up to exploit the gold and silver mines of that continent.

Disraeli borrowed heavily to finance his speculation: a thousand pounds from an uncle, around £1,500 from a money-lender called Robert Messer, more from his publisher friend John Murray. He agreed with Murray to set up a Tory newspaper, to be called *The Representative*, as *The Times* in the early 1820s was

seen by Tories as politically unreliable. How different from our
own day.

In December 1825, the City suffered a disastrous crash.
Disraeli, just turned twenty-one, was ruined, his mining shares
worthless. He owed many thousands of pounds – a considerable
sum in those days, though the exact amount is not known.
Because he had been under twenty-one when he had purchased
the shares he could not be held legally liable for his debts, but this
did not stop his creditors pursuing him. He spent much of the
next two decades avoiding them and running up further debts.

Adding, now, to his political ambitions was the knowledge that
a Member of Parliament cannot be imprisoned. Disraeli was
unable to pay his promised share of the start-up costs of *The
Representative*, and fell out with his friend Murray, who went
ahead without him. The paper failed after six months.

Partly as therapy, partly as a means to pay off his debts, Disraeli
resorted to writing a novel loosely based on his financial
misadventures. But *Vivian Grey*, which appeared anonymously
soon after, parodied too closely Disraeli's former friends and
business associates, and the secret identity of its author was soon
revealed. Society was appalled and fascinated in equal measure at
his apparent peddling of confidences. Duels were threatened, but
never fought. Disraeli had made his name and bought a valuable
breathing space from his creditors. A sequel was hastily brought
out the following year, 1827.

Soon after its publication, the stress of the past two years took
its toll. Disraeli was sitting in his room one evening, when he
heard a loud ticking noise. Checking his watch, he realized the
sound seemed to come from within his head. He slept badly, and
the following morning was unable to write. The noise returned in
the evening. 'I could compare it to nothing but the continuous
roar of a cataract,' he later wrote. With his debts still unsettled, his
nervous condition worsened. He languished in Bloomsbury doing
nothing. Doctor after doctor was called. 'I was bled, blistered,
boiled, starved, poisoned, electrified, galvanized; and at the end
of a year found myself with exactly the same oppression on my
brain.'

Ten years later, a doctor diagnosed his condition as 'chronic
inflammation of membranes of the brain.' Disraeli later admitted
he had suffered 'exhaustion of the nervous system'. Today we

might call it a nervous breakdown.

Slowly, and with rest, he recovered. In 1831, with his creditors increasingly vocal, he felt fit enough to embark on a sixteen-month grand tour around Europe and the Middle East. He travelled as far as Constantinople and enjoyed several audiences with the Sultan. As for what Disraeli did on these travels, we have few details other than the highly fictionalized material in his novels. But we do have some clues. Back home in 1833 he was attending dinner parties dressed in 'green velvet trousers and ruffles' and shocking guests with his passion for the East, which, according to the painter Benjamin Haydon, 'seemed tinged with a disposition to palliate its infamous vices . . . I meant to ask him if he preferred Aegypt, where Sodomy was preferment, to England, where it very properly was Death.'

Jane Ridley suggests Haydon was hinting at a little-discussed aspect of Disraeli's nature. He was a dandy, and dandies were notoriously effeminate, but Disraeli, she believes, went further. 'Like his political Radicalism, it was an attitude Disraeli found no difficulty in reconciling with the more conventional frameworks of Toryism or heterosexuality; bisexuality came as naturally to Disraeli as did Tory Radicalism,' she says.

An image of Disraeli at this time was provided by the Countess of Montalembert who thought him 'an egregious coxcomb . . . outraging the privilege a young man has of being absurd'.

This is all very speculative. Being a dandy in those days meant aping the dress and manner of a set, some of whose members would have been bisexual or gay, but that does not mean that all who followed these fashions were themselves bisexual or gay.

It was certainly heterosexual affairs which landed him in trouble over romance. Disraeli sounds as though he was in love at least with the idea of love. After dalliances with a series of women, most of them older than him and some of them married, he became involved with Henrietta Sykes, the daughter of a wealthy sporting Norfolk brewer. Their affair became a public scandal. Henrietta had been married for eleven years to the sickly Sir Francis Sykes, by whom she had four children. Bored, tempestuous, voluptuous, and significantly older than Disraeli, she would sign her letters to him 'your mother'.

They would be seen at parties and the opera together, but although gossip was rife, it suited Sir Francis to turn a blind eye for the time being. He was busy in adultery with the married Clara Bolton, who happened to be one of Disraeli's former lovers. But Clara was less willing to ignore Disraeli's affair. Resentful that she had been discarded by Disraeli, she encouraged Sir Francis to break the pair up. By 1836, when they parted, this suited Disraeli well enough. His prospects of a political career were brightening.

A year later, Henrietta's husband found her in bed with a new man. Late one night he shut Henrietta out of the house, refused to allow her to see her children, and then placed an advertisement broadcasting her adultery.

It could so easily have been Disraeli. Even now, he did not emerge unscathed. At the time Disraeli was making his fifth attempt to enter Parliament, standing for the winnable seat of Maidstone, and rumours dogged his campaign.

Although he finally won the election, his appearance, at the age of thirty-three, on the hustings in dandified dress astonished the people of the town. They howled abuse, and there were cries of 'Shylock' and 'Old Clothes' as the mob offered him stinking lumps of ham and bacon.

His Commons career began badly. He was nervous, he was, at first, an unsuccessfully pretentious orator, there were rumours about his dalliances with married women, and he was still seriously in debt. A Maidstone lawyer, Charles Austin, accused the newly elected MP of promising bribes to the voters of Maidstone during the election, bribes which he had failed to honour. (Bribing electors was a common practice, but a gentleman paid the bribes he promised.)

Austin's claim is probably true, but Disraeli's handling of the affair shows his genius – and shows why, in these pages, he joins the ranks of those who got away.

Instead of ducking, Disraeli went on to the offensive. Taking Austin's onslaught as an attack on his honour, he wrote a letter to *The Morning Post*, alleging worse by Austin. Rather than challenging Disraeli to a duel, as Disraeli had expected, Austin instead sued for libel. Disraeli was allowed to apologize flamboyantly in court. Though he had incurred costs, he had succeeded in switching the issue from that of his unpaid election bribes to his libel. Fortunately his legal bill was paid by the latest older woman in his life: Mary Anne Wyndham Lewis, the widow of his deceased running-mate in the Maidstone election.

Disraeli had written in a private letter dated December 1837, soon after his election: 'I am not married, but any old, ugly and ill-tempered woman may have me tomorrow.' Mrs Wyndham Lewis was a good deal more attractive than that, and though she was twelve years older than Disraeli, she was also rich. Disraeli's haste to conclude the match appeared almost crude, but their affection for each other seemed genuine. She was to act as a stabilizing influence over him for the rest of her life.

He despaired of Maidstone shortly after his election, and began searching for a cheaper seat with fewer voters requiring fewer bribes. He chose Shrewsbury for the 1841 election. His need to remain in Parliament became evident the moment the dissolution was called. A handbill was plastered over the town, listing the judgement debts against him during the past three years. They totalled over £21,000. In the list were included

the names of unhappy Tailors, Hosiers, Upholsterers, Jew Money Lenders (for this Child of Israel was not satisfied with merely spoiling the Egyptians), Spunging Housekeepers, and, in short, persons of every denomination who were foolish enough to Trust him . . . He seeks a place in Parliament merely for the purpose of avoiding the necessity of a Prison, or the benefit of the Insolvent Debtors Act.

In the end most of the debts were, if not settled, made subject to agreements. The others he brushed off, with some success, as collateral raised for other people. The voters of Shrewsbury accepted his excuses and his money, and elected him.

Disraeli's political career began to prosper. As middle age approached, the MP made headway against his debts with his wife's assistance. He could concentrate on the pursuit of power. By the time his wife died of cancer, in 1872, he had already been Prime Minister once.

When the widower returned to power in 1874, his curious relationship with the widowed Queen Victoria began. Disraeli had learnt how to flatter lonely middle-aged women without appearing over-familiar. He addressed the delighted Queen, who had just produced a slim volume of her own, with the phrase 'we authors, ma'am'. Early lessons were paying off.

Early lessons in risky speculation did not, however, seem to have been learned. Disraeli was still a gambler. But this time his gamble succeeded. Disraeli bought almost half the Suez Canal without Parliament's authority. A patriotic journalist in the area informed the Foreign Office that the extravagant and spendthrift ruler of Egypt, the Khedive Ismail Pasha, was keen to sell. The Foreign Office, identifying no tangible gain for Britain, could not justify the purchase. Disraeli however saw a bargain and at the end of December 1875, with Parliament in recess, he borrowed the money from his friends the Rothschilds and boldly bought shares for the government. Fortunately Parliament, sunning itself in the enhanced national prestige, approved the purchase in the New Year.

Disraeli was an uncensorious man. Once, when Palmerston was in power, the seventy-nine-year old Prime Minister was cited as co-respondent in a divorce case involving a Mrs O'Kane (prompting the inevitable popular joke: 'she was Kane but was he Able?'). Disraeli remarked that it was a pity this had got out, as Palmerston would now sweep the country at the next election. He did.

The story Jane Ridley tells runs rather counter to the course of much political scandal. The more common tale is of the idealism of youth giving way in a politician to cynicism and corruption – and ending in scandal. But Disraeli started in scandal. As a young man he was reckless and amoral, and very nearly ruined himself. He remained an artful pragmatist for the rest of his career, but it may be argued that, burned by his early experience of debt and disgrace, the mature Disraeli had learned something. His personal difficulties had lent him a certain alienation from the herd. His 'One Nation' Toryism steered the Conservative party away from class politics and away from unthinking opposition to reform. Cynicism is not always a degrading force. Disraeli became cynical about the rich, about privilege, and about the Christian Establishment in nineteenth-century Britain. He learned both to use and to despise 'the system'. His alienation may have saved him – and his party – from too deep an attachment to faction, class and privilege. A brush with scandal can be a redeeming experience.

'Youth is a blunder, manhood a struggle, old age a regret,' Disraeli wrote in *Coningsby*. But the blunders of youth arm us for the struggle, and need be no cause for regret.

GEORGE HUDSON – 1849

The Railway King

'In society but not of it,' said Lady Dorothy Neville of George Hudson, in her celebrated memoirs. Those looking to make a quick buck out of railway privatisation would do well to read Hudson's tale. The massive expansion of the railway network in Britain during the middle of the last century gave many men the chance to make their fortunes, but the greatest fortune of all was rapidly won – and spectacularly lost – by George Hudson MP, the 'Railway King'.

Born in 1800 near York, Hudson became a draper in the town. In 1828 he inherited £30,000, invested heavily in the North Midland railway and threw himself into politics. He bought three estates, served as Deputy Lieutenant for Durham and was thrice Lord Mayor of York. At forty-five he was elected Conservative MP for Sunderland.

In the years 1847–8 Britain was experiencing 'railway mania'. Hudson acquired railway companies until he came to exercise more power in the industry than anyone before or since. And he used his seat in Parliament ruthlessly in the expansion of his business empire. This was not unusual: at the time, 155 MPs were directors of railway companies and it cannot have been a coincidence that their services had been so sought after. But Hudson went too far. He bribed other MPs to support the private bills authorizing his railway purchases.

Once, he advised the Duke of Wellington's two sisters to sell their large holdings in a railway company he knew to be rotten, and they did so, shortly before they would have lost a fortune in its downfall. The grateful Wellington asked whether there was any way he could repay the MP. Hudson replied that his daughter, whom he had sent to an expensive private school, was being victimized for her humble origins. Could Wellington help? The great man responded by a personal call, with flowers, and an outing to tea, so that her reputation among schoolfriends and staff was swiftly secured.

Hudson's dream was to build up a unified system, based on his home-town, that covered the whole of the country. An early slogan he used was 'Mak all t' railways cum t' York'. And certainly, as the 1840s neared their end, he found himself well on his way to achieving that aim. He controlled 1,450 of the 5,000 miles of track in England, and was in charge of the Midland, the York and North Midland, the York, Newcastle and Berwick, and the Eastern Counties companies. His empire stretched from Bristol to Berwick.

To achieve this level of control, he had sought to gain influence wherever it might be of use to him – legitimately or otherwise. As well as being elected to the Commons in 1845, he was Lord Mayor of York and served on the magistracies of York, the North Riding, and Durham. He was part proprietor of the *Yorkshire Gazette*, the *Sunderland Times* and the *Railway Chronicle*.

In the financial field, Hudson used the York Union Bank (he was chairman) to borrow heavily in the City, to fund his operations. Moreover, he influenced prices on the London and York Stock Exchanges by buying and selling shares whose prices he wanted to move. He falsified accounts and fraudulently paid dividends out of borrowed capital instead of profits, in order to give an impression of greater success than was actually being achieved. Of great assistance to him in these deceptions was the fact that he kept all the accounts in his head.

But like Maxwell's a century and a half later, Hudson's deceit caught up with him. He was not alone in using creative accounting to drum up cash for his investments, and his core businesses were mostly bona fide. In Hudson's day (as in ours) the perpetrators of many potential financial 'scandals' were rescued by the ultimate profitability of their ventures and Hudson may have been the visible tip of a parliamentary iceberg. But what did for him was geometry. Hudson was conveying passengers from Newcastle and York to London via Derby and Birmingham, piggy-backing on George Stephenson's line. Edmund Denison took the straight line down the East coast. A railway between Cambridge and Lincoln to shorten Hudson's route failed, and his prospects faded.

By the beginning of 1849 Hudson's empire was crumbling. He

OFF THE RAIL.

'Off the Rail', *Punch*'s cartoon of the fall of Hudson, 1849

had overstretched himself. Keen-eyed shareholders, who had become suspicious and started to study the accounts, found discrepancies. In February the York, Newcastle and Berwick Company set up a committee of investigation. Its report two months later signalled the end of the reign of the Railway King. In October 1846, Hudson had recommended to the company that they buy shares in another company, the Great North of England. They agreed, and put Hudson himself in sole charge of the purchases. What Hudson hadn't told them was that earlier in the month he had bought some GNE shares himself, in a personal capacity. So he sold his own shares to his own company. He sold them at £23 10s per share, while their true market value was only £21. In the age of the directors' share option, we can only marvel at his restraint.

Hudson was forced to buy back the shares, and repay the £9,000 which he had defrauded from the company. *The Yorkshireman* newspaper, in the lapel-clutching prose of the day, took up the case: 'Mr Hudson shall not escape us. The thousands he has duped, and the breaking hearts from whence spring curses both loud and deep, shall have ample satisfaction for the injuries they have suffered and the torments they have endured.'

Another of Hudson's companies, the Eastern Counties, set up their own committee. Until now Hudson had been the hero of the company, having 'rescued' it from near bankruptcy in 1845. But now it was discovered that of the £545,714 he had paid out in dividends between 1845 and 1848, £320,572 had come not from profits but from capital. The committee found that as well as stealing the company's money to pay his own hotel bills, Hudson and David Waddington (another MP on the company's board) had stolen £9,000 with which to bribe other MPs into supporting Hudson's purchases of other companies. The committee petitioned Parliament.

Hudson was lost. He was forced to resign all his chairmanships. His brother-in-law, Richard Nicholson (a co-accused) killed himself in shame. Nine days later, Hudson was forced to make a Commons reply to the allegations of bribery. He was in such a state that for several moments he could not even speak. Even when he did start, building up to a defiant performance, his fellow MPs heard little to impress them. From now on he was to be an outcast (but, as an MP, an unarrestable one) in the Commons and outside it. In the months that followed, he was forced to pay back the sums he had stolen from his various companies. In York he was particularly unpopular – he didn't even dare show himself there. His name was removed from the Aldermanic roll, and the new approach to York train station, which had been named Hudson Street, was given the rather plainer title of Railway Street.

The following year his co-swindler, James Richardson, sued *The Yorkshireman* for libel over an article condemning him and Hudson. He lost, so damning Hudson even further. But Hudson was determined to stay in the Commons, a determination based less on stubborn pride than on the legal protection his status as an MP gave him.

In the 1852 election he managed to avoid defeat, largely because two years earlier he had secured the opening of a new dock in his Sunderland constituency. But even while he sat as an MP, he would always flee to Paris when Parliament was in recess, in order to escape his creditors. He lost his Sunderland seat in 1859 and spent the remaining years of his life in litigation, in Boulogne, making efforts to operate financially outside England. He died in 1871, virtually penniless.

We must not be too hard on George Hudson. He wasn't a Maxwell, more an improviser who moved money on casters. The statue planned for him outside York was replaced by one of George Leeman, his chief tormentor, the sort of high-toned creep who inspires in us a sneaking affection for men like Hudson.

ROBERT LOWE -- 1873

An Albino Chancellor with an 'Unhappy Knack'

Robert Lowe, Chancellor of the Exchequer in Gladstone's first government, cut a curious figure. An albino, with one eye malformed and the other so sensitive to light that he had to keep his eyelids almost shut, he was described by *Punch* as having an 'unhappy knack of offending his subordinates and quarrelling with all with whom he comes into contact'. His desire to 'get things done', without due regard to the niceties of the rule book, led to two financial scandals in quick succession. His cantankerous refusal to apologize spoiled his rehabilitation.

Lowe was born in Nottinghamshire in 1811. From Winchester he went on to University College, Oxford, where he taught for a time. Called to the Bar in 1842, he emigrated the same year to Sydney, Australia. He built up a lucrative practice there and played a major role in the state legislative council from 1843 until 1850.

Home again in 1850, Lowe began writing editorials for *The Times* and in 1852 he entered the House of Commons, holding office under both Aberdeen and Palmerston. He led the renegade wing of the Liberal Party which opposed their own Prime Minister, Lord Russell, over his moderate attempts to widen the franchise. Lowe's grouping became known as the Adullamites. John Bright, who supported household suffrage, had called them the 'Cave of Adullam' because everyone who was discontented or in distress resorted there. Despite this disloyalty, Gladstone later chose Lowe as his Chancellor in 1868. His abilities were so conspicuous as to outweigh his disobliging manner and bizarre appearance. He was still at Number 11 when his first scandal came to light in March 1873.

In recent years the newly nationalized telegraph service had been expanding rapidly with a trebling in the number of stations. Rates had been reduced and standardized. The man Lowe had placed in charge of this task, the ultra-efficient and hard-working civil servant Frank Scudamore, was widely credited for this success. Unfortunately, Scudamore's success had been partly financed by illegal borrowing. In order to pay the often unpredictable bills for expanding the network of telegraph lines, he had been dipping into the savings of working men in the Post Office Savings Bank. In 1871 he borrowed £171,775; the following year it was £400,000.

The man who should have spotted this, the Financial Secretary William Baxter, was kept out of the picture by Lowe. Like Scudamore, Lowe was a doer, and considered Baxter too pedantic. The request for Treasury funds to pay back the savings accounts went straight to Lowe, who agreed to them straight away, without inquiring too closely why Scudamore needed these funds.

When Opposition MPs revealed in the Commons what had been going on, the ambushed Lowe had little choice but to promise an investigation. Although it found that the payments had been due to over-enthusiasm rather than fraud, the press were hard on him. He was not popular.

Hot on the heels of this affair came the exotic-sounding Zanzibar scandal. The Sultan of Zanzibar, a keen patron of the slave trade, had been the subject of growing public protest. To dissuade him from permitting slavery, the British government promised him a mail service from Zanzibar to Aden and the Cape Colony.

But who would provide it? It was not a commercial proposition. The Union Steamship company offered to take the franchise for a mere £5,000, as long as their subsidized government contract for the Britain to Cape Town service was renewed. In fact there was no need for a subsidy on this latter route: a Mr Donald Currie had started a service unsubsidized.

Lowe knew that the nit-picking Baxter would insist on a tendering process, so he didn't tell him, but signed the contract and told the Union Steamship Company to commence the service immediately – ignoring the requirement for prior parliamentary approval. Parliament, Lowe promised, would ratify the contract later.

When Mr Currie learned that the Union Steamship Company's contract had been renewed without a tender, he protested, forcing the government to look into the matter. The contract with Union for the England–Cape run was thrown out.

Lowe was now fighting for his political life. Without the subsidy of the England–Cape service, he settled with Union on £26,000 for the Zanzibar to Cape run. But so mistrusted was the Chancellor by now that it became clear he was unlikely to get parliamentary support for this either. He used a procedural device to postpone a vote, thus gaining a ten-day delay.

When he returned for the second debate, Lowe refused to apologize and plead human error. Backbenchers would have accepted nothing less. He made unconvincing excuses for his procedural short-cuts. The Commons demanded a commission of inquiry, which finally shaved £6,000 off Union's contract.

Both scandals simmered on into the summer. It became obvious that the cantankerous Lowe would have to depart. Gladstone wanted this to happen quietly after the heat had died down. Baxter wrote to Gladstone in fury about the Zanzibar affair, offering his resignation. Gladstone was forced to bring forward his reshuffle. Lowe was demoted to Home Secretary, a post he held until the election the following year. He never held office again.

Lowe was created Viscount Sherbrooke in 1880 and died twelve years later.

GLADSTONE – 1880

'When you're out saving fallen women, save one for me'

. . . So Disraeli is reputed – almost certainly inaccurately – to have remarked to his rival. William Ewart Gladstone was a great statesman – strong, grave, deeply religious, the personification of Victorian respectability. But frequently, the Grand Old Man of Victorian politics would leave the Dispatch Box and turn his remarkable rhetorical skills on a different audience. Four times Prime Minister, he would stalk the seedier pavements of London in search of prostitutes, driven by a craving he had battled against since university days.

Precisely what that craving was we shall never be quite sure. How far he satisfied it we do not know. There are many views, and from the story which follows the reader may form his own. Mine is that – despite evidence which any modern tabloid newspaper would interpret in the obvious, crude way – it is entirely possible and on the whole likely that Gladstone, an immensely complicated man of almost unfathomable depth, never slept with the prostitutes whose company he sought. Professor H. C. G. Matthew quotes W. E. Gladstone (on Leopardi) thus in *Gladstone: 1875–1898*:

> There is scarcely a single moral action of a single man of which other men can have such a knowledge, in its ultimate grounds, its surrounding incidents, and the real determining cause of its merits, as to warrant their pronouncing conclusive judgement upon it.

Gladstone was tortured by questions of morality and fascinated by sin. He was undoubtedly capable of resisting temptation. He exerted cruel self-discipline. He seemed to enjoy tormenting himself. I believe that Gladstone was in the curious, twisted business of arranging temptation, enjoying it, and resisting it.

45

He had plenty to choose from. Late-nineteenth-century London was said to boast one prostitute for every eight 'gentlemen' and, over a forty-year period, Gladstone got to know a fair few of the former. He made no secret of this. He was so unashamed he even brought some of the gaudily dressed women back to 10 Downing Street. Sympathetic biographers say that, once there, he recited passages from the Bible to them. No one knows whether the fierce moralist and respected lay preacher actually had sex with those he called his 'erring sisters', whether he paid them anything, or if so how much.

The risks were enormous. Cabinet colleagues begged him to stop. At first many of his contemporaries were content to believe his protestations that his aims were purely charitable and he did find a sizable number of his harem honest employment. Yet it emerged seventy years after his death, with the publication of Gladstone's fourteen volumes of diaries, that he was not himself convinced of his charitable aims. In one passage he explains how his motives were partly 'carnal or the withdrawal of them would not leave such a void'. He never much interested himself in the political movement for the reform of the laws on prostitution, or prostitutes' rehabilitation.

His wife Catherine, whom he married in 1839, knew about his interest in prostitutes. How much she knew, or cared to know, about his feelings and motivations is unclear. H. C. G. Matthew, whose study of Gladstone and his diaries has been as meticulous and thoughtful as any we are likely to have, writes: 'What she knew of her husband's sexual temptations, we do not know. Had she seen the scars on his back when in the 1840s and 1850s he used the scourge after meeting prostitutes?' Wracked by guilt he would flog himself with a vicious scourge. Even then he could not prevail. As a student he had written (probably of masturbation) about 'this besetting sin' which returned 'again and again like a flood'.

In his diaries the whipping sessions were recorded thus: ♄ His diaries suggest this self-administered justice was retributive rather than deterrent, although even retribution seems questionable as an explanation. Might it have been recreational? He seemed to enjoy it. In 1843 when he had just entered Robert Peel's government, he wrote:

Has it been sufficiently considered, how far pain may become the ground of enjoyment? In which case be it observed not only are the pleasure and the pain simultaneous and the first superior, but the latter is actually the occasion, the material, the substratum of the former.

Prostitutes had bewitched Gladstone since his Oxford days in the late 1820s. The anguish returned in the 1840s when he joined Peel's government. The pressures of ministerial life and the financial problems of his wife's family, from whom he had inherited Hawarden Castle in Flintshire, created a 'severe psychological crisis whose expression took a sexual form', according to one biographer.

In 1843 Gladstone, a high-church Tory, and at this time President of the Board of Trade, wrote in his diary: 'Fearful is the guilt of sin returning again and again in forms ever new but alike hideous.' He saw all sexual temptation as evil and a cause for guilt. At first he had sated his desires by reading what he regarded as pornography: Restoration poems, French verse fables, and classical authors such as Petronius!

In his diaries Gladstone gives a partial but revealing account of his encounters with more than French literature. On 13 July 1851, he wrote: 'Went with a note to EC's [Elizabeth Collins was a prostitute he saw regularly] – received (unexpectedly) and remained two hours: a strange and humbling scene – returned and *ß*.' It is clear by this time that Gladstone was forsaking the comforts of home very often.

15 July 1851: 'Fell in with EC and another mixed scene somewhat like that of forty-eight hours before – afterwards *ħ*.'
23 July 1851: 'I then in a singular way hit upon EC: two more hours, strange, questionable, or more: followed by *ħ*.'
7 May 1852 [about to become Chancellor of the Exchequer]- 'Saw E. Collins: bad: and there must be a change.'
1 April 1856 [back in Opposition]: 'Saw a Spaniard: and had a warning.'

Who was the mysterious Spaniard? What was the warning? Gladstone clearly never heeded it. During this time he was subjected to at least one serious blackmail attempt in 1853 while still Chancellor. A man named William Wilson was astonished to see him in furtive conversation with a prostitute near Leicester Square. He saw a chance to make a few farthings. Gladstone's response to the blackmail attempt was swift: he immediately turned Wilson over to the police. Wilson received twelve months hard labour.

The press reported the incident briefly and factually. There was not even a hint of scandal. But thirty years later, when Victorian morality was more rigid, the Grand Old Man, now the Liberal Prime Minister, was forced to accept that he faced a political, if not a moral, problem.

In 1880 the Prime Minister, now turned seventy, was visiting brothels in pursuit of his 'rescue work'. In a sort of 'back to basics' [see pp.308–21] moral climate – his own leadership had helped foster it – his ministers intervened and implored him to stop. They feared a scandal. The government was in peril.

Rumours that Gladstone was a philanderer had persisted throughout his career. Earlier he had enjoyed what was, at the very least, an emotional, intense and sexually charged relationship with a courtesan called Laura Thistlethwayte. In his early letters to her, he began 'Dear Spirit'. She had showered him with gifts, and as her general extravagance was ruining Captain Thistlethwayte, her husband, Gladstone came to fear that their friendship might eventually be probed in the courts. 'What,' asks H. C. G. Matthew, 'was [Catherine Gladstone's] view of the regular letters to and from Laura Thistlethwayte and the visits [to her London town house] and later to Laura's cottage in Hampstead?'

Gradually, his relationship with the woman he called 'Mrs T' cooled. His friendship with the actress Lillie Langtry was probably sexually innocent, but it raised eyebrows. It may have been acceptable for the Prince of Wales but not for the Prime Minister of the world's greatest imperial power. There had also been rumours in the 1870s that a close political friend, Madame Olga Novikov, upon whom Gladstone relied for advice and information about Russia, was a mistress. Modern biographers regard these rumours as absurd. What is more likely is that Gladstone's powerful sex drive allowed shrewd women like Novikov to tease his susceptibilities and gain political influence with him.

In 1882 Lord Rosebery, a junior Home Office minister, who was to succeed Gladstone as premier, demanded an urgent audience. Agitation over Irish home rule had led to threats on Gladstone's life. He now received round-the-clock police protection. Rosebery saw the potential danger and spelt out the risk of a badly paid bobby passing on the secrets of the bordellos to a press far more hostile than it had been thirty years earlier.

Despite the grave risks, the Prime Minister still could not break the spell. Three months after the warning, and with gossip running through the Palace of Westminster, Rosebery's worst fears were realized. A Tory MP spotted Gladstone talking to a prostitute.

Colonel Tottenham MP seized on an opportunity to discredit the Prime Minister. The news spread like wildfire through Westminster and respectable society. It became the talk of the Victorian chattering classes. But, lacking hard evidence, the press never ran the story. Gladstone denied impropriety: 'It may be true that the gentleman saw me in such conversation but the object was not what he assumed or, as I am afraid, hoped.' Gladstone survived. But to the amazement of his colleagues and his long-suffering wife he had not learned his lesson.

Two years later there was a temporary halt after another desperate plea, this time from his private secretary Edward Hamilton, but Gladstone only took the hint after a final showdown in July 1886 when Hamilton presented the newly re-elected Prime Minister with compelling evidence that a strong blackmail case was imminent. Gladstone, who was by now seventy-seven, made a solemn promise to Hamilton. According to his diaries he kept it.

'15 and 17 June '92 are the penultimate examples of encounters with prostitutes,' writes Professor Matthew. 'Significantly, Gladstone refers to being "accosted", i.e. the initiative was the prostitute's, not, as in the past, his.'

Still with years of public life ahead, Mr and Mrs Gladstone celebrated their golden wedding anniversary in 1889. Of their four sons and four daughters, two became MPs, one became a baron, one became a clergyman, and another married the Dean of Lincoln. Two years before he died, still troubled by guilt, he tried to set the record straight when he gave his son, Stephen, who had taken holy orders, the carefully worded statement that he had 'not been guilty of the act which is known as that of infidelity to the marriage bed'. This may be partly borne out by the nicknames bandied around the brothels during the 1880s: 'Old Glad-eyes' and 'Daddy-do-nothing'. But his diaries are littered with contradictions. When writing in his diary of one prostitute's second visit to his home, he felt he had been 'certainly wrong in some things and trod the path of danger'.

The man Queen Victoria called 'old, wild and incomprehensible' died at the age of eighty-four in 1898, having left office four years previously for political reasons unconnected with scandal. The country mourned, as the great Victorian Prime Minister was buried with full honours in Westminster Abbey. *The Times* wrote:

> Gladstone's extraordinary career owed much to his happy domestic surroundings and the sympathy and watchful care of his wife . . . Mr Gladstone has known the truest blessing and joys of family relationships. He could truly have repeated the saying of Edmund Burke that once he crossed the threshold of his home all the troubles he had encountered outside would vanish.

Others thought differently. 'Gladstone . . . founded the great tradition . . . in public to speak the language of the highest and strictest principle, and in private to pursue and possess every sort of woman,' wrote one commentator, Peter Wright – his remarks occasioning a libel action from Gladstone's sons, after the old man's death.

In general, it may be said that attempts to discredit Gladstone failed. It is a testament to his enormous personal moral authority – an authority which perhaps no British Prime Minister had achieved before or could ever hope for now – that Gladstone was enabled to prevail against so powerful a tide of national rumour. The rumour continues to this day; he still prevails against it. It is quite an epitaph.

CHARLES STEWART PARNELL – 1880–90

'This man is wonderful – and different'

'In leaning forward in the cab to say a good-bye a rose I was wearing in my bodice fell out into my skirt. He picked it up and, touching it lightly with his lips, placed it in his button-hole' – thus wrote Mrs Kitty O'Shea of her first encounter with Charles Stewart Parnell.

Parnell was a remarkable Irish phenomenon. He had a political party at Westminster named after him. He united his divided homeland behind his dream of Home Rule, made and unmade ministries and mercilessly obstructed the British Parliament. He won over one of the century's great statesmen, Gladstone, to his dream. By 1890 it was in sight. It had taken Parnell fifteen years to get this far. And for the last ten of them he had been living with another man's wife.

The lady was born Katherine Page Wood in Essex in 1846, but would gain notoriety forty-four years later as the adulteress, Kitty O'Shea. Kitty's father had once been chaplain to Queen Caroline, and her upbringing was comfortable but modest. An uncle, Lord Hatherley, was Lord Chancellor in Gladstone's 1868 government (a connection which later proved useful).

In January 1867, on the eve of her twenty-first birthday, Kitty married the dashing twenty-six-year-old British army captain William O'Shea. Dublin-born and a Roman Catholic, he had joined the 18th Hussars at the age of eighteen but retired from the army before his marriage. A vain man, with little income from his estate, he soon squandered the money his solicitor father had left him.

The O'Sheas had three children, but their marriage sank quickly into one of convenience. It was in the husband's interest to continue the pretence: he took generous hand-outs from his wife's rich aunt, Mrs Benjamin Wood. Fluent in French and

51

Spanish, O'Shea had relatives in both countries and spent long periods abroad, including one in which he bought and managed a sulphur mine in Spain which, like most of his business ventures, failed. In 1874, when he had been gone for eighteen months, eighty-two-year-old Aunt Ben, concerned for the children, bought her niece Wonersh Lodge, near her own home in Eltham, Kent.

Thereafter Kitty O'Shea lived in Eltham. Her husband, when not abroad, stayed at their London flat in Victoria. Partly to keep up appearances she would make the trip to London, hosting suppers for her husband's business associates at Thomas's Hotel, Berkeley Square. As the decade wore on, when O'Shea turned to politics, his guests would include the leading Irish politicians of the day. One of his targets was the rising political star among the new crop of Irish MPs elected in 1875: the member for County Meath, Charles Stewart Parnell.

Born in Wicklow, the son of a Protestant landowner, Parnell enjoyed an impeccable anti-British pedigree. His mother was the daughter of Commodore Charles Stewart of the United States Navy, a hero of the US war against the British in 1812 whose own parents had emigrated from Belfast before the American Revolution. The prevailing anti-British sentiment in the Parnell household did not stop his parents sending their son to school in England, where he hated everything except the cricket. Passionate in this un-Irish activity, he sustained his own XI.

He gained a place at Magdalen College, Cambridge, but never finished his degree. In 1869 Parnell got into a drunken street fight, the first of many quarrels. The fiery Irishman thought his victim was a pompous 'swell student'. In fact he turned out to be a respectable Cambridge merchant, who sold manure. About to be arrested, Parnell followed standard procedure and offered the policeman a bribe 'to settle the affair'. In his drunkenness he handed over a shilling, thinking it was a sovereign. Underbribed, the policeman persisted with an arrest for assault. Suspended by his college, Parnell turned his back on Cambridge.

And England. He returned to Ireland – a land now seething under Britain's coercive attempts to keep control. The revolutionary Fenians stood for armed resistance to British rule. Parnell was a striking, handsome and forceful presence, and a powerful recruit to the cause. He favoured a hard-nosed assault through securing the election of anti-British MPs to Westminster. In 1870 the Irish Home Rule League was established. Mostly Catholic, it succeeded in getting fifty-six MPs elected to Westminster in the 1874 election. The following year Parnell joined them.

Within two years he distinguished himself through his radical oratory. He cared little for Commons tradition but had a careful eye for Irish nationalist sensitivities. With other Home Rulers he used the obstruction of debates in the Chamber to draw attention to Irish concerns. In 1877 the Home Rule Confederation of Great Britain elected Parnell their president. He was now thirty-one and already the most conspicuous figure in Irish politics. William O'Shea recognized Parnell's growing strength and sought his friendship and support. At first he seemed to meet rebuffs.

In 1878 Ireland faced another famine. There were cases of families, unable to pay rents to absentee landlords, being mercilessly evicted from the countryside. Parnell saw his chance. He identified himself with their plight and the violent methods of the Irish Land League, which was resisting evictions and making rent-collection a life-threatening occupation.

Parnell thus became the centre of the 'new departure' in Irish nationalism: agitation at home and obstruction in the Commons. At the General Election in the spring of 1880, he was comfortably returned along with eighty-five other Home Rulers. One of these was Captain O'Shea, whose dinner parties in his Victoria flat had paid off. Elected MP for County Clare, O'Shea supported Parnell when he was voted leader of his party in Parliament. O'Shea was anxious to cement a close relationship with the powerful Parnell. He sent his wife to Westminster with a dinner invitation for his leader.

In her memoirs, Kitty gives her own account of that fateful first meeting when both were thirty-four:

He came out, a tall, gaunt figure, thin and deathly pale. He looked straight at me smiling and his curiously burning eyes looked into mine with a wondering intentness that threw into my brain the sudden thought: 'this man is wonderful – and different'.

After taking the rose that had fallen from her bodice, and placing it in his buttonhole, he then sealed it in an envelope on which he wrote her name.

He accepted the dinner invitation. The following year he moved in with her at Wonersh Lodge. Her husband later denied any knowledge (at this stage) of their affair. But he challenged Parnell to a duel in 1881, after arriving at Eltham to find the Irish leader's portmanteau in the house. Parnell accepted the challenge, whereupon the captain backed down. 'From the date of this bitter quarrel,' wrote Mrs O'Shea, 'Parnell and I were one, without further scruple, without fear and without remorse.' O'Shea threatened divorce, but when his wife listed O'Shea's own infidelities, the threat subsided. He was still dependent on Aunt Ben's money.

Parnell's politics were as stormy, opportunistic and intuitive as his capture of Kitty. His success at obstructing Parliament had led to the suspension of thirty-six Irish MPs, wringing from Gladstone the 1881 Land Act, giving Irish tenants 'the three Fs' – fixity of tenure, fair rents and free sale.

The Land Act presented Parnell with a problem. He was not the only Irish politician to note his compatriots' preference for martyrdom over results, where these involved compromise with the English. He had done business with the English and, though the 1881 Land Act, dragged from Parliament, was a significant concession, it did not challenge British rule. This could have compromised him.

With rural Ireland in near-anarchy after four years of agrarian protest, Parnell cleverly set about testing the new law by putting cases to the Land Commission the Act had created, and he travelled through the countryside talking up sedition. As a result he was sent to Dublin's Kilmainham gaol on 13 October 1881. Biographers have suggested that imprisonment was his aim all along.

Now Parnell's ascendancy was assured. He was a nationalist hero, imprisoned for his cause. Inside Kilmainham he could not be held responsible for subsequent events: the suppression of the Land League and a winter of widespread terror against British rule. But he was also separated from his beloved Mrs O'Shea, who was now expecting their first child. Claimed by O'Shea as his own, the baby lived only two months, dying in April 1882, before Parnell's release.

Gladstone's government realized that Parnell was the only man who could restore order in the countryside. With Captain O'Shea as the intermediary, the government began negotiating with Parnell. The resulting Kilmainham Treaty guaranteed further concessions to Irish tenants in return for Parnell's promise to quell the agitation.

On 2 May 1882, Parnell was released. Four days later the Chief Secretary, Lord Frederick Cavendish and his (Catholic) senior civil servant, Thomas Burke, were gunned down by Fenians as they walked through Dublin's Phoenix Park. The murders affronted the nationalist movement, as the IRA bombing in Warrington was said to have done a century later. Parnell, dissociating himself from the killings, used them to bring the nationalist movement under his control at Westminster.

He was put under twenty-four-hour police surveillance, something which caused news of his unconventional domestic arrangements to filter back to the Cabinet. Gladstone already knew, as throughout the 1880s it had been Mrs O'Shea who had drafted Parnell's letters to Gladstone and she had met the Liberal leader on three occasions. On 17 May, Lord Harcourt, the Home Secretary, warned his colleagues that the Kilmainham Treaty would not be popular 'when the public discovered that it had been negotiated by Captain O'Shea, the husband of Parnell's mistress'. The Home Secretary revealed how O'Shea's earlier divorce threat had only been silenced by the potential exposure of his own affairs.

Kitty and Parnell settled down to something not far from domesticity, given their adultery. Two daughters, Clare and Katharine, born in 1883 and 1884, were undoubtedly Parnell's. Christmas 1883 saw the couple in Brighton at a rented house. To their surprise the husband turned up. With only moments to spare, Parnell clambered down the fire escape. Composing himself outside, he then presented himself at the front door ten minutes later. The ignominy (when the story was related years later by Mrs O'Shea's cook during the divorce case) diminished Parnell's standing. Cartoonists sketched Parnell clinging to an outside stairway. An enterprising toy maker created a miniature Parnell clattering down a fire escape.

Parnell had never acknowledged O'Shea's efforts in negotiating his release from gaol and O'Shea grew increasingly resentful and distrustful towards his party leader and cuckolder. Though O'Shea pretended he did not know of the affair, a pretence in which his wife and Parnell colluded, tongues wagged. Aunt Ben, however, continued signing cheques. In the election campaign of 1885, Parnell was pointedly questioned about matrimonial fidelity in front of a noisy crowd. He refused to answer.

That election saw O'Shea re-elected, with the support of the radical Joseph Chamberlain. Chamberlain was hostile to Parnell's Home Rule, but talked alternatives with O'Shea – perhaps aiming to split the Irish party. O'Shea, re-elected as a Home Ruler, refused to sign a pledge supporting Parnell, but Parnell was still riding high, in Ireland as well as England. Gladstone's Reform Bill in 1884, giving agrarian workers the vote, increased his support. In 1886 Gladstone formed his third government, reliant on Parnell's backing, with the specific pledge to 'pacify Ireland'.

Parnell was now pivotal in British as well as Irish politics. Gladstone needed the votes he could deliver. Home Rule for Ireland depended upon him too. Only illness, or scandal, could threaten Parnell. It was now that his health began to deteriorate, and the likelihood that his adultery would be exposed started to grow.

In 1886 the *Pall Mall Gazette* ran a report headlined 'Mr Parnell's suburban retreat'. The MP had been involved in a slight accident with a market gardener's cart on his way 'home'. The

---

MR. PARNELL'S SUBURBAN RETREAT.

Shortly after midnight on Friday evening, Mr. Parnell, while driving home came into collision with a market gardener's cart. During the sitting of Parliament the hon. member for Cork usually takes up his residence at Eltham, a suburban village in the south-east of London. From here he can often be seen taking riding exercise round by Chiselhurst and Sidcup. On Friday night as usual his carriage met him at the railway station by the train which leaves Charing-cross at 11.45. As he was driving homeward a heavy van was returning from Covent-garden market, and this came into collision with Mr. Parnell's conveyance, damaging it, but fortunately causing no serious injury to its owner, who after a short pause continued his journey.

Pall Mall Gazette, 24 May 1886

paper added that Parnell often slept at Eltham when Parliament was sitting. Disingenuously, O'Shea demanded an explanation from his wife. She claimed the report was an invention of Parnell's enemies. Letters between the O'Sheas were becoming more bitter.

Gladstone, pledged to 'pacify Ireland', tried to introduce a limited version of Home Rule. But times were changing. The ageing statesman had not heard the new voice of Protestant Ulster, nor grasped Britain's sense of imperial ascendancy, as Chamberlain had. As Britain prepared for Victoria's silver jubilee, all classes united behind Empire. The mood was not for relinquishing territory.

Parnell backed Gladstone's Home Rule Bill. A miscellany of Whigs and Radicals led by Chamberlain quit the party rather than support it, joining the Tories in the No lobby. The bill fell. The Liberal party split. A Conservative and Unionist government took over. The argument over Home Rule was becoming a cruel tug-o'-war, and the looming scandal over Parnell was to give perhaps the decisive tug. The last century of Irish history may have been shaped by its brush with Captain O'Shea's bruised ego.

We know from correspondence that from 1886 until he filed for divorce in December 1889, O'Shea was well aware of the living arrangements in Eltham. We also know he was close to Chamberlain. O'Shea was embarrassed by his wife's antics. Newspapers dropped hints. In October 1886 the Sussex *Daily News* reported that Parnell had been staying with Mrs O'Shea in Eastbourne. Parnell was now adopting aliases (such as 'Mr Fox') as a shield against snooping.

In April 1887 a further bombshell hit. *The Times* published a letter, ostensibly signed by Parnell, expressing support for the Phoenix Park murders of 1882. Parnell's position as the unchallenged leader of nationalist opinion in Ireland was in jeopardy. He denounced the letter as a forgery but it took nearly two years for his name to be cleared: a needy Irish journalist called Richard Piggott, accused of composing the forgery, collapsed under cross-examination, and soon afterwards committed suicide. Not many years later, G. B. Shaw remarked: 'Put an Irishman on a spit and you can always get another Irishman to turn him.'

That summer, 1889, with Parnell wronged, judged harshly, then fully vindicated, the prospects for Home Rule and peace in

Ireland looked brighter than for many years. Furious negotiations continued through August.

A few days before Christmas Parnell went to Hawarden for talks with Gladstone, now Leader of the Opposition, returning triumphant with the promise of a Home Rule bill. The next election, due in 1892, might have delivered a majority for Gladstone, and thus for his hugely controversial Home Rule. The historian G. M. Trevelyan comments:

> No one can ever tell what chance there was of a solution of the Irish question by that generation of men, nor whether Civil War or Settlement would have resulted from a decisive majority for Home Rule at the polls. The question was never put to the test, owing to the downfall of the Irish Chief.

Captain O'Shea filed for divorce on 24 December 1889, citing Charles Stewart Parnell as co-respondent.

Had the Captain's patience finally snapped? Or had the financial inducement shifted? Aunt Ben had died in 1889, leaving her huge fortune to Kitty, his wife; O'Shea, always skint, was now interested in the estate. Other relatives contested the will and O'Shea saw the opportunity to join them, bidding for a share for himself rather than continued dependence upon his wife. This too may have precipitated the divorce. Or was his motive political? O'Shea may well have been acting for Chamberlain, hostile to Gladstone's and Parnell's Home Rule. This was a chance to sink their alliance.

The divorce would not be heard for nearly a year. Parnell, his health deteriorating, remained optimistic throughout 1890, but Gladstone wrote: 'I fear a thundercloud is about to burst over Parnell's head and I suppose it will end the career of a man in many respects valuable.' Parnell's supporters dismissed the rumours as just the latest slur.

Mrs O'Shea had no defence but her husband's own infidelities (she had listed seventeen). The evidence against her and Parnell looked stronger. The 1886 cutting from the *Pall Mall Gazette* was produced in court. The cook told of the fire escape episode. As the ignominy grew, the lovers chose to stay away from court. Unchallenged, Captain O'Shea emerged cruelly wronged by a deceitful wife. The divorce was granted, and he gained custody of the children, including Parnell's. Parnell gained his Kitty and lost his reputation.

'Do you believe in Mr Parnell?' is the question which will be asked on every hustings. And if there is not one solitary Englishman left among us, from Mr Gladstone downwards, who could answer that question in the affirmative, how dare we ask the nation to trust him in an affair involving the integrity and future prosperity of the realm?

wrote W. T. Stead, editor of the *Pall Mall Gazette*, at the time. (As will be seen later, such indignation was his trademark.) The *Methodist Times* summed up Nonconformist opinion:

This man has been guilty of deadly sin, and no healthy and honest Christian could accept him as a leader. Mr Parnell admits that he has been guilty of immorality of the grossest type . . . If the Irish people deliberately accept such a man as their representative, they are morally unfit to enjoy the privilege of self-government. We do not for a moment believe that the Irish people will really degrade themselves at this momentous crisis. But if they took the unscrupulous and obscene advice which has been given them they would sacrifice the support of the most powerful section of the Liberal Party, and the moral sympathy of the civilised world.

Back in Ireland he lost the Catholic Church, too. The Archbishop of Ardagh thundered: 'I cannot but look forward with dismay to our interests, religious as well as civil, being placed under the guidance of a convicted adulterer.'

Mrs O'Shea was portrayed as an evil behind-the-scenes manipulator. *Vanity Fair* wrote: 'The political princess O'Shea who must be obeyed' (a pun on Rider Haggard's best-selling novel). The last straw was when the Irish *Freeman's Journal*, which had always supported Parnell in the past, turned against him.

Gladstone, collusively allied to Parnell, tried to remain aloof. 'It is no part of my duty as the leader of a party in Parliament to form a personal judgement on the moral conduct of any other leader or fellow member.' The following Sunday in sermons up and down the country Nonconformist churches – the backbone of Liberal opinion – came out against Parnell. By now Gladstone had only one choice: Parnell or Home Rule? he asked the Irish MPs. Cecil Rhodes cabled Parnell from S. Africa: 'Resign. Marry. Return.'

But Parnell would not resign. Facing Gladstone's ultimatum, the Irish parliamentary party met for six days in committee room 15 at the Commons. Exhausted by their differences, forty-five MPs left the room on 6 December 1890, to found their own party under a new leader. Inside the room, Parnell looked about him: only twenty-five had stayed.

Ireland now had two bitterly opposed parties committed to Home Rule, one for Parnell and one against him. He commuted between Eltham and Ireland to fight hopeless by-elections for his own faction. His message became increasingly revolutionary, and although rejected by the majority of voters, it left a deep impression on the young.

In the summer of 1891 he and Kitty married in a simple register office ceremony in Sussex. Lovers for more than a decade, their marriage was not to last long. Parnell's health was fading.

Shortly after their honeymoon, he was forced to return to Ireland to support a candidate in a by-election in Cregas. Ignoring doctors' orders, he addressed the crowd. Refusing an umbrella, he stood bare-headed in the wind and rain, railing against the anti-Parnellites: 'We shall continue this fight. We fight not for faction but for freedom, . . . the fight my friends throughout Ireland are now waging and waging so bravely. I honour them for their courage and I will not leave them until they get a better leader.' Parnell had lost the suitcase his new wife had packed for him, and sat up in his wet clothes all night, chatting to a journalist. Ill, he left Ireland the next day, 30 September 1891, telling his ragged army in Dublin they would soon see him again. They did, a fortnight later, but not as he expected.

In England, at Brighton, Kitty nursed her forty-five-year-old husband for a week. Parnell had contracted rheumatic fever. Her account of his death on 6 October is moving:

Late in the evening, he suddenly opened his eyes and said: 'Kiss me, sweet wifie, and I will try to sleep a little.' I lay down by his side, and kissed the burning lips he pressed to mine. The fire of them, fierce beyond any I had ever felt, startled me, and as I slipped my hand from under his head he gave a little sigh and became unconscious. The doctor came at once but no remedies prevailed against this sudden failure of the heart's action, and my husband died without regaining consciousness, before his last kiss was cold upon my lips.

As the lid was closed on Parnell's coffin, his wife dropped inside the withered rose he had kept since their first meeting eleven years earlier. Kitty Parnell, whom Ireland considered the ruin of her lover, was advised not to accompany his corpse to Dublin. Public disapproval, the bane of their lives together, pursued her even now.

Dublin, loyal to the end, gave him a magnificent funeral.

It was a decade before Irish politics recovered from the split. Kitty, financially ruined by the divorce, published her memoirs in 1914, moved often and never remarried. Norah (her daughter by O'Shea) wrote: 'She has never stopped mourning Parnell.' Before her mother's death in 1921 at the age of seventy-six, Norah observed: 'She has the happy delusion that Parnell comes back to her at night, when things are worse, and draws her out of the black waves as she lays dying.'

CHARLES DILKE – 1885–6

'He taught me every French vice'

'In the case of a public man a charge is always believed by many, even though disproved,' wrote Charles Dilke, one of the most prominent Liberal politicians of his day – before his fall. He was to star in a bedroom farce of such fiendish complexity that the story might be offered to trainee tabloid journalists as an Advanced Level examination question, to see if they can render what follows in more easily grasped outline than can I.

Sir Charles Wentworth Dilke was elected MP for Chelsea in 1868. By 1883 he was in the Cabinet, as President of the Local Government Board, a position he retained until Gladstone's election defeat of 1885. Many saw him as a potential Prime Minister.

But the promising career of this doctrinaire radical with Republican sympathies collapsed on Saturday 18 July 1885. Returning home at midnight he innocently opened a letter from his friend Mrs Christina Rogerson. She had 'grave information' to impart.

Early the following morning the lady ushered him into her drawing room and dropped a bombshell. Her lawyer brother was acting in the divorce case of a Mr Donald Crawford. Crawford's twenty-two-year-old wife, she explained contemptuously, was intent on destroying Dilke. Virginia Crawford was related to Dilke by marriage: his deceased brother's widow was one of her sisters. Virginia was an extraordinary and colourful woman, in many ways more interesting than Dilke. She had a history. The daughter of a Tyneside shipowner, she had been forced to marry a man (Crawford) twice her age, and with a sister, Helen, had for years secretly enlivened her married life in the arms of medical students from a nearby hospital. She and Helen also frequented a Knightsbridge brothel, where both women had been conducting an affair with a certain Captain Henry Forster.

Virginia was now claiming that the forty-two-year-old Dilke had been her lover from February 1882 to the late summer of 1884. Their secret trysts, she alleged, had been conducted at his Sloane Street flat and her home in Kensington. For good measure she threw in more: claims that Dilke had a string of other lovers, including one of his maids, Sarah, and her own mother, Mrs Eustace Smith. Unfortunately for Dilke, this last allegation was true.

Mrs Rogerson then relayed the name of the next lady on Crawford's list: it was her own. Dilke gasped: 'Are there any more?' There were. Mrs Rogerson had left the worst till last. Crawford was claiming she had been coerced into three-in-a-bed romps with Dilke and Fanny Stock, a buxom serving girl at his Sloane Street address (also referred to by some contemporaries as Fanny Grey). Crawford was later to allege that, tucked up in bed with Fanny and herself, the MP 'taught me every French vice . . . He used to say that I knew more than most women of 30.'

It was clear to Dilke that Mrs Crawford had created the web of deceit to throw her own husband, Donald, off the scent. She was portraying him as what would now be called a 'sex beast'. If Virginia had a serious lover at all, though, it was not Dilke, but Captain Forster and, consumed by jealousy, her middle-aged husband had hired private detectives to report on his wife's infidelities. When he had confronted her she said that her only lover had been Dilke. He had filed for divorce.

It has never been established whether Dilke, undoubtedly a ladies' man, had enjoyed the kind of affair alleged, or any affair, with Virginia Crawford. Something about his self-defeating attempts to prove his innocence suggests that these allegations, at least, really were not true. But because he was known as single and susceptible, her choice of him to name would have been shrewd, whether true or not. It has been suggested that Crawford was anxious for a divorce anyway, but anxious also to protect Captain Forster; and that she had resented Dilke's affair with her mother. There was gossip that she had also been encouraged by Mrs Rogerson to frame Dilke – because Rogerson was bitter, believing herself to have been jilted by the politician.

Others have suggested that Dilke was framed for political reasons: he was a rising Liberal star; he was controversial; he was a republican. Queen Victoria, it was said, was amused.

Framed or not, Dilke saw at once how serious these accusations were. To have one affair might be manageable: but to bed so many, and to stoop below the stairs, and then get caught, was a bed too far.

As it happened, Dilke was himself engaged to be married. He wrote a painful letter to his fiancée, the upright widow Emilia Pattison. 'In my belief the conspiracy comes from a woman who wanted me to marry her – but this is guesswork. I only know that there is a conspiracy, from one of two women, perhaps from both.' Then, boiling with rage, he went to Mrs Crawford's house, insisting she withdraw the farrago of lies. She refused.

Dilke was in despair. His diary entry two days later says:

'Left for the last time the House of Commons . . . A sudden fall indeed! Such a charge – even if disproved – which is not

Sir Charles Dilke and his second wife (courtesy of Roy Jenkins *Sir Charles Dilke,* HarperCollins and of Hulton Deutsch)

easy against perjured evidence picked up with care, is fatal to supreme usefulness in politics. In the case of a public man a charge is always believed by many, even though disproved, and I should be weighted by it throughout life. I prefer therefore to at once contemplate leaving public life for ever.'

Even from a Liberal, to split an infinitive in 1885 indicated immense personal strain.

His wedding went ahead in Chelsea on 3 October under the shadow of the Crawfords' impending divorce case. Gladstone was re-elected Prime Minister four months later but, famous for his virtue, could not risk giving Dilke Cabinet office with the divorce hearing only ten days away.

At the hearing on 12 February 1886, Dilke was represented by the newly appointed Attorney-General Sir Charles Russell. (It was acceptable in those days for government law officers to take private briefs.) Joseph Chamberlain sat by his friend's side. The only substantial evidence offered by Crawford was his wife's confession. It had no legal force so Dilke had no case to answer.

The Attorney-General refused to put Dilke in the witness-box. Then he blundered badly. Without Dilke's permission, he told the court: 'In the life of any man there may be found to have been possible indiscretions.' He was, of course, referring to Dilke's affair with Crawford's embittered mother. The Crawford team had employed four people to muck-rake. The newspapers had a field day omitting the crucial word 'possible' and instead speculating entirely on Dilke's 'indiscretions'. Mr Justice Butt compounded the MP's misery when he granted Crawford his divorce. If Crawford's wife had not slept with Dilke, why was the divorce granted?

It was at this point that the *Pall Mall Gazette* swung into action. The editor, W. T. Stead, who was later mercifully to drown in the *Titanic*, shrewdly combined the sensationalism needed to sell papers with a self-appointed role as guardian of public morals. The previous year, in order to expose child prostitution, he had bought a thirteen-year-old girl for £5 from her parents: a criminal offence (though his behaviour toward her was unimpeachable) for which he received three months' imprisonment. He served his sentence ostentatiously, and every year thereafter wore his prison uniform in public on the anniversary of his conviction. His protest did succeed in getting the age of consent raised from twelve to sixteen in 1885. Now, after Dilke's court appearance, Stead called on the MP to clear his name. Dilke responded. He asked the Queen's Proctor to use his powers to annul Crawford's decree nisi before it was made absolute.

The Proctor granted his embattled friend's request and ordered a second hearing that July. Dilke was confident of success. By now he had tracked down the infamous Fanny Stock, who was happy to deny the three-in-a-bed claim. He also had proof of Mrs Crawford's adultery with Captain Forster, which she was still denying.

Even before the trial started, things began to go wrong. Dilke had been cleared at the first hearing; he was a witness, not a defendant, at the second. His lawyers could not therefore demand to cross-examine the treacherous Mrs Crawford.

Dilke's problem was therefore an almost intractable one in law: without the key witness, he had to pin all his hopes on counsel to prove a negative: that he had never slept with a named individual, whom he could not call as a witness.

Just eleven days before the trial Dilke suffered a further humiliation when he was rejected

Virginia Crawford (courtesy of Roy Jenkins *Sir Charles Dilke,* HarperCollins)

by the electors of Chelsea in a massive swing against the Gladstone government.

The trial started on 16 July 1886. The courtroom was packed. Rarely had a simple divorce case attracted such massive public interest. Dilke was at an immediate disadvantage by being called first to the witness-box. Mrs Crawford had the benefit of hearing Dilke's evidence before responding. Although she was forced to admit her adultery with Captain Forster, she stuck resolutely to her claim that Dilke had been her main lover.

The case lasted a week. The jury took only fifteen minutes to reach their verdict – the decree nisi was *not* contrary to justice. Such an outcome did not absolutely imply that Dilke was Mrs Crawford's lover, but it was enough for chattering tongues. Dilke's political career was finished and he immediately wrote an address to the electors of Chelsea:

> As far as public life goes, I have no option but to accept the verdict, while protesting once more against its justice. I can only, gentlemen, assure you, as I have already often assured you, and with equal solemnity sworn in court, that I am innocent of the charges brought against me, and respectfully and gratefully bid you farewell.

Dilke's plea of innocence received substantial but belated backing from a committee established by his supporters. They uncovered convincing evidence (which they published in a pamphlet in 1891) that Mrs Crawford's affair with Captain Forster was much more involved than she admitted at the second trial. There was also evidence of other lovers, and they established strong alibis for Dilke on three of the nights she had claimed to have spent with him. But all this was too complicated, and it was too late.

In 1892, Gladstone was elected Prime Minister for the fourth time. Reeling from Parnell's adultery, the new Premier wanted no further suspicion of infidelity in his administration. Although Dilke had been re-elected by the burghers of the Forest of Dean, this gifted politician was never again rewarded with public office. He held his seat until his death in 1911.

Historians generally doubt that any adulterous relationship between Dilke and Crawford ever took place. Virginia herself was by no means finished. She survived until 1948, becoming a public figure in her own right: as a writer and thinker, a Labour councillor, and so ferocious a campaigner against fascism that Mussolini blacklisted her.

LORD ROSEBERY – 1894

An Abominable Rumour – or a Snob Queer?

One of the most intriguing, yet unproven, scandals of the Victorian age involves the Liberal Prime Minister, Lord Rosebery. It is alleged that when he was Foreign Secretary in Gladstone's last government, he had a homosexual affair with his twenty-seven-year-old private secretary, Viscount Drumlanrig. Fear of exposure led, it was said, directly to the young man's suicide in 1894. Drumlanrig's father was the odious 8th Marquess of Queensberry. This half-mad Scottish peer, famous for introducing new rules for boxing, certainly believed the Foreign Secretary had seduced his son.

Queensberry had plenty to worry about. His younger son, Lord Alfred Douglas, was, as they say, romantically linked to Oscar Wilde. After the playwright's public exposure it was rumoured that the Foreign Secretary had known about and condoned the liaison between Douglas (his private secretary's brother) and Wilde. There were strong suggestions that the government's determined and surprising persecution of Wilde, through two trials, was intended to scotch this rumour.

Lord Rosebery had succeeded his grandfather as 5th Earl in 1868 at the age of twenty-one. Though an impressive speaker, this learned and bookish man has been remembered less for his political than for his literary skills. He published works on Pitt, Peel, Napoleon and Chatham and became Lord Rector of Aberdeen, Edinburgh and Glasgow universities. In 1878 he married the heiress, Hannah Rothschild, who died after twelve years of marriage, aged thirty-nine.

Rosebery entered Gladstone's government in 1881 as a junior Home Office minister. He was probably better known as the owner of a Derby winner. When the party split two years later over Irish Home Rule, Rosebery followed Gladstone, who later rewarded his loyalty by making him Foreign Secretary in 1892.

It was around this time that young Viscount Drumlanrig, a good-looking, hard-working but fairly dim twenty-five-year-old, was introduced to Rosebery, then a forty-five-year-old widower. A fellow Scot and heir to the Queensberry title, Drumlanrig had just left the Coldstream Guards, where he was a lieutenant. He was unmarried. Though lacking qualifications for the post, he was soon found a position as Rosebery's private secretary. The Foreign Secretary, impressed with Drumlanrig's hard work, sought advancement for his young charge as a Lord-in-Waiting to the Queen. As such he needed to be made an English peer in his own right, for Drumlanrig's father, the Marquess of Queensberry, had not been re-elected as a representative peer since 1881, and could not sit in the House of Lords.

The Marquess was a wealthy and hot-headed atheist, well-known in cycling circles, and had enjoyed his fair share of scandal. His first wife won a divorce from him in 1887 on grounds of his adultery with a lady called Mabel in Camden Town. He remarried very soon after, but this union lasted only a few months before it too was dissolved. When he heard of Rosebery's plans to elevate his eldest son to the peerage his reaction was startling, and strange. Queensberry sent angry letters to Rosebery and Gladstone. He even wrote to the Queen, complaining of the Foreign Secretary's 'bad influence' on his son: he seems to have meant in the direction of homosexuality.

To no avail: Drumlanrig became Baron Kelhead on 22 June 1893, and Lord-in-Waiting to the Queen. From this moment on he almost never spoke to his father, who was outraged. In August the Marquess pursued Rosebery to the Hessen resort of Bad Homburg in Germany where the Foreign Secretary was holidaying with the Prince of Wales. Queensberry took with him a dog whip. He was found, whip-in-hand, near Rosebery's hotel. The Prince of Wales persuaded the Chief Commissioner of Police to intervene, thus saving the forty-six-year-old politician from a painful thrashing. The Commissioner was able to report to Rosebery the next day: 'The Marquess of Queensberry, in consequence of the entertainment I had with him, found it advisable to depart this morning with the 7 o'clock train for Paris.' Rosebery told the Queen he found one of the more taxing parts of his job was 'to be pursued by a pugilist of unsound mind'.

Queensberry's attempted assault started society gossip about the nature of the relationship between Rosebery and Drumlanrig. Many suspected that the Foreign Secretary was indeed homosexual. He opened all his letters himself. Lewis Harcourt, the son of Rosebery's political rival Sir William Harcourt and no stranger himself to scandal (see pp.84–6), later wrote that this was not surprising 'considering some of the things which, to my knowledge, some of them must contain'.

The following March, 1894, the eighty-four-year-old Gladstone finally gave way to a younger man. Rosebery, at forty-six, began his undistinguished sixteen months as Prime Minister. He was more successful on the turf than he was in Parliament: both that year and the following his horses won the Derby, which only served to make him unpopular with the Nonconformist wing of his party. Virtually every piece of legislation the Rosebery government introduced was blocked by the Conservative-dominated House of Lords.

During the summer Drumlanrig was engaged to a young woman by the name of Alix Ellis. On the weekend of 18 October he accepted an invitation for a weekend's shooting at Quantock Lodge near Bridgwater, the home of his new fiancée's uncle, the MP Edward Stanley. At one point he left the other shooters and went into the next field. After a few minutes his companions heard a shot. They ran and found the twenty-seven-year-old Viscount lying dead with gunshot wounds. Suicide was widely believed, although the newspapers the next day reported a 'shooting accident' and the coroner recorded a verdict of 'accidental death'. Later the dead man's nephew, the 11th Marquess, told the writer H. Montgomery Hyde that he was 'positive' that his young uncle had 'taken his own life in the shadow of a suppressed scandal'. Another possibility is that he could not face the prospect of marriage.

Oscar Wilde's biographer, Richard Ellmann, believes the young man was being blackmailed. Nine years earlier the Labouchère amendment – 'the blackmailer's charter' – had been slipped through during a late-night sitting of the House of Commons. The Criminal Law Amendment Act of 1885 made, for the first time, all forms of male homosexual activity illegal, on pain of imprisonment for up to two years with hard labour.

Despite their estrangement, Drumlanrig had been the only one of Queensberry's sons whom he seemed to love. He wrote in grief and rage to his ex-wife's father – the young man's grandfather, who had arranged the first meeting between his grandson and Rosebery – Alfred Montgomery, on 1 November 1894.

Queensberry Estate Office

> Comloncon Castle
> Ruthwell, N.B.

Sir

Now that the first flush of this catastrophe and grief is passed, I write to tell you that it is a *judgement* on the whole *lot of you.* Montgomerys, the Snob Queers like Rosebery and certainly Christian hypocrite Gladstone the whole lot *of you* set my son up against me indeed and made bad blood between us, may it devil on your own heads that he has gone to his *rest* and the quarrel not made up between him and myself. It's a gruesome message: if you and his mother did not set up this business with that cur and Jew friend (?) *Liar* Rosebery as I always thought –

At any rate she [Lady Queensberry] acquiesced in it, which is just *as bad.* What fools you all look, trying to ride me out of the course and trim *the sails* and the poor Boy comes to this untimely end. I smell a tragedy behind all this and have already *got Wind* of a more *startling* one. If it was what I am led *to believe,* I of all people could and would have helped him, had he come to me with a confidence, but that was all stopped by you people – we had not met or spoken frankly for more than a year and a half, I am on the right track to find out what happened, *Cherchez la femme,* when these things happen. I have already heard something that accounts *for it all.*

QUEENSBERRY

Having lost one son in a homosexual scandal, Queensberry was now determined not to lose a second. It is perhaps helpful to remind ourselves that homosexuality was not then seen so much as an inescapable orientation to which some were prone, but more as a dangerous habit into which someone might be led by another more wicked than himself. The parallel is more with an addictive drug than with a personality trait. The whole thing could be seen as Rosebery's fault.

At the moment of Drumlanrig's death, some believe, Wilde had been intending to leave the spoilt and indiscreet Douglas for good, and announce it to Queensberry. But after reading the papers that morning in Brighton where the couple were staying, he felt such 'infinite pity' for his 'Bosie' that he did not catch his intended train back to London.

Queensberry now plotted his final revenge against the author. By bringing down Wilde's reputation as a playwright, which was riding high, Queensberry hoped to revive his own, which had been battered by his divorce and the suicide of his favourite son. On the opening night of *The Importance of Being Earnest* (14 February 1895) the Marquess planned to barge into the theatre and make a speech denouncing Wilde, but the author got wind of this and had guards block his entry. Queensberry contented himself with leaving a bouquet of vegetables for the author at the stage door.

Queensberry then left his calling card at Wilde's club, something which was to lead to the author's imprisonment and exile. On the card Queensberry had written, with aristocratic misspelling, 'To Oscar Wilde posing as a Somdomite'. Queensberry had finally committed himself to paper. Wilde, who understood Queensberry to have meant 'ponce and sodomite', was persuaded to sue, not wisely as it turned out, for criminal libel.

Though his family were embarrassed by their father, Lord Alfred Douglas's surviving brother agreed to pay half the costs, while his mother, Lady Queensberry, would provide the other half.

Wilde lost the Old Bailey case, but what made his subsequent prosecution for gross indecency so certain? Some have suggested

that this was because Rosebery's and Gladstone's names came up
during the six-day hearing. In fact at the start of the trial, Wilde's
counsel, Sir Edward Clarke, seemed preoccupied with this. He
accidentally called Queensberry 'Lord Rosebery'. The case was
going badly for Wilde. Young men had been found who would
confess to having had homosexual relations with the author. In a
last desperate effort, Clarke attempted to demonstrate the fragile
state of the Marquess's mental health by releasing recent letters
he had written. One of these he sent to his ex-wife's father, Alfred
Montgomery, on 6 July 1894, complaining of Lady Queensberry's support for the continuing friendship of 'Bosie' and
Wilde. The angry Marquess wrote: 'Your daughter must be mad
by the way she is behaving . . . I am now fully convinced that the
Rosebery–Gladstone–Royal insult that came to me through my
son, that she worked that.' [*sic*]

British newspapers chose to ignore the existence of the names
of senior politicians. The Continental press, however, were less
inhibited. They repeated what Queensberry had been suggesting
all along: the Prime Minister, taking a benign view of Lord Alfred
Douglas's relationship with Wilde, had created a top-level
conspiracy to silence the father.

After Wilde lost his libel case against Queensberry, it was a
matter of hours before he was arrested and charged with indecency.
The evidence Queensberry had unearthed, including damning
statements from a number of young men, had condemned the
playwright. With Rosebery himself the target of homosexual slurs,
accused of having supported Wilde against Lord Alfred Douglas's
father, the authorities could not now be seen to go lightly on Wilde.
Yet the Prime Minister did consider trying to do something to help
Wilde. His Home Secretary, Herbert Asquith, warned him: 'If you
do, you will lose the election.'

Wilde's first trial began on 26 April 1895. The large crowd
which gathered outside Bow Street Magistrates Court was hostile
to the middle-aged champion of aesthetics. They jeered Wilde as
he arrived. But inside the court the jury could not agree a verdict.
In the febrile atmosphere of the day, this increased suspicions that
they had been influenced in order to protect Rosebery and his
cohorts.

Tim Healy, the Irish nationalists' leader at Westminster, who
had successfully challenged Parnell after the O'Shea divorce case

(see p.58), begged the Solicitor-General, Lockwood, not to try his countryman a second time. The law officer replied: 'I would not but for the abominable rumours against Rosebery'.

Fearing accusations of a cover-up, Lockwood had a further reason for ordering a second trial. The name of his own wife's nephew, Maurice Schwabe, had come up. One of the chief prosecution witnesses, the self-confessed male prostitute, Fred Atkins, claimed at the first trial he had seen the Solicitor-General's nephew-in-law in bed with Wilde.

At this point, with the second trial looming, the *New York Herald* chanced its arm. On 20 May it reported that 'there is still a continued prevalence of gossip concerning well-known people whom it is attempted by current rumour to connect with the case.'

Sir Edward Hamilton, Gladstone's former private secretary, wrote in his diary the next day:

> The Oscar Wilde and Taylor cases have been brought forward again; and unless there is some cantankerous jury-man a verdict is confidently expected this time. A verdict of guilty would remove what appears to be a wide-felt impression that the Judge and Jury were on the last occasion got at, in order to shield others of a higher status in life.

This time Wilde was found guilty. On 25 May 1895, he was sentenced to two years with hard labour. There was no mercy shown. All of the author's possessions, including his children's toys, were auctioned to pay his debts.

In the General Election the following month, Rosebery's Liberal Party was heavily defeated. He resigned the Liberal leadership the following year but remained active in the House of Lords for a further decade, and lived on until 1929, publishing historical works and arguing for imperial federation. One of his horses brought him further triumph at the 1905 Derby. The former Liberal Prime Minister grew increasingly out of step with his party and by 1909 was considered an Independent or Conservative. In 1911 he was created Earl of Midlothian. His elder son, a keen cricketer and huntsman, succeeded him as 6th Earl. His younger son was killed in Palestine in 1917. In his later years Rosebery spent ever more time in his Italian villa at Posillipo near Capri – a resort, it has been pointed out, which was popular with homosexuals at the time.

After his release from Reading Gaol, short of cash in 1897, Wilde spent the remaining three years of his life in France and Italy. The guest of a M. Dupoirier, he said of the hated wallpaper in his room 'one of us will have to go'. He died in Paris on 30 November 1900, at the age of forty-four, a broken man.

In 1896 his one-time lover, Lord Alfred Douglas, had written to a French magazine to complain of Wilde's treatment:

> I am confident that the Government did not wish to let the prosecution of Oscar Wilde take its regular course . . . Why did the Crown take the very irregular course of having a second trial – why was the prosecution conducted with this extraordinary animosity; briefly why did the Crown manifest so eager a desire to obtain a verdict of guilty? The reason is very simple. The Government was intimidated; the second trial was the result of political intrigue. I would wish to ask Mr Asquith, the then Home Secretary, that if a second trial was not instituted and a verdict of guilty obtained against Mr Wilde, the Liberal party would be removed from power. The fact is that the Liberal party then contained a large number of men whom I have referred to as the salt of the earth [homosexuals]. The maniacs of virtue threatened a series of legal actions which would have created an unprecedented scandal in political circles. If Oscar Wilde was found guilty the matter would be hushed up. This was the cause of the second trial, and the verdict of guilty. It was a degrading *coup d'état* – the sacrifice of a great poet to save a degraded band of politicians.

There can be no doubt that such a view was held by many at the time, and that – even though it was endorsed by the unreliable Alfred Douglas – it was a reasonable suspicion. What is hard to establish is whether or how far the political establishment actually did act to secure Wilde's conviction; there is no question that the conviction suited them. It was at the point of decision whether to order a second trial that figures in the government could have exercised a decisive influence.

Rosebery once described politics as 'this evil smelling bog'. For many, a faint whiff is discernible here.

THE MARCONI SCANDAL – 1912

From Whitewash to Won't Wash: the Marconi Octopus

Though the mere mention of a minister in a divorce case was enough to warrant immediate resignation before the First World War, ministerial misbehaviour in the world of financial wheeling and dealing was regarded as a lesser offence. That is, until the Marconi 'octopus' wrapped itself around Asquith's Liberal government in 1912. Three senior ministers, including the Chancellor of the Exchequer, secretly cashed in (or tried to) on the boom in radio telegraphy.

The wireless was much in focus at the time, a symbol of progress. In 1910, radio captured the public imagination when the captain of a transatlantic liner off the coast of Quebec signalled Scotland Yard that a certain Dr Crippen was on board, the first time the recent invention had been used in police work. In 1912, impressed, the government awarded the English Marconi Company a huge contract to build six radio stations linking Britain to the Empire.

Rufus Isaacs, the Solicitor-General in the Liberal government, was impressed too. Before the award of the contract, he surreptitiously bought 10,000 shares in the sister company, American Marconi, from his brother, who was its managing director. These shares were not due to go on the market for several days. Although expected to do well anyway, they were given a huge boost when the stricken *Titanic* sent out SOS signals on the new wireless at 2.20 a.m. on 15 April. Seven hundred people were saved from certain death. Two days later, the Solicitor-General sold 1,000 shares to two of his friends, David Lloyd George, the Chancellor (see pp.86–92 to find out how else Lloyd George raised money), and Alexander Murray, the Chief Whip.

On 19 April the American Marconi stock opened at 65 shillings and closed the day at 80 shillings. But the three ministers tried to ride the boom for too long and lost their profits.

Although the government contract with English Marconi was widely known, there was a series of conflicts of interests though a less clear link with any hoped-for financial gain. In terms of 'standards in public life' the position was actually rather confused. However, Isaacs, as Solicitor-General, was responsible for the legal side of the deal and Lloyd George as Chancellor controlled the purse strings. Rumours spread that ministers of the Crown had exploited their position in the run-up to the flotation.

On 8 August, *Eye-Witness* broke the story. It got it only half right. In an anti-semitic outburst the magazine named (wrongly) Herbert Samuel, the Postmaster General, and (correctly) Rufus Isaacs, as beneficiaries of inside information. The Prime Minister, H. H. Asquith, rashly dismissed the allegations claiming that 'scurrilous rubbish was best ignored'.

But *Eye-Witness* had no intention of dropping its investigations. Meanwhile, *Outlook*, another magazine, dragged the Chancellor of the Exchequer into the controversy for the first time. The national press was forced to follow. Lord Northcliffe, the owner of the *Daily Mail*, launched a strident attack on the 'Welsh solicitor and the Jew barrister' (Lloyd George and Isaacs).

When Parliament reassembled after its summer break on 11 October, the growing scandal dominated the first day's proceedings. In a highly charged debate Rufus Isaacs, the Solicitor-General, denied that any ministers had bought shares in 'that company': English Marconi, the beneficiary of the government contract. He failed conspicuously to add that they had tried to get rich by an early raid on associated shares: those of the American sister company. MPs were unimpressed. Asquith, ruing his offhand dismissal of the reports, was forced to concede a Select Committee to examine the affair.

It proved a meagre concession. The committee was given an inbuilt government majority of three, and one star witness had disappeared. Alexander Murray, the Chief Whip, had clearly tired of the pressures. He had left politics and was on business in Colombia, beyond the reach of even the new wireless. He was fourteen days' mule ride from the nearest telegraph office.

In February 1913, Leo Maxse, editor of the *National Review*, appeared before the committee and seemed well informed about the case. Isaacs decided that he and Lloyd George should come

THE MARCONI OCTOPUS.

LIBERAL PARTY. "ANOTHER TENTACLE OR TWO AND I'M DONE!"

Punch, 18 June 1913

clean about their purchases of the American shares. When the committee accused them of having misled the Commons five months earlier, Isaacs and Lloyd George feebly protested that to explain the distinction between the two Marconi companies would have been too complicated. Both men had offered their resignations to Asquith when the scandal first broke, but he had refused to accept them. Now he was privately enraged. On 4 April he told George V that their actions were 'lamentable' and 'difficult to defend'.

Then further news broke about Murray, the former Chief Whip. MPs – their intelligence and trust already insulted – were mortified to learn that Murray had launched a solo investment exercise, gambling £9,000 of Liberal Party funds on the shares.

The findings of the Select Committee with its government majority became known as the Whitewash Report. A minority report issued by Lord Robert Cecil concluded:

> The acceptance by a public servant of a favour of any kind from a government contractor involves so grave and obvious a danger of corruption that if the . . . action is to be condoned by parliament we feel that a wide door will be opened to corruption in the future.

The official report, far milder in its conclusions, was now dubbed by Punch as the 'Won't Wash' report. However it was this, not Cecil's version, which was discussed for two days by the Commons. It was finally rubber-stamped on 19 June. No one resigned. Shortly afterwards, Rufus Isaacs was rewarded with the post of Lord Chief Justice of England. Lloyd George went on to become Prime Minister.

> 'More whitewash!' said the Falconer,
> Doing the Party trick,
> 'Throw it about in bucketfuls;
> Some of it's bound to stick.'
> 'Very poor art!' the public cried;
> 'You've laid it on too thick!'

> *Punch*

HORATIO BOTTOMLEY – 1922

'The greatest swindler of the century'

Horatio Bottomley could have been anything he wanted, said his *Daily Mail* obituary in 1932: a brilliant journalist, a first-rate lawyer, a powerful industrialist. Instead, the former Liberal parliamentarian came to be remembered as undoubtedly the greatest confidence trickster ever to boast the initials 'MP' after his name, and arguably the greatest confidence trickster, in or outside politics, of his age. He is reckoned to have amassed at least £50m in today's terms, from scheme after scheme of shameless, ceaseless and compulsive deceit.

Some seventy years later, and long after abandoning a political career, Robert Maxwell crashed to the tune of larger sums, but his losses arose from real business ventures, albeit failed ones. Maxwell left significant companies and publications behind and it can be argued that his deceits only multiplied, born of desperation, as his honest ambitions grew too grandiose to sustain. But Bottomley was a cheat from the start. Bottomley's enterprises were always and by design hollow, he never seriously tried to build anything genuine, and he left nothing useful behind. Knowingly, he took £150,000 from the poor alone, plus tens of thousands more from any board of directors that happened to be passing. His gifted oratory lubricated him through a diverse career – from professional gambler to jingoistic war recruiter.

We may argue the toss as to which man – Bottomley or Maxwell – was fatter, which more colourful, or which the more brazen public performer; but for sheer moral contumely, Horatio Bottomley leaves Robert Maxwell standing. A useful review of his career by the late Gerald Rawling published in *History Today* (vol. 43) provides a timely reminder that twentieth- century political sleaze was off to a flying start by 1922: in a style and on a scale that later politicians have emulated but never matched.

It is apt that Horatio Bottomley's verbal skill was first celebrated when he defended himself so cleverly against fraud charges (before a jury and the notoriously severe Mr Justice Hawkins) that, to public amazement, he walked coolly away. Hawkins took Bottomley aside and urged him to read law. If he had, he might never have found – and lost – a seat in Parliament, risen into – and fallen spectacularly from – public grace, and ended up in Wormwood Scrubs.

Bottomley's story is a classic snakes and ladders tale. Born in 1860, he was orphaned at the age of four (though authorities suppose his real father to have been not William Bottomley, but a neighbour and Freethinker, Charles Bradlaugh). After five harsh years at an exceptionally cruel Birmingham orphanage, young Horatio escaped to a nearby aunt, Mrs Praill, who accepted him on condition he buckle down to hard work. This he did, and then at fourteen he went to London where an uncle found him employment as an errand boy.

It was when he moved to a Coleman Street solicitors' practice and began working as an office boy that Bottomley had his first recorded introduction to the swindler's art: the managing clerk was coining a living from those city firms he induced to pay non-existent county rates. Bottomley learned well and by fifteen knew thoroughly the intricacies of the Lord Mayor's court at the Guildhall and was *au fait* with the swearing of affidavits and serving of writs: knowledge which would later prove useful.

At twenty-four Bottomley was making progress. He had for some time been working on *Secularist* and *Freethinker*: newspapers published jointly by Bradlaugh – whom Bottomley came to see as his 'political and spiritual mentor' – and his guardian and uncle, George Holyoake. He had excelled at shorthand while working as a court reporter with a company in which he became a partner. Now married (and unfaithful) to Eliza Norton, he began to produce transcripts of local political and municipal speeches in his *Hackney Hansard* and *Battersea Hansard.*

Next was born his *Financial Times* (no relation!) which came on stream and began to pay just as his *Hansards* went into liquidation. The official receivers took action leading to his first run-in with the courts. Bottomley was to say later: 'I hold the unique distinction of having gone through every court in the country – except the divorce court.' This last was a tribute only to

Eliza's forbearance. The legal tangle, centring around kickbacks from overpriced property transactions, was but the first from which he walked sweetly away, saying: '... though not of an advanced age, I see that I have committed 21 pages of crimes.' With £600,000 unaccounted for from £1m capital, his guilt has never been seriously disputed.

Bottomley careered off into newly discovered Australian gold, made a mint floating companies only to liquidate and wind them up, leaving the shareholders deftly diminished. To his increasingly crooked holdings he added what he called his 'stable'. This did not house his horses (for which indeed he had an expensive passion) but solicitors, accountants and retired boxers acting as 'heavies'.

In 1906 he ran successfully for Parliament under the Liberal banner in South Hackney. After a previous unsuccessful attempt in Hornsey, he unleashed a box of dirty tricks directed by Tommy Cox – friend, campaign director and general claque-leader for any Bottomley project – who defaced rival posters. One vote-puller was Bottomley's line of horses trotting down the High Street with saddlecloths reading: 'Vote for my owner.'

But *John Bull* was Bottomley's business *par excellence*: an early draft of the *Sun*. This vulgar, cheeky, populist newspaper carried the slogan: 'Politics without Party – Criticism without Cant'. With or without cant he was soon in court again, over the collapse of his goldmining activities and the location of monies from the sale of almost ten million elegant five-shilling shares, with forged certificates. Again he defended himself; again he walked away. It is difficult, at a century's distance, to credit the survival and growing success of such an obvious and complete fraud.

Louder and stouter by the month, Bottomley successfully recontested his seat in 1910. At a key constituency meeting organized by the Tory challenger, Cox recruited fifty men to march out in steel toe-capped boots, drowning out the speaker. But then Liberals have long been known for the inventiveness of their campaigning methods.

His political career was soon to be thwarted, however. In 1912 he went bankrupt with liabilities of £233,000. Obliged to give up his seat in the House and lose his Pall Mall flat, Bottomley's career in scandal was only just hitting its stride. He now flung himself into lotteries, which had to be routed through Switzerland to remain within the law.

"I COULD NOT LOVE THEE, DEAR, SO MUCH,
LOVED I NOT HONOURS MORE."

Punch, 26 July 1992

With the outbreak of the Great War, *John Bull* became ever more jingoistic, and Bottomley a prize recruiter of fighting men. For £200 and a percentage of the gate, he would take to the stage and rant for England. He returned to the post-war Commons as an Independent, with a majority of 8,315 and a temporarily clean financial slate.

Through *John Bull* Bottomley had sold government Victory Bonds at £1 each, against Whitehall's price of £5. The enticement to buy from Bottomley was the opportunity of a £20,000 prize in a sweepstake. But instead of buying Victory Bonds with the money customers gave him, he spent nearly £42,000 on two other newspaper projects, both of which ran at a loss.

Truth magazine began to expose Bottomley. Characteristically, the MP's instinct was not to take cover, but to renew battle. He began an action against a former colleague, Reuben Bigland, who had circulated pamphlets denouncing the Victory Bonds obtainable through *John Bull*. Bottomley was advised by friends not to sue – and indeed it proved a lawsuit too far. Its indirect result was that the Director of Public Prosecutions now brought action against him for fraudulent conversion in Victory Bonds.

For once, oratory could not save him, though in court he did manage to persuade the prosecution to adjourn each day at 11.30 a.m. so that he, now an alcoholic, could drink a bottle of champagne. The prosecution may well have reckoned it helpful to their chances. Another favour he sought was that the name of Peggy Primrose, his favourite mistress, who worked as an actress, be kept out of the proceedings though she had received £1,000 in bonds. Nevertheless, the prosecution dissected Bottomley, revealing that he had received up to £4,000 a week from receipts at his recruiting meetings.

He served five of seven years after good behaviour. Peggy Primrose remained devoted to him after his wife Eliza's death, and backed his unsuccessful second attempt at a comeback. Still regarded as a phenomenon, the would-be Lazarus toured the Empire, lecturing. But when he reached the Windmill Theatre in London in 1932, he collapsed. A second heart attack killed him several months later.

Horatio Bottomley is remembered for his reply to a prison visitor who, finding him sewing mail bags, inquired 'Sewing, Bottomley?' 'No,' was the grim reply, 'reaping.'

LEWIS HARCOURT – 1922

'Loulou'

Lewis (later 1st Viscount) Harcourt, known to his friends as 'Loulou', was the only surviving son of the great radical Liberal statesman Sir William Harcourt (1827–1904) who was Home Secretary, later Chancellor of the Exchequer. Sir William is best remembered as the man who introduced Death Duties in 1894 with the words 'we are all socialists now'. A celebrated orator, Sir William would probably have succeeded Gladstone as Prime Minister, if the Queen had not tipped the balance in favour of the erratic Rosebery.

Loulou was a sickly child: his mother died soon after his birth and he was passionately attached to his father. Until the age of forty his career consisted in being his father's private secretary. When Sir William died, Loulou entered Parliament, where he was to sit in Cabinet from 1905 to 1916, initially as First Commissioner of Works (he was responsible for giving London's parks much of their present aspect) and, from 1910, as Colonial Secretary. He left the government in sympathy with Asquith in 1916, ascending to the peerage the following year. After the war, his house remained a notable political salon.

In 1899, Loulou had married the fabulously rich American heiress Mary Burns, niece of the banker Pierpoint Morgan. Her parents' wedding present was a magnificent double house in Brook Street, which Mrs Harcourt decorated in the eclectic, ornate style then fashionable in New York. The decor, dubbed *'Loulou Quinze'* by visitors of the day, has been retained by the Savile Club which has occupied the building since 1927 – only a few years after Harcourt's death and the family's departure.

If the outward trappings of Loulou's life and career were conventional, the private side was less so. The Harcourts were an apparently contented couple with a son and two daughters, but Loulou's true romantic and sexual interests lay elsewhere. He was an enthusiastic practising paedophile, absorbed by children of both sexes. A great friend was Reginald (Reggie) Brett, 2nd

Viscount Esher, Edwardian *éminence grise* and professional *confidant* – not least – of the King, as well as many prominent politicians. They saw much of each other: Reggie was Secretary to the Board of Works while Loulou was Commissioner. Reggie shared his friend's sexual tastes but preferred boys to girls. He had a long affair with his own second son, Maurice, who also supplied a number of Eton schoolfriends. Loulou seduced Maurice too, as well as Reggie's young daughter Dorothy (the 'Brett' of D. H. Lawrence), putting her off men for life. (Loulou was not a physically attractive man; many found him repulsive.)

Reggie became concerned about his friend, believing his indiscretion and high public profile might lead to eventual exposure. Both men were Fellows of Eton, and, according to James Lees Milne's excellent biography of Esher, *The Enigmatic Edwardian* (1986), boys there were warned to avoid taking walks alone with either Lord Harcourt or Lord Esher.

Some time during the autumn of 1921, Loulou pounced on an Eton boy who, with his mother, was visiting Nuneham Court, the Harcourts' country house in Oxfordshire. The boy was Edward James (the future millionaire homosexual aesthete, patron of Betjeman and the surrealists, and owner of Monkton Hall). James recalls in his memoirs that he fought off Loulou's advances ('a hideous and horrible old man') and told his mother what had happened. She gossiped indignantly about the assault among friends in London society, and the story slowly made the social descent until it reached the police.

On the morning of 24 February, Loulou, who had been looking preoccupied for days, was found dead by his valet in his dressing room at 69 Brook Street – where he had been sleeping since ceasing relations with his wife some years earlier. (The room is currently Bedroom no. 1 at the Savile, but in late 1995 will become the library room of the Flyfishers' Club.) He had swallowed a whole bottle of the sleeping draught known as Bromidia.

Every effort was made to achieve a British standard of graceful untruth. At the inquest held a week later, Loulou's doctor claimed he had been in precarious health and the overdose might not have killed a man with a strong heart. Lady Harcourt also gave evidence and insisted that her husband had been 'most cheerful' the day before his death. The coroner concluded that 'there was not the slightest motive for suicide' and (according to

The Times of 1 March 1922) brought in a verdict of death by misadventure. Loulou's *Dictionary of National Biography* entry, by his friend Lord Onslow, claims he died suddenly at his country house after being unwell for some time, adding nothing more about the circumstances.

Political society evidently knew the truth about what was unquestionably the great politico-sexual scandal of the 1920s. Meanwhile, Esher quickly went through Loulou's archives to extract his child pornography collection, said to be the best in the world, which he carried off to his own house. Its ultimate fate is unknown.

The family, including the new Viscount, aged thirteen, left London soon afterwards and proceeded to live quietly on their estate in Oxfordshire.

This scandal, famous at the time but only ever among 'people who know', was kept out of the newspapers and has rarely appeared in print. I stumbled on the story quite by accident, while dining with the retired Labour MP and psycho-political writer, Leo Abse, at his club, the Savile. Leo mentioned the club's link with Harcourt, and gave me the outline. A friend and historian, Michael Bloch, supplied from his own research the details set out above, and I am grateful to him.

DAVID LLOYD GEORGE – 1922

The Honours Scandal: Lloyd George Knew My Father

Many of today's peers have David Lloyd George to thank for their position. Lloyd George knew their fathers, or grandfathers, and they gained something from the acquaintance. They took advantage of the Prime Minister's great post-war liquidation sale when honours were available for retail.

'Lloyd George spent his whole life in plastering together the true and the false and therefrom extracting the plausible,' commented Stanley Baldwin of the great man's career. Lloyd George had survived the Marconi scandal of 1913, and the war had disposed of Asquith, making him Prime Minister in 1916. At the head of a coalition government after the war, he enjoyed – in the fullest sense – the Prime Minister's gifts of patronage.

The sale of honours was nothing new in the early part of this century. As today, a generous party benefactor could find himself rewarded with an honour he might not have received on the basis of his good works alone. What made Lloyd George's abuse a full-blooded scandal was its brazenness: the sheer scale of the operation, with its permanent office hawking titles.

Money always had charm, but before Lloyd George cash alone had not usually been enough. The recipient of an honour had to have the right background and social trappings. There was an element of subtlety, coupled with a care that the practice didn't go too far. Things carried on pretty nicely for all concerned. Unfortunately, no one told Lloyd George, who came to rely on the widespread sale of honours as income. Liberal funds were under the control of the Asquithian wing of the party, while those of the Conservative Party (led by Bonar Law) were reserved for their own use. Hence Lloyd George found himself in need of what would effectively be a personal campaign fund to fight a general election.

To raise this money, he simply increased the sale of honours to audacious levels. The need for those purchasing honours to have the tedious 'cover' of a plausible claim was dispensed with. Anyone with the cash could purchase the desired honour in what became an effective, if seedy, marketing operation.

In charge of proceedings were the Liberal Chief Whip Freddy Guest (replaced in March 1921 by Charles McCurdy) and Lloyd George's crass, cigar-smoking press agent, Sir William Sutherland. But the real driving force, enlarging the scandal to its ultimately calamitous proportions, was the man they in turn appointed as 'broker' – a colourful character: one Maundy Gregory.

Gregory, the son of a Southampton clergyman, had failed as a teacher, actor, playwright and theatre impresario, and had served ingloriously in the war. But in this new guise a natural talent for fraudulent impersonation and deception flowered. Established in offices in Parliament Square, and claiming to be powerful and well-connected, he began selling honours to anyone who was interested, and who had the requisite (and very large) amounts of cash. For he *was* powerful and well connected.

A price list for honours offered knighthoods at £10,000. A baronetcy would set you back £30,000 (dearer because it was hereditary). A peerage cost upwards of £50,000.

Like any good businessman, Gregory proved adept both at creating products and developing his market. He would seek out possible customers himself, not wait for an approach from them. The OBE was invented specially at this time: in four years over 25,000 were awarded. Gregory would also scrutinize the list of those in the running for honours for legitimate reasons – and persuade some to pay up, unaware that they would have received the award anyway!

An example of this skilful marketing was cited in the debate in the House of Lords, after the scandal had broken. The Duke of Northumberland quoted from a letter sent by a government tout (probably Gregory):

> There are only 5 knighthoods left for the June list – if you decide on a baronetcy you may have to wait for the Retiring List. It is not likely that the next Government will give so many honours, and this really is an exceptional opportunity, but there is no time to be lost if you wish to take it. It is unfortunate that Governments must have money, but the party now in power will have to fight Labour and Socialism, which will be an expensive matter.

Trade grew brisk. Peerages were awarded at the previously unheard of rate of fifteen a year, while the same annual number of baronetcies meant that the average of the previous twenty years was doubled. Between December 1916 and July 1922 over 1,500 knighthoods were awarded. By 1922 Lloyd George had amassed more than £2 million.

Not surprisingly, quality of recipient was in inverse proportion to burgeoning quantity. Gregory was tolerant about the background of his clientèle. Money alone talked. Richard

Williamson, who received his CBE for 'untiring work in connection with various charities', turned out to be a Glasgow bookmaker with a criminal record. The 1921 New Year list saw Rowland Hodge become a baronet 'for public services, particularly in connection with shipbuilding'. No mention was made of his 1918 conviction for hoarding flour, sugar, bacon and other foodstuffs. In June 1920 John Stewart, a Dundee whisky distiller, received a baronetcy for 'public services'. It cost him £50,000. In 1924 he committed suicide with a shotgun, leaving debts of £500,000. The money he had paid for his honour was returned to his creditors.

Besides selling honours, Lloyd George gave some away – to newspaper barons. Between 1918 and 1922 Fleet Street received forty-nine Privy Councillorships, peerages, baronetcies and knighthoods. For a while it worked. But by 1922 Viscount Northcliffe (owner of *The Times* and the *Daily Mail*), Viscount Rothermere (*Daily Mirror* and *Sunday Pictorial*), Lord Beaverbrook (*Daily Express*) and Sir George Riddell (*News of The World*) were to turn against Lloyd George, and the days of his premiership would be numbered. The gods who had cherished him, and been rewarded, abandoned him.

Such widespread and shameless corruption could hardly escape public notice. London became known as the 'City of the Dreadful Knights', while music-hall comedians christened the OBE the 'Order of the Bad Egg'. In some Pall Mall clubs, when a newly honoured member entered the room, others would sing under their breath (to the tune of *Onward Christian Soldiers*) 'Lloyd George knows my father, Father knows Lloyd George.' In P. G. Wodehouse's *The Inimitable Jeeves*, Bingo Little refers to a peerage costing 'the deuce of a sum. Even baronetcies have gone up frightfully nowadays, I'm told.'

By February 1919, even the unfastidious Freddy Guest warned Lloyd George that the belated New Year's list was a 'grave risk' because 'the bulk of the recommendations' were for '(a) the press, (b) the trade, and (c) the capitalists'. Lloyd George took little heed, and the business flourished.

Patience was now running thin at the Palace. King George V objected strongly to the abuse of the honours system. He had begun holding up some awards for a year or so, agreeing to others with the utmost reluctance. As the abuse grew, so did the

monarch's anger. Sooner or later, patience must snap. And it did
– at the July 1922 Honours List. Published on 3 June, it
contained awards brazen by even Lloyd George's standards. Sir
John Drughorn, a shipowner recommended for a baronetcy, had
in 1915 been convicted of trading with the enemy. Sir William
Vestey, recommended for the same honour, was a wartime tax
dodger.

But the most notorious name on the list was Sir Joseph
Robinson. The eighty-two-year-old South African businessman
had been fined £500,000 for defrauding the shareholders of his
mining companies. His appeal had been turned down by the
Judicial Committee of the Privy Council as recently as the
previous November. No one in either the South African or British
governments would accept responsibility for nominating him.

Not surprisingly, there were massive public protests. Members
of both Houses of Parliament complained, while King George V's
verdict was that 'the Robinson case must be regarded as little less
than an insult to the Crown and to the House of Lords'. Despite
his efforts to avoid it, Lloyd George was forced to concede a
debate in the Commons.

It took place on 17 July 1922. His long and rambling speech
brought derision from MPs. Claiming that the war had been the
reason for the award of so many honours, he said that the sale of
honours to the highest bidder was a 'discreditable system. It
ought never to have existed. If it does exist, it ought to be
terminated, and if there is any doubt on that point every step
should be taken to deal with it.'

It is interesting to compare these public words to those Lloyd
George uttered in private to J. C. C. Davidson (a respected
adviser to the government and later a Conservative MP): 'You
and I know that the sale of honours is the cleanest way of raising
money for a political party. The worst of it is you cannot defend
it in public.' He further commented (also in private) that 'a man
gives £40,000 to the party and gets a baronetcy. If he comes to
the leader of the party and says, I subscribe largely to the party
funds, you must do this or that, we can tell him to go to the devil.'

Whatever defences of the practice he offered in private, Lloyd
George was determined that public scrutiny of matters should be
limited to the minimum possible. Two hundred and seventy-nine
MPs had signed a motion calling for a Select Committee, but he

prevailed with the tenuous argument that, as the Royal Prerogative was involved, a Royal Commission (with, as it happened, less extensive powers) would be more appropriate for conducting the investigation. His will prevailed. Further, the commission was instructed to examine general procedure for the future, not specific events of the past. (An interesting parallel with the similar limitation placed on the Nolan Committee's remit seventy-two years later (see pp.328–9).)

Somehow, Lloyd George managed on the whole to avoid direct blame for the affair. Revisited today, it stands out as far worse than many other parliamentary scandals at which society has blanched and enjoyed itself. It is hard at this distance to understand why the scandal never quite blew itself into the storm which the facts – perfectly well known – justified.

It seems the abuse had become so well known that a certain cynical tolerance had set in. Shock thresholds had been levered gently upwards, and too many people had become involved for Lloyd George alone to be identified as the moving force. Then again, many numbers of the Establishment had come either to owe their position to the sale of honours or to have close friends or associates who did. They were hard-faced men who had done well out of the racket.

The scandal did, however, help destroy an already discredited administration. Lloyd George resigned in October (the commission reported a month later). His successor, Bonar Law, accepted the need for change. A Political Honours Scrutiny Committee (comprising three Privy Councillors), and the 1925 Honours (Prevention of Abuses) Act which made it a criminal offence to traffic in titles, were consequences. Stable doors were bolted. Horses within whinnied; horses without grazed in tranquillity.

And Sir Joseph Robinson had to be persuaded to decline his peerage. When the messenger arrived in his Savoy hotel room to deliver the bad news, the almost totally deaf businessman thought at first that more money was being requested, and grudgingly reached for his cheque-book.

Further down in the undergrowth, the seedy Maundy Gregory had maintained his network of connections within the honours system and actually managed to continue for a while trading in honours. But in 1933, he offered a knighthood for £10,000 to

Cdr Edward Billyard-Leake, who went straight to Scotland Yard. In his resultant prosecution under the 1925 Act, Gregory was persuaded to plead guilty and remain silent in exchange for a quarterly pension. There were no doubt many prominent people, from those with humble OBEs up to men in strawberry and ermine, who found it in the national interest that Gregory was enabled to avoid a long and revealing trial. Some of their descendants sit in the Lords today.

RAMSAY MACDONALD – 1929

Prime Minister and Pornographic Love Poet

This is the slightest of stories yet curious indeed: a Prime Minister being blackmailed by a Viennese lady in Horseferry Road, over his pornographic love poems to her. The affair never reached the newspapers – never even reached the dinner tables of 1930s political society. It has been published only once, by the one surviving parliamentarian privy to the secret. Robert (now Lord) Skidelsky, in his book *Interests and Obsessions*, recounts the tale as Sir Oswald Mosley related it to him. Mosley is our only source and so before the story is accepted as history, the appropriate caveat should be entered.

Mosley (the future fascist leader) was a Labour minister at the time of the episode: Chancellor of the Duchy of Lancaster in Ramsay MacDonald's government. MacDonald went on to break with the Labour movement, head a coalition government in 1931, and end his career in personal political failure; but at this point, in 1929, he had just formed a government.

A Viennese woman of mature years, living near Victoria Station in Horseferry Road, was threatening to blackmail the Prime Minister over pornographic poems she said he had written to her. She was short of money and MacDonald had refused, she said, to provide for her.

Mosely was asked by the PM to act as secret mediator as Mosley and his wife Cynthia had introduced MacDonald to the woman while they and MacDonald were on holiday together in 1928. MacDonald had found her 'agreeable'. The Mosleys had been pleased to see MacDonald, a widower, with a companionable lady, and as pleased, some time later, to encounter the two of them together at a house party in Cornwall. Mosley told Skidelsky that it seemed MacDonald and the lady had interests in common: in particular he was told that MacDonald liked to read poetry to her. It was only after the election that Mosley discovered what kind.

In response to the blackmail threats, Mosely visited her flat in Horseferry Road. She had been threatening to sell MacDonald's letters to the French press. He did not see them, but persuaded her to delay action. Later she resumed her threat. When the issue was finally settled – she was paid £20,000 for the correspondence – the letters were in Paris, where it fell to the British Ambassador, Sir Charles Mendl, to retrieve them. Sir Charles read and destroyed the correspondence. He confirmed to Mosley its pornographic nature, but gave no further details.

The world may to this day read and enjoy MacDonald's *Socialism and Culture* and his *Labour and the Empire*, as well as the memoir he wrote of Margaret, his wife; but at the Prime Minister's talents in Lord Rochester's field, we can only guess.

T. I. MARDY JONES – 1930

MP Loses Seat on Train from Pontypridd

It is hard not to feel sorry for the obscure Labour backbencher T. I. Mardy Jones, who made a humiliating and unceremonious departure from Parliament weeks before the financial crisis which triggered the Great Depression. The House of Commons, poor Mr Mardy Jones discovered, can put on quite a show of retributive and socially selective justice, especially where a breach of its own privileges is concerned.

Thomas Isaac Mardy Jones had followed his father down the coal mines at the age of twelve. His father died in a pit disaster – frequent in those days. The son rose through the ranks of the Labour Party to become the MP for his home town, Pontypridd, in July 1922.

Once, MPs received no wages. Labour had successfully fought to secure small salaries – its working-class MPs had few other sources of income – and the socialist government of 1924 had secured a further privilege: MPs were eligible for vouchers which they could exchange for rail tickets between London and their constituencies. These were not transferable to friends or family. It was a clear rule. Mr Mardy Jones broke it.

He sent two rail tickets to his wife Margaret, and their twelve-year-old daughter, on 19 December 1930. Mrs Mardy Jones and the little girl, who made only rare excursions to the capital because of the cost, boarded the steam locomotive at Pontypridd, excited at the prospect of seeing the bright lights of London.

A first class single in 1930 cost £1 12s 9d (19s 8d 3rd class). An MP's salary was £360. The price of such a ticket was thus about 20 per cent of his week's earnings. Mrs Mardy Jones and her daughter took their place in a first-class carriage when disaster struck. They were challenged by three ticket collectors.

Mr Mardy Jones had been careless. One of the tickets was six weeks out of date. There was an altercation during which a tearful

Mrs Mardy Jones insisted that the tickets must be in order because her husband had said so, and he was an MP, so he must be right. The conductors from the Great Western Railway, a private company, were not impressed. They passed the distraught woman's name and address to the GWR police.

Christmas must have been a miserable affair in the Mardy Jones household as they anxiously awaited the knock on the front door of their small terraced home. The MP tried to get in touch with the general manager of the GWR but was refused a meeting. The GWR police waited until 6 January before calling. Mr Mardy Jones did not flinch from the truth. 'She had not got sufficient cash. I was short too. I am paid quarterly, and the cheque was not due until the end of December.'

The GWR showed no mercy. Charges were pressed. The day before he went to court on 6 February, Mr Mardy Jones, after consulting the Labour whips and his constituency officials, resigned from the House of Commons. He pleaded guilty to transferring two non-transferable tickets to his wife, and helping her to travel without paying a fare. His wife pleaded guilty to using non-transferable tickets and intending to travel without paying a fare.

In his defence, the former MP said he had needed important papers from his home in Wales and had been stranded in Westminster because the Labour government had been defeated the night before. He was involved in protracted negotiations to reduce the working day in the coal mines, a subject close to his heart. 'I was at my wits' end,' he told Marylebone court. 'My wife was there so I decided to get her to bring me the papers. Knowing I could not get tickets in time for her to travel next day, I sent her the two tickets I had in my pocket.'

Mr Mardy Jones might have got away with it if he had sent only one ticket for his wife, but Mrs Mardy Jones refused to leave their twelve-year-old daughter in the house on her own.

Imposing fines of £2 on each defendant, the magistrate, Mr Hay Halkett, compounded the former MP's ignominy. 'It is rather disgraceful to find an MP involved in a case like this,' he said to the reporters packing the public gallery. 'However disgusting this case is, and I think it is very disgusting, we have to remember that Mr Mardy Jones has risen to his present position from a coal mine.' The magistrate then ordered the former coal miner to find costs of £31 10s or face the prospect of forty-two days in jail. Mr Mardy Jones found the money. He had lost his seat.

J. H. THOMAS – 1936

Cabinet Minister Turns Budget Tipster

Budget purdah was abolished in 1993 by the Chancellor of the Exchequer, Kenneth Clarke. Before then the rule had prevented ministers discussing any aspect of economic policy which might touch on the forthcoming Budget. The very existence of the Chancellor's famous battered briefcase could barely be mentioned. But even after Mr Clarke's relaxation, Jim Thomas would still have been out of order. A popular and racy speaker, Thomas was a big, ruddy-cheeked former railwayman as renowned for his witty asides as he became for his unfortunate loose tongue.

Born in Newport in 1874, James Henry Thomas started work at the age of nine as an errand boy. At twelve, he took up his first full-time job cleaning locomotives on the Great Western Railway, eventually earning seven shillings a week. He earned his spurs in the growing trade union movement when he led his first strike at the age of fifteen. Aged thirty-six, he was elected MP for Derby – among forty Labour MPs returned in the 1910 election: the new party was taking wing.

As a young MP he was a victim of the vicious alcoholic wit, F.E. Smith. Thomas asked him the way to a toilet in the Commons. 'Downstairs,' said Smith, 'turn right and on the third door on your right you will see the sign "Gentlemen". But don't let that put you off.'

Thomas was by nature a moderate. He became general secretary of the National Union of Railwaymen at the end of the war, and his conciliatory stance helped settle the 1926 general strike peacefully. In the first Labour government in 1924 Thomas held Cabinet office as Colonial Secretary. He seemed to be on his way up.

Seven years later he was less popular among his old friends, having followed Ramsay MacDonald into coalition with the Conservatives. But by 1936, Colonial Secretary again, and quite at home with his new-found Conservative colleagues, J. H. Thomas was still regarded as potential Foreign Secretary material. That was until he breached what had become one of Parliament's more sacred traditions.

In the 1930s, the Chancellor of the Exchequer would normally announce details of the budget to the Cabinet twenty-four hours before he addressed the Commons, but with the Easter recess imminent, Chancellor Neville Chamberlain broke with convention and told surprised Cabinet colleagues on 19 April 1936 that he was planning the biggest tax rise since the war. Stanley Baldwin, the Prime Minister, felt ministers would require the full Easter break to recover from the shock: Chamberlain planned a threepenny rise in income tax and a hike in tea duties.

It was political dynamite. Coming a full thirteen days before the Budget statement there was an inevitable risk of a leak. Over Easter, Colonial Secretary Thomas shared his secret with his good friend Alfred Bates during a round of golf. When the Stock Exchange reopened a few days later the minister's golfing chum exploited his inside information and sold shares he thought were most sensitive to the tax increases. Days later he compounded Thomas's sin by taking out insurance policies against a threepenny rise in income tax. Betting on the Budget was a common practice during the 1930s but most punters insured themselves against a general tax rise. Bates got better odds by putting all his money on a startlingly precise figure.

On the morning of 21 April, Budget day, Sir Alfred Butt, the Conservative member for Balham and Tooting, went for tea and biscuits with his friend J. H. Thomas. It was a profitable meeting. As the Colonial Secretary lifted the teapot he told Butt to make the most of his cuppa as the price was set to soar. Before Chamberlain stood up to make his speech, Sir Alfred had

Punch, 10 June 1936, with headlines from the *Daily Mail*, 23 May 1936

obtained highly specific insurance cover.

Less than forty-eight hours later, with the country still reeling from the punitive tax rise and with housewives jostling each other in the stampede for pre-Budget-priced Brooke Bond, a keen-eyed MP, Sir Assheton Powell, asked the Speaker's permission to make a grave allegation to the House. MPs sat up. Powell told a hushed Commons he had detected an unseemly interest by a certain member of the public in insurance immediately prior to the Chancellor's speech. The unthinkable had happened. The Budget had leaked.

Baldwin was mortified. An immediate tribunal was set up to find the culprit. All eyes were on the handful of civil servants and government printers, but after eight days of exhaustive interrogation, much to the embarrassment of the government and the quiet contentment of the Opposition, the tribunal vindicated Whitehall's loyal public servants. Sensationally all the evidence pointed to a leak from within the Cabinet.

Butt and Bates were hauled before the tribunal. Neither could provide a convincing explanation for their windfalls. When recent social engagements were examined, the finger of accusation pointed at their mutual friend, the Secretary of State for Colonial Affairs. It was only surmise and would never have stood up in court; but shock rippled through Westminster. With his political reputation now annihilated, Thomas did the honourable thing and resigned before the tribunal damned him.

Meanwhile, some merry sideshows to the main event were uncovered. Thomas, it seemed, was a would-be author with a taste for insider-gambling. His golfing friend Bates had advanced him £15,000 for his autobiography which the Cabinet minister had not even started. And it emerged that using his Tory friend, Butt, as an intermediary Thomas had earlier gambled on the date of the election now behind them. Having placed a £1,000 bet on the country going to the polls some time in 1935, they netted a £600 profit from the venture. Sir Alfred Butt had no choice but to follow J. H. Thomas into the political wilderness.

On 11 June the former Colonial Secretary made a moving eight-minute resignation speech to the House and left Westminster for ever. He spoke of the 'humiliation and stain' of the tribunal's report. Thomas's forced departure from public life gave him time to write his by-now much-trailed autobiography,

My Story, which appeared in 1937. Not uncomfortable in his disgrace, he busied himself with his job as Chairman of British Amalgamated Transport Ltd and Vice-Chairman of Crystal Palace. He went to his grave in January 1949 protesting his innocence and insisting that he 'never consciously gave a Budget secret away'.

ROBERT BOOTHBY – 1940

'It never occurred to me'

Robert Boothby was one of those enhanced personalities who had seemed destined for high office. A supporter of Churchill's when few others would back him in the 1930s, his role at the forefront of British public life seemed assured. His *political* judgement in essentials was splendid. One of the earliest political disciples of Keynes and a day-one abominator of Nazism, he represented an enlightened and humane brand of Conservatism: a proto-Wet. But a scandal involving an undeclared conflict of interest in 1940 resulted in his resignation, and (until he took up the campaign for homosexual law reform twenty years later) estrangement from politics. He threw himself instead into television.

His biographer Robert Rhodes-James agrees with contemporaries that Boothby was an impulsive, rumbustious, easy-going and generous man. According to his cousin, Ludovic Kennedy, he had fathered at least three children by the wives of other men (two by one woman, one by another). He had a long love affair with Harold Macmillan's wife. Kennedy wrote in his autobiography: 'I once told him [Boothby] to his face that he was a shit of the highest order, at which he rubbed his hands, gave a deep chuckle and said: "Well, a *bit*. Not entirely".' Yet he was, said Kennedy, 'a companionable man of great charm'.

The cause of his downfall was his friendship with Richard Weininger, a businessman who had gained and lost a million dollars on the US stock market before the First World War. In 1923 Weininger became a Czech citizen, living in Munich and Berlin and with business interests in both Czechoslovakia and England. Horrified by the Nazis' persecution of the Jews in Kristallnacht, he had left Berlin for Prague. Boothby and Weininger both shared a concern for Czechoslovakia and in August and September 1938 Boothby – Conservative MP for East Aberdeenshire since 1924 and for four years the Parliamentary Private Secretary to Winston Churchill – visited the Republic and was greatly alarmed at its vulnerability.

Boothby's weakness was his gambling, made worse by not having enough money. It was his undoing. By 1939 previous investments had made his financial standing unstable and to ease his burden he got a temporary and unsecured loan from Sir Alfred Butt (see J. H. Thomas, pp.97–9) in August 1938. Here his problems began.

In January 1939 Weininger became concerned that his wife's personal assets, estimated at £200,000, were tied up in Czech banks. Weininger asked Boothby if there was anything he could do to negotiate their unfreezing. Boothby was currently working in the City as a banker and said he would try to help. This was to be a 'personal transaction' between client and banker, in which Boothby would take 10 per cent of any assets recovered. Rhodes-James says Weininger made the offer. The Zota Company was set up to secure the release of the funds and Boothby was given £1,000 expenses by Weininger to visit Czechoslovakia.

When Germany invaded Czechoslovakia on 15 March 1939, the trip was abandoned, and Czech bank balances in Britain were closed. The Bank of England swiftly set about trying to find the number of British holders of funds in Czechoslovakia and Weininger's wife put in a claim of £240,000 for herself and her daughters.

On 18 April a Committee for Claimants against Czech Assets was set up, representing most claimants in Britain. It was natural that Boothby would be proposed as Chairman, and he agreed. He omitted to mention his interest in one of the claims. It is here that he has been judged to have crossed the unstated and imprecise line in such matters. It was probably less clear at the time. Regulations governing members' interests were vague: they implied that an interest had only to be declared if a Commons vote was involved. The only payment Boothby received from the Committee was a small cigarette case presented in gratitude for his work on it. Nevertheless, rumours that Boothby was being paid for his work as Committee Chairman circulated in the City. Reputation counts there and such rumours were damaging. Blithely, Boothby dismissed them.

Interests became increasingly tangled. On 1 April 1939, for example, Boothby wrote to Weininger saying he would be staying the weekend with the Financial Secretary to the Treasury and that he would 'bring pressure to bear in that quarter'.

On 3 May Boothby received a letter from the Zota Company saying Zota would give Boothby 10 per cent of any assets recovered (about £24,000). The timing suited Boothby as creditors were pressing: on 30 June he wrote to Alfred Butt stating that the 10 per cent of the Czech assets would pay off the debt. Meanwhile Boothby badgered the Treasury to get a speedy decision on compensation for the lost Czech assets. He was assured that Zota's application was proceeding duly.

That same day he wrote to Sir John Simon, the Chancellor, enclosing a letter from Weininger and saying that British holders of assets in Prague should be compensated as soon as possible. Under pressure to settle his own debts, he wrote again on 31 May, pressing for an early settlement of the Czech claims. The clash of interests was now indisputable.

The efforts of the Committee were hampered by the fact that it did not speak for all the claimants. In fact the largest London claimants, the Petschek brothers, had not joined the Committee. This arguably weakened their case, and certainly undermined the Committee's standing. Boothby was understandably eager to get the Petscheks into the fold. He asked his lawyer, Colonel Harry Nathan, a Labour politician, to write to the Petscheks to encourage them to join the Committee. A letter was also enclosed from Weininger to the brothers. The brothers considered these letters threatening. They showed them to Sir Edward Reid, a prominent figure in the City. For Reid this confirmed suspicions about Boothby.

The matter was brought to the attention of the Chancellor, who interpreted the letters, writes Rhodes-James, as a 'form of improper pressure' being brought to bear upon the Petscheks. On the basis of the letters, Sir John Simon, who knew of Boothby's private interest, summoned the MP and accused him of using his position as Chairman to make money. Boothby, completely unprepared for such accusations, was dumbstruck, a silence later interpreted by Simon, according to Rhodes-James, as 'dejection'.

After leaving Simon, Boothby wound up the Committee and cancelled a cheque from Zota, but Sir Alfred Butt was threatening writs. Boothby gave him a £5,000 cheque. Shortly after this his father came to the rescue and paid off the rest of the debt; but the damage had been done.

Boothby carried on. He spoke twice in the House, on the Czechoslovakia (Financial Claims and Refugees) bill, about the special consideration which should be given to all claimants resident in Britain. He kept negotiating with the Treasury on Zota's behalf, still not mentioning that he expected his cut from any payment made to Weininger. By 9 August, Boothby was able to repay £3,000 of a £6,300 loan to Weininger, to whom he wrote 'I am hoping to receive a substantial amount when the second half of the Czech assets is paid.' On 17 August 1940, he wrote again on Ministry of Food notepaper complaining about the delay in the pay-out.

His fall came soon after. When the Emergency Powers (Defence) Act came into force, many innocent foreigners were put in gaol, Richard Weininger among them. Before his arrest he phoned Boothby and asked him to look after his papers. When the police arrived, Weininger's secretary phoned Boothby who said the secretary should hand over any papers – 'scarcely the act of a man with a guilt-laden conscience', writes Rhodes-James.

The seized papers were brought to the attention of Prime Minister Churchill and on 17 October 1940, he announced a Select Committee investigation into Boothby's activities. By then Boothby had been appointed a junior minister in the Ministry of Food. It was he who introduced the free milk ration for schoolchildren that would be removed some thirty years later by the Minister of Education, Mrs Margaret Thatcher.

The investigation was a disaster for Boothby. The Chairman was a pro-Munich Chamberlainite (Boothby was a Churchill ally), while Boothby's lawyer got hopelessly out of his depth. The

Select Committee concluded that Boothby should have declared his special interest in Weininger's holdings. This was hardly disputable. What, however, can be maintained in Boothby's defence is that his omission was innocent, or no more than negligent, or at least only marginally culpable – something widely believed at the time. What was so damaging to Boothby was that the Committee went on to remark that 'Mr Boothby's conduct was contrary to the usage and derogatory to the dignity of the House and inconsistent with the standards which Parliament is entitled to expect from its members.' In the view of Rhodes-James, the report, and the subsequent destruction of Boothby's career, turned on the malice of a political enemy.

Boothby resigned from the Food Ministry. He had the sympathy of most MPs and Downing Street let it be known that it would oppose any effort to expel him.

On 28 January 1941, the report was debated in the Commons. Boothby made his resignation speech. Churchill wrote later that Boothby gave a 'remarkable Parliamentary performance that perceptibly affected the opinion of the House'. The speech was certainly remarkable in its candour: 'Looking back, the whole unfortunate business seems so unnecessary. A post-script in a letter, a sentence or two in a conversation or a speech – which could have altered neither the facts nor the course of events nor my conduct in relation to them are all, it seems, that were required. But it never occurred to me that they were necessary. It may be that I was thoughtless . . .' He echoed similar thoughts in his autobiography, years later: 'The single sentence "I have an interest to declare" would, it seems, have cleared me. I can only say that it never occurred to me to say it.'

He had been, after all, working for many people; and was paid by only one, a close personal friend. It is hard to see how non-disclosure affected his conduct.

Boothby remained in public life, although not in the way he might have anticipated. In 1958 he became the 1st Baron Boothby of Buchan and Rattray Head.

He had a flair for the bold gesture and enjoyed publicity. Even as an MP he had raised smiles by a weekly dispatch of herrings to his friend Noël Coward, as part of his campaign to popularize the fish. 'Lord Boothby remembers the frisson,' writes Coward's biographer, 'that swept through his office in the City when a telegram arrived addressed to him: MEET ME TONIGHT IN DREAMLAND 10.00PM – NOEL COWARD.' Dreamland in Margate was one of Coward's beloved amusement parks. Boothby also turned himself into what we were learning to call a television personality. But scandal of a sort was again to seek him out. Boothby became a prominent homosexual law reform campaigner, championing the cause when it was taboo in the press. Michael Foot described him as a 'non-playing captain'. Others say different. He may have played for both teams.

A speech in 1954 started off his personal campaign and he began putting down Parliamentary Questions on the subject. He went to see the charmless Home Secretary, Sir David Maxwell-Fyffe, who replied: 'I am not going down as the man who made sodomy legal.' But Maxwell-Fyffe referred the matter to a committee headed by Sir John Wolfenden. It is upon Wolfenden's work that twentieth-century homosexual law reform can be said to have been founded.

Years later, on 11 July 1964, scandal broke. The *Sunday Mirror* splashed: 'Peer and a Gangster: Yard Probe Public Men at Seaside Parties'. The front-page article alleged that Scotland Yard was investigating a homosexual relationship between a peer and a London thug. The following Sunday the same paper again splashed the story, claiming it had a photo: 'The Picture We Must Not Print'.

In fact a photo did exist: of Ronnie Kray, who was homosexual, and Boothby in the latter's flat. By not printing it, the paper inflated its importance. The article described it as 'of the highest significance and public concern', but in reality it was not. An outraged Boothby wrote to *The Times* on 31 May 1964, explaining all. Kray had been to his flat to discuss a business arrangement, but nothing came of it and no deal was struck. Before he left, Kray, who was in the habit of getting himself photographed with famous people, asked for a photo with Boothby, who obliged. Boothby maintained he did not know about Kray's gangster connections. Whether or not he did, the sexual innuendo may have been spurious.

A letter from Boothby was printed in full and without comment. The *Sunday Mirror* acknowledged there was no truth in the allegations and Boothby received a full apology. The paper's editor was sacked, and Boothby was paid £40,000 in compensation. The case never even went to court.

Reviewing Boothby's life in his sympathetic *Bob Boothby, A Portrait*, Robert Rhodes-James believes Boothby was unlucky. He is one of those unfortunate men whose reputations have become a smudge in public memory: 'some sort of scandal, wasn't there?' we murmur, remembering perhaps that there was something about his cut from a financial deal involving Czechoslovakia, something about homosexuality, and something about the Krays. Yet when each matter is viewed separately, as each ought to be, the vague impression of monolithic scandal, like some great rock, apparently glimpsed through a fog, scatters; and we see only shards of flotsam.

SIR PAUL LATHAM and WILLIAM FIELD – 1941 and 1953

Two Routes to Oblivion

When in 1941 King George VI invoked an ancient procedure which had not been used since 1815 to inform Parliament that a member who served in the army was to face a court martial, Sir Paul Latham, MP and officer in the 70th (Sussex) Searchlight Regiment, Royal Artillery, was recovering from attempted suicide.

Thirty-six-year-old Latham had been charged in June 1941 with improper conduct with three gunners and a civilian man, his behaviour having been discovered when a letter written to him by one of the gunners was opened in his absence. 'Well, there's only one answer: a motorbike,' the rich young officer, who owned Hurstmonceux Castle, had replied to a fellow-officer who had urged him to 'stick out' his difficulties.

Hauling his artificial leg over the saddle of a motorbike, he roared off and hit a tree. He was found by the roadside with serious head injuries. Much good it did him! Eton and Oxford-educated Sir Paul was charged with fourteen offences (to which the charge of attempted suicide – then a crime – was added), convicted of eleven, cashiered, and sentenced to two years' imprisonment. He was forced to resign his seat as Conservative MP for Scarborough and Whitby.

It seems, in retrospect, astonishingly brutal. The MP (2nd Baronet of Crow Clump) had three years earlier announced that he would not be seeking re-election for Scarborough and Whitby – 'for family reasons'. His marriage to Lady Patricia Doreen Moore, the only daughter of the 10th Earl of Drogheda, had since been dissolved. Until his death in 1955, Latham lived quietly, farmed, and worked for others.

When, twelve years later, William James Field, Labour MP for North Paddington, appeared at Bow Street Magistrates' Court charged with importuning men for an immoral purpose, his occupation was recorded as 'biochemist'. That is what, in a panic, he had told the police constable who arrested him in a public lavatory at Piccadilly Circus tube station. Much good it did *him*. He was forced to resign

William Field put up more of a fight than Latham had. The forty-three-year-old MP initially admitted his occupation to the officer arresting him. But at the police station, on being asked whether 'you want that to go in as your occupation? Have you got some other occupation you could put down?' he came up with 'biochemist'. He also changed his plea to 'not guilty', and appealed against his initial conviction (on 7 January 1953). He said the suggestion that he describe himself as a biochemist had put in his mind the idea that the matter could be quickly disposed of, and that was why he had at first pleaded 'guilty'. This annoyed the judge, who accused him of dragging matters out.

The first court had heard he had been seen to visit toilets in Piccadilly Circus tube station and Leicester Square five times between 9.25 p.m. and 10.14 p.m. 'During these visits he stood beside or in front of various young men, smiled at them, and looked in the direction of their persons. None of the persons [sic] in the urinals appeared to be affected by his conduct'. In his defence, the biochemist MP said he had been worried about political matters and his mother's health; that the House of Commons was not open and he did not belong to any West End clubs. He went to the toilet for perfectly natural reasons, he said, after a meal at the Corner House in Piccadilly Circus. He added that it had been a very cold night. He was found guilty and fined £15 with £21 costs.

In the run-up to a final appeal, Field's woes mounted. His Hammersmith house was burgled and jewellery and silver plates were stolen. The appeal was dismissed on 30 October. Field took the Chiltern Hundreds and left the Commons a few days later.

GARY ALLIGHAN –1947

'Approaching the fringe of semi-sobriety'

Who, do you suppose, was the last MP to be expelled from the House? A rapist? A murderer? A war-traitor? An international crook? No. It was a man who admitted in print that MPs leak stories to journalists for reward, favours or drinks. He also suggested that MPs get drunk. The House was outraged. The full wrath of an affronted legislature came down upon his head.

Gary Allighan was both an MP and a journalist. The Labour MP for Gravesend had started his career working for Horatio Bottomley (see pp.79–83) as an assistant editor, and worked on the *Luton News*. He had also been a news editor of the *Daily Mirror*. He had served two masters – press and Parliament – and when it came to the crunch, Allighan devoted his loyalty to the wrong one.

He was hauled up before the Commons Privileges Committee after writing an article in the *World Press News* 'exposing' the means lobby correspondents were using to obtain leaks and insider information. The technique, he said, was to ply MPs with drink until they collapsed into the proverbial 'well-placed source'. This was what enraged his colleagues, but what gave them the stick with which to beat him was the discovery that he was, himself, just such a source.

Under the headline 'Labour MP reveals his concept of how party news gets out. Public that pays is entitled to know', he wrote:

> Every newspaper on Fleet Street has anything up to half a dozen MPs on its 'contacts' list . . . some of the contacts are on a retainer, some get paid for what they produce, some are content to accept 'payment in kind' – personal publicity. I, as news editor of the *Daily Mirror*, used to 'OK' payments to several regular MP contacts, both for stories, info' and tip-offs. At least two of them were prominent MPs – one is a Cabinet minister of such prominence as to be in the first four of potential premiers.
>
> That is one way any enterprising newspaper gets what the Party calls 'leaks'. Another way more accurately justifies that description. MPs leak around the bar. Being no less human than subs, some MPs 'knock 'em back' at the bar and, being less absorptive than reporters, become lubricated into loquacity.
>
> No worthwhile reporter could fail to get the stuff. If he knew no other way, and had no other contacts, all he would have to do would be to spend his time, and the paper's money, at the bar and if he did not pick up enough bits and pieces from MPs in search of refreshment to make a first-rate story, he ought to be fired. Herbert Morrison is not half the Party 'boss' he is accused of being – if he were he would put the bar out of bounds to Labour MPs, some of whom have succeeded in approaching the fringe of semi-sobriety.

Herbert Morrison was on the Privileges Committee. A motion was put to discharge Allighan for contempt.

The committee called in the editors of every daily title to give evidence. They were all sworn in, except Peter Zinkin of the *Daily Worker*, who affirmed. The *Evening Standard* editor admitted that he paid £330 a week to the *Trans-Atlantic News Agency* for political reports and that two detailed accounts of a private Labour Party meeting over the lowering of the length of National Service that had recently appeared in his newspaper were authored by Gary Allighan. Allighan, who admitted having a controlling interest in the news agency, though a nominee was registered as proprietor, told the gathering he had supplied reports of the meeting out of journalistic duty which he had seen ('wrongly' he said) as higher than his duty as a politician. (At the time, twenty-two MPs were members of the National Union of Journalists.) Allighan's article had appeared in the *World Press News* on 3 April 1947. The committee's inquiry began at a time when full details of the meeting were splashed across ten evening and daily newspapers.

The plot thickened when the editor of the *Evening News* admitted paying £35 weekly to an MP source, though he would not reveal whom. It was not Allighan.

The Privileges Committee Report, censuring the MP severely, said Allighan had aggravated his contempt by trying to cast suspicion on other MPs beside himself.

Allighan let off steam in the *Evening Standard*:

> Who could have taken the speeches down? I reply: anyone of the score or more MPs who can be seen at every Party meeting making voluminous notes. On one occasion – here I 'leak' – the chairman had to appeal to them to restrain their note-taking energy.

He admitted he had occasionally leaked a couple of reports, and called for the private meetings to be opened, saying 'secret diplomacy' was evil.

Next, the committee received a letter from Allighan's doctor, saying the MP was on the brink of a nervous breakdown and had made arrangements to travel to South Africa to rest.

On 4 August, Evelyn Walkden, Labour MP for West Riding, rose up nervously to make a 'personal statement' to the House. He admitted giving information to the *Evening News*, whose reporter had 'protected' him as a source. He described how he would receive the £35 payment more or less each week, sometimes over a cup of tea with the lobby correspondent. However, the former trade union official said that he had disclosed his £35 to the Inland Revenue. He survived.

On 30 October the same year, with the Privileges Committee Report on the table, the Commons voted to expel Gary Allighan, who thus became, in 1947, the most recent MP to be expelled from the House. He moved to South Africa, where he became Principal at the Premier School of Journalism in Johannesburg and wrote numerous books.

Allighan said that on the eve of his election in 1945, he, Hector McNeil and Michael Foot had made a solemn promise never to drink alcohol in the House. Perhaps if he had drunk a little more, and published a little less under his own name, he would have stayed the course. Dozens of other MPs quietly altered their arrangements with the press as a result of this episode, and some (though not all) of the practices Allighan alleged were swiftly and silently ended.

TOM DRIBERG – 1942–76

One That Got Away

'Sex is only enjoyable,' said the professionally outrageous left-wing Labour MP Tom Driberg, 'with someone you have never met before and will never meet again.' From the 'cottages' (public lavatories) of London, to the large underground urinal behind the Metropole Hotel in Moscow – the delights of which he revealed to the spy Guy Burgess – and his regular trips to Westminster privies with House of Commons kitchen staff, Driberg had, in his own words, 'a chronic, life-long, love-hate relationship with lavatories'. Tom Driberg was an early but enthusiastic apostle of the doctrine that there is no such thing as a heterosexual male, but some are a bit abstinate

This was one great scandal which, ever hinted at, never functioned as a scandal. It is only thanks to Driberg's frank but unfinished, autobiography, *Ruling Passions*, published after his death in 1976 that a wider public can share a secret which was common knowledge at Westminster. Indeed, even beyond. After I joined the Foreign Office in 1976 I was asked to compile a guest list of 'cultured' MPs to accompany the Foreign Secretary, Jim Callaghan, when he entertained his Scandinavian counterpart at the opera at Covent Garden. It struck me that Driberg was suitable and I included his name. My head of department struck it out. I asked him why. 'Can't say,' he said, 'but don't ever include Driberg. On anything.'

Everybody who needed to, knew. But somehow knowledge never went wider. Driberg had friends in Fleet Street and contacts in MI5 and MI6. His veiled threat to expose other gay parliamentary colleagues would, if carried out, have kept the headline writers occupied for years and taken us further 'back to basics' than we quite wish to go.

During his adult life it was rare for the MP for Maldon in Essex (and later for Barking) to go more than a few days without sex. Even two happily married Labour leaders were not safe from Driberg's voracious sexual appetite.

He had started early. At the age of ten, his first fumblings with another boy in the cubicles at school encouraged him to explore the local public lavatories. His first true sexual experience soon followed: 'the impatient sperm would not be contained and the coming was a good deal hotter and faster than that of the Magi', he recalled, with characteristic restraint, in his autobiography. At Oxford, seducing a don, he 'managed what I have experienced, otherwise, only once in my life – an exercise in soixante-neuf culminating in exactly simultaneous ejaculations'. He left Christ Church without taking a degree.

From 1933 to 1943 he wrote the William Hickey gossip column on the *Daily Express*, 'These Names Make News'. At the time he had his closest brush with scandal. He picked up two unemployed miners in the street and took them back to his flat. He later insisted that the reason they all ended up in his bed was that there was nowhere else for any of them to sleep. One of the

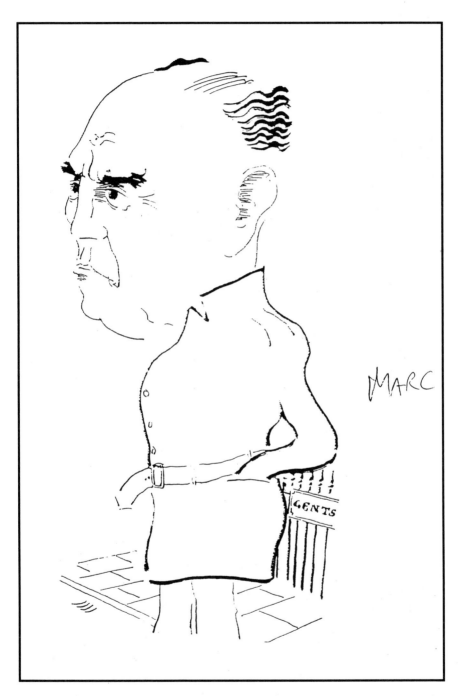

Tom Driberg by Marc

men began to doubt Driberg's altruism when a straying hand stroked his groin. He went hotfoot to the nearest police station. Driberg's subsequent trial for indecent assault, at which he was found not guilty, was kept out of the press only after Lord Beaverbrook, proprietor of the *Daily Express*, brought his considerable influence to bear on the whole of Fleet Street.

It was 1942 when Driberg was first elected – as Independent MP for Maldon, at the age of thirty-seven. (He took the Labour whip in January 1945.) Early Essex man was kept in the dark from the very start about the bachelor MP's proclivities. 'In the often ridiculous document called an election address, which every candidate issues, such details as *Married, with two children* are usually included . . . I should have had to put *Homosexual, promiscuous*. I don't think there would have been many votes in that.'

At Westminster Driberg was less circumspect. How he avoided public scandal has long been the subject of debate among his contemporaries. Chapman Pincher suggests: 'Driberg's long relationship with MI5 solves the mystery of why such a notorious homosexual, who was repeatedly caught in the act publicly by the police, was never successfully prosecuted.' Driberg had a more down-to-earth explanation. He boasted to friends that no government would dare allow prosecution, because they could never be certain how many of Driberg's conquests would be revealed on their own benches. He also claimed that any British police constable would take a bribe if it were large enough and in cash. The trick, he said, was to keep a substantial roll of banknotes on one's person at all times.

Driberg recalled only two close shaves during his time as an MP. The first was in Edinburgh during the Second World War, when he accompanied a Norwegian sailor to an empty air-raid shelter. He was just about to attend to the man's 'long, uncircumcized, and tapering, but rock-hard erection' when 'we were caught, almost wet-handed' by two policemen. The quick-thinking MP remembered that at his 1935 trial a policeman had told him that if he had known that Driberg was William Hickey of the *Express* he would never have arrested him. Driberg flourished his press card at the bobby. 'Good God, man, I've read ye all of my life! Every morning,' said the bobby. The danger having passed, Driberg got talking to the policeman; 'I liked him and thought him attractive, but judged that it would be going too far, in the circumstances, to make a pass.'

His second scrape was in one of his favourite public conveniences in Jockey's Fields, off Theobalds Road, London. His chosen mate turned out to be a policeman posing as an *agent provocateur*. Using the same approach as in Edinburgh, Driberg achieved the same result. He reinforced the message with 'an assurance that any charge would be hotly resisted, with benefit of learned counsel and the evidence of a genito-urinary specialist, if necessary in court after court'.

Columnist George Gale once pointed out that it was not only Driberg's own reputation which was at risk from his behaviour. His sexual appetite remained as strong as ever at party conferences, so that 'in a town crawling with delegates, reporters and photographers, he risked his own career, the success of his cause and the welfare of his party all for the sake of a snatched few seconds of mutual masturbation'.

Few attractive men were safe from Driberg's attentions. He was a regular at Ronnie Kray's flat, where as one biographer put it, 'rough, but compliant East End lads were served like so many canapés'. He once propositioned Mick Jagger with the line: 'Oh my, Mick, *what* a big basket you have!' The rock star did nothing more than blush. Francis Wheen, in his biography of Driberg, tells the story of the night when the MP met a uniformed policeman walking across Hungerford Bridge, and 'without a word, after the merest glance of consent, I knelt down and fellated him.'

One of his few dislikes – he shared it, as so little else, with Mrs Thatcher – was a horror of beards. The *Times Literary Supplement*, reviewing his autobiography, noted that 'men with beards were immune from his passions. This may explain the high incidence of beards on the Labour Left.' Driberg paid a high price for his one-man crusade to convert every clean-shaven male in the Palace of Westminster. He was denied the ministerial office his intelligence might have merited. He knew very well why, branding Attlee and Wilson 'deeply prejudiced puritans'. This seems a little harsh.

The announcement in 1951 of his intended marriage to Ena Binfield caused disbelief at Westminster. Churchill, shown a picture of the strikingly plain bride-to-be, remarked, 'Oh well, buggers can't be choosers.' A policeman at the Commons expressed sympathy for Binfield: 'Poor lady, she won't know which way to turn.' Evelyn Waugh, unable to attend the wedding, wrote to Driberg: 'I will think of you intently on the day and pray that the church is not struck by lightning.'

In his spare time, Driberg carved a reputation as a fairly serious figure on the Labour Left. He passed for a wit. Woodrow Wyatt says he could never take the Speaker seriously when he declared 'The Clerk will now proceed to read the Orders of the Day' after Driberg had dug the newly-elected Wyatt in the ribs and, *sotto voce*, sung the lines to the tune of *John Brown's Body.*

He supplemented his MP's pay in the early 1970s by anonymously compiling the crosswords for *Private Eye.* One puzzle, fairly typical of his output, contained the clues 'seamen mop up anal infusions' (enemas) and 'sounds as though you must look behind for this personal lubricant' (sebum). The £2 prize on this occasion was won by a Mrs Rosalind Runcie of St Albans, Hertfordshire. It is not clear whether she had any help from her husband, the local bishop, later Archbishop of Canterbury.

One London cabbie, at least, had a lucky escape. On 12 August 1976, when Driberg was dashing to a lunch in the City, he keeled over in the back of a taxi and died from a heart attack. His autobiography had been started. Seventy thousand words had been written. Friends feared the worst. He had told colleagues that both the style and content would be forthright and explicit. When it finally appeared nearly a year after his death it provoked outrage from politicians, but they were lucky. The *Sunday Times* noted that he did not get beyond his entry into Parliament in 1942. 'Sadly, the author took the saucier secrets of the Palace of Westminster to the grave with him.'

Walter Terry, political editor of the *Sun*, labelled it a 'devastating, stomach-turning document. Probably the biggest outpouring of literary dung a public figure has ever flung into print.' Lord George Brown called it 'beastly' in the *London Evening News* and the usually restrained *Economist* titled its review: 'Pederast's Progress'. The *Sunday Telegraph* condemned Driberg's 'vicious life'. Immorality in high places was nothing new, the paper said, but 'Driberg's autobiography surely sets a new low which is unlikely to pass unnoticed in the rest of the world'.

The inconvenient timing of his death robs us of confirmation of two of Driberg's most daring alleged exploits. Francis Wheen, in

Tom Driberg: His Life and Indiscretions, claims Driberg knelt to administer oral sex on his hero Nye Bevan in the Labour Leader's office at the Commons. The fiery Welshman is alleged to have shouted enthusiastically: 'Tell me a story, Tom, tell me a story!' – a request Driberg was in no position to grant. Driberg bragged that he could disprove the rumour that Bevan was a eunuch – his penis was, said Driberg, 'long, but a trifle thin'.

Woodrow Wyatt, in his 1985 memoirs, recalled a story told him, he said, by the former Labour Prime Minister, Jim Callaghan. Driberg and Callaghan were returning to London after a meeting, and stopped to urinate by the roadside. Driberg grabbed Callaghan's penis and commented, 'You've got a very pretty one there.' Callaghan retreated fast. Later he denied the story. Wyatt now refuses to comment. Both are in the House of Lords, while the late Mr Driberg is probably in the other Hades.

JOHN BELCHER – 1948

'A gift from some of John's acquaintances'

John Belcher has the dubious distinction of being the only minister in Clement Attlee's astonishingly clean post-war government to resign after a scandal. We look back from an era of 'cash-for-questions' scandals (see p.324) to an era of post-war rationing, and a 'groceries-for-questions' affair. Sherry, burgundy, whisky, meals out, lunch and a suit featured among the gifts from an unscrupulous lobbyist, 'the Spider of Park Lane', with more than one government minister on his books.

John Belcher was the first minister fingered. With Britain still in the grip of rationing, Mr Belcher's crime was allowing himself to be showered with gifts by one of Westminster's first political lobbyists. The junior Trade minister accepted a holiday for his family in Margate, another in Bournemouth, a £68 gold cigarette case, a three-piece suit, lavish entertaining at Harringay dog track and boxing matches at Bethnal Green. The gifts came from the Spider, Sydney Stanley, king of the fixers in the thriving black economy under post-war austerity. Belcher met him in April 1947, a year after becoming a minister. Within a month he was being rewarded in Margate.

Polish-born Stanley, alias Kohsyzcky, Rechtand or Wulkan, was an undischarged bankrupt with a 1933 deportation order outstanding against him. Despite his physical appearance (one writer described him as 'five feet three . . . portly and ill-formed . . . a wide flat face and deep-set eyes') he persuaded the distrustful business community that it could work with the new socialist government, and that he could be a bridge. He spent more than £60,000 a year on entertaining to prove his point. Belcher, a former Great Western Railway clerk, had been elected MP for Sowerby in Yorkshire in 1945, and made a minister within a year.

Star, 3 February 1949

He was quickly ensnared in the web of the Spider.

Forty-three-year-old Belcher was keen to establish good relations with the business world. His 'door was always open'. Open, for instance, to Sir Maurice Bloch, head of the Glasgow distillers, Bloch Brothers Ltd. In a two-month period Bloch gave Belcher fifty-six bottles of sherry, burgundy and whisky – unimaginably precious commodities in post-war London – in return for three import licences for 'essential' business supplies.

None could match the generosity of the Spider. For Belcher's birthday, Stanley threw a dinner party at the Garter Club. The bill for half a dozen people was £89, lavish at the prices of the day. At the same time, Stanley was promising businessmen that his friend the minister could open doors for them. Belcher's and Stanley's undoing was the increasingly exaggerated nature of these promises: promises the minister was unable to fulfil.

In August 1948 two business contacts became suspicious. Stanley had persuaded Harry Sherman, head of Sherman's Football Pools, that he could get Belcher to drop a prosecution against the company that had resulted from Sherman's breach of the paper-rationing regulations in the production of coupons. Another company, Stagg & Russell Ltd, had paid Stanley £10,000 for an import licence for amusement arcade machines. Harry Sherman complained to an official in Belcher's office; Stagg & Russell went to the police.

On 30 August Harold Wilson, then President of the Board of Trade and Belcher's boss, was told about Sherman's claims. He informed the police, the Prime Minister and the Lord Chancellor. A tribunal was set up under Mr Justice Lynskey and Belcher was asked to go on leave for the duration as the twenty-six-day tribunal heard about the extent of the 'cash-for-favours' scandals.

Other government ministers were named. Charles Key, the Minister of Works, had progressed from lunches and bottled beverages from Stanley, to a first fitting for a suit! George Gibson, a director of the Bank of England, was censured for abusing his position with Stanley to gain material advantage.

Lynskey's 50,000-word report was published in January 1949. It was withering in its denunciation of Stanley: 'a man who will make any statement, whether true or untrue, if he thinks that it is to his own advantage'.

Belcher was found guilty of using his influence as a minister in return for 'small gifts and hospitality'. His constituency party scheduled a meeting to consider his future as an MP for 26 February (he had already resigned as a minister during the tribunal's inquiry). He saved them the trouble and resigned on the day the report was debated in the Commons: 3 February 1949.

His wife, Louise (known as 'Lulu') insisted she had never accepted any gifts. Tracked down in a West End restaurant, she held up her hands in reply to reporters' questions, and declared: 'Those are the hands of a working woman – not hands ready for gifts from anyone.' With quiet pride she claimed she had saved £20 out of her housekeeping to buy herself what in those days was called a 'costume'. Suddenly she hissed: 'But now how can I buy it? How can I escape the censure of women whose eyes tell me they believe it was a gift to me from some of John's acquaintances!'

There was little sympathy for the couple. Humiliated, Belcher had to return to his former job as a railway clerk. In 1960, Harold Wilson intervened personally to help his former minister, who faced prosecution for tax arrears. Belcher retired from the railways in 1963, and died the following year.

It was after this case that Attlee set up a committee to look at the problem of middlemen and consultants. It reported in October 1949 that 'common sense and vigilance' were the only necessary safeguards against corruption, an observation of quite blinding futility.

CAPTAIN PETER BAKER – 1950

'I've been ill for a long time'

The Times of Wednesday, 1 December 1954, carried a photograph of the Queen in full regalia walking through the Royal Chamber at the Lords, to open the Parliament. But the new Commons session was to be without its member for South Norfolk. A headline above and just to the left of the Queen and her robe-carriers offers a brutal summary: 'MP Sent to Prison – Seven Years for Forgery'. Captain Peter Baker, at thirty-three the youngest MP in the House, was bound for Wormwood Scrubs, forged bills of exchange for thousands of pounds flying in the breeze behind him, his companies sinking, brandy and anti-depressants now his only comfort.

This would not be Captain Baker's first experience of being held captive. The son of an army major, his career had begun in the Royal Artillery and he had earned a Military Cross in the Second World War after working for the Dutch resistance movement, when he was twice captured and twice tried to escape. Elected in 1950, he was already running numerous businesses when he entered the House. Captain Baker had energy to spare. In his short parliamentary career he had had a dozen run-ins with the Tory whips, including the then Chief Whip, Edward Heath, over diverse issues. Each time he had been headed back into the fold. Party managers strained to control him: but neither his heart specialist, abdominal specialist, neurologist or three auxiliary doctors who 'drugged me, injected me, massaged me and cajoled me' could persuade him to rest. Sorrow in the whips' office at his jail sentence will have been mitigated.

When finally brought in to the Old Bailey, Baker blamed liquor, exhaustion, and his increasingly volatile mental state, for both his fraudulent actions and his inability to recall them: his failure, for instance, properly to remember the forging of signatures such as those on twelve bills of exchange worth a total of £13,200; or the letter which accompanied them, supposedly written by Sir John Mann, partner in the brewery, which Baker had simply dictated to his typist. The letter authorized him to use the Bills as he chose, and helped secure an £8,500 loan from the Edgware Trust. Sir John was wholly unaware of it.

This is just a detail in a tangled picture, for which Baker was to apologize in an abject letter to the House; and on which he was to expand later in his autobiography, finished two days before he pleaded guilty at the Old Bailey. He called the book *My Testament*.

Testimony was certainly called for. Captain Baker had tried to combine his role as politician with the chairmanship of a raft of companies, including four publishing houses, a wine merchant, an aircraft company, a whisky company, and television, radio, investment and property companies based off Pall Mall and in their heyday employing over 500 people. Publishing was a fascination this MP shared with, for instance, Robert Maxwell and Horatio Bottomley. Indeed Baker dealt with Maxwell, selling him his British Book Centre in New York, and considering the then unknown businessman 'a remarkable character.' The interest that publishing holds for MPs is curious. Michael Heseltine also began his business career in this way.

And it was publishing which most agitated Baker's finances and his health. In July 1950 his publishing houses were over-spending and under-selling. 'While publishing was the cause of many of my subsequent worries and certainly a contributory cause to my ill-health, it also brought me more happiness than any other activity except politics,' he wrote. At one stage his secretary was a Mrs M. Spark, who has included Baker in one of her novels.

Within three years, and facing a liquidity crisis, his business conduct turned seriously fraudulent. Four thousand pounds from the Edgware Trust loan went to his Falcon Press, and £2,500 to his father who, the court heard, was now a major creditor of many of his son's seventeen companies. Between December 1953 and May 1954, six of the Bills of Exchange matured and were paid. But on 9 June an attentive cashier noticed irregularities in the seventh signature. The bill was not honoured.

Baker then went to the Bank of America for £3,000. Asked for guarantors (the bank was not content with his father's word) Baker went back to his secretary's typewriter, producing a guarantee 'signed' by Bernard Docker, an industrialist, and another by one Owen David. He obtained a £2,500 overdraft. Next came a loan for £49,000 from Barclays, secured on three forged signatures – Docker, Mann and a Mr Reynolds. From this Barclays account Baker transferred £11,000 to his earlier creditor, the Bank of America, £4,500 to a firm of solicitors involved with his businesses, and £33,000 to the Peregrine Press account at the National Provincial Bank. Out of this £33,000 he drew £18,000 over ten days for his own Provincial account. Then he spent £12,000 on a controlling share in a whisky company. Barclays never saw its £49,000 again.

Baker's bizarre business activity was taking place against the backdrop of an ever more complicated political life. His mind was beginning to float off course. According to Baker, 'There were whole weeks in 1953 and 1954 that I cannot remember. Often I had to check up in *Hansard* to make sure I had attended the Commons and voted.' He may not have attended as assiduously as he should. Challenged in the Smoking Room by Sir Charles McAndrew, who as a Deputy Speaker ought to have known every MP but could not recall Baker, the MP replied: 'Please don't apologize, I have no idea who you are either.' This would have been funnier if it had been meant as a gibe.

In *My Testament*, Baker explained:

Falcon proved a constant worry, and in Parliament, the Budget and the Finance Bill brought me the worst all-night sittings on record . . . for four days and nights in succession . . . with all-night sittings at the House and Board meetings during the day, I never went to bed. However, I needed a flask of brandy always by me to see me through it. Despite sedatives, sleeping pills and draughts, I had practically no sleep during these years, however tired I became.

It was a wonder he ever went into politics at all. 'I could not reconcile myself to the policies of either of the main parties,' he wrote, perhaps rather late in the day.

He corresponded with the whips several times, offering to resign, but was dissuaded. Persuaded to vote with his party for German rearmament, he said to the whips' office: 'I shall vote with you for three reasons. Firstly, because I believe that a rearmed Germany, with a European Defence Community, is just the least of four possible evils. Secondly, because I want my summer holidays. And thirdly because without a German Army, you [the Tory whips] would be the last survival of Prussianism in Europe.'

And still his businesses sank deeper into loss. In the end the banks lost a total of £102,000, of which £22,720 was traced directly to Baker. It was not, however, suggested that money was being diverted for his personal enrichment. Unlike Horatio Bottomley (see pp.79–83), Baker's crooked dealings were designed to shore up real but failing businesses: not as fronts to rob the public.

On 28 May Baker was summoned to an important meeting by the industrialist Bernard Docker and Sir John Mann. Docker waved a phantom guarantee at Baker. Baker paused, and said: 'I've been ill for a long time.' The breakdown had come at last.

He was arrested at the Holloway Sanatorium by a Chief Superintendent he already knew socially and he spent the night in a cell with drunken women and prostitutes. 'During the last twelve months before entering a Nursing Home I had at least thirty daytime blackouts and was twice taken to hospital after half-hearted attempts at suicide. My mind varied from unreliable pin-sharp brilliance to complete inability to record events and conversations. The rest that I had refused to take was bound to force itself upon me.'

Baker's first reaction was to plead not guilty at a Bow Street committal, but at the Old Bailey he admitted six charges of forgery. He received seven years. When Baker was ushered away, the prison escort whispered: 'Seems like a long time to me,' at which Baker hissed: 'Sounds a bloody sight longer to me.'

His term began at Wormwood Scrubs before he was transferred to Leyhill Prison Without Bars in Gloucestershire. In prison he wrote another book, *Time Out of Life*. Baker, who was married with two daughters, was released in 1959 and discharged from bankruptcy in 1962. In 1963 he petitioned unsuccessfully for a Queen's pardon and died in Eastbourne in November 1966.

IAN HARVEY – 1958

'The 11th Commandment:
thou shalt not be caught'

Thus wrote Ian Harvey. 'Tory MP Caught in Bush with Guardsman', the headlines would proclaim today. '£5 fine on Ian Harvey. He will pay to end of life,' rumbled *The Times* on 11 December 1958. They were right. Ian Harvey was a minister. Fined for indecency with a young Coldstream Guard, he knew his parliamentary career was over. He was the first in a depressing roll call of Macmillan's ministers brought down by scandal.

Harvey had started playing with fire and guardsmen five years before becoming MP for Harrow East in 1950. Now, living in fashionable Trevor Square, off Hyde Park, he was well placed to pick up troopers from the Knightsbridge barracks of the Household Cavalry. From a young age he had known he was homosexual, but ambition had dictated pragmatism and in 1949 he had married Clare Mayhew, sister of the Labour MP and broadcaster Christopher Mayhew, now a peer. The union satisfied his constituency supporters who, as he recalled in his autobiography, *To Fall Like Lucifer*, 'thought it was a mistake to have a candidate who was a bachelor and over thirty'. Glamorous Mrs Harvey was wheeled in. It worked and the following year her husband was elected MP for Harrow East.

Mr Harvey did not let marriage or political office interrupt his forays into Hyde Park. 'I discovered a very convenient place near the Peter Pan statue in Kensington Gardens. J. M. Barrie, unlike some of his predecessors, would hardly have approved. Peter Pan had his back to us so I could not be accused of polluting the young.'

Harvey, who had been singled out as a serious talent, was taking a great risk. In 1958 the maximum sentence for any form of homosexual conduct was five years in prison. 'In view of my undoubted political ambitions this conduct could well be adjudged as verging on insanity. Every time it was over I pretended to myself that this was definitely the last time. I knew perfectly well . . . exactly what would happen if I were caught.' He would be back in his usual spot the very next night.

In 1953 he was given a stark reminder of what could lie in store. The Labour MP William Field, fined £15 for importuning in a public lavatory (see pp.107–8), was forced to resign. 'This should have shown me the red light,' said Harvey.

Born in Surrey in 1914 seven months before the outbreak of the First World War, Harvey enjoyed a comfortable middle-class upbringing. He attended Fettes College (Tony Blair's old school) in Scotland and Christ Church College, Oxford, where he was President of the Union. After a distinguished wartime career he went on to a successful job in advertising and wrote a noted book, *Techniques of Persuasion.*

He moved into politics, serving his apprenticeship in local government. His wartime service enabled him to make his mark in Parliament as a member of a Commons Select Committee whose advice reinforced draconian punishments for practising homosexuals in the armed forces. He rapidly became known as one of Macmillan's abler young supporters. In 1956 he was a popular choice as Parliamentary Secretary at the Ministry of Supply. When Macmillan became Prime Minister the following year, Harvey was promoted to the Foreign Office. Two years later, he fell like Lucifer.

After dinner at the Polish embassy on Wednesday 19 November 1958, temptation proved too strong. Just after 11 p.m. when the guardsmen would be returning from the pubs to the Wellington Barracks, Harvey followed his normal routine and walked along the Mall, another favourite pick-up point. A teenage guardsman in uniform caught the minister's eye. He caught up with him and they went into St James's Park. They had no intention of feeding the ducks. A few minutes after they disappeared into a bush the harsh glare of a torch beam interrupted them. A policeman and park-keeper had heard a rustling noise in the bushes. *The Times* reported: 'They saw two men standing under a tree misbehaving.'

Harvey panicked and on the way to Cannon Row police station attempted to make a run for it. But ministerial life had already taken its toll, he tired, and was swiftly recaptured. At first he gave the duty sergeant a false name and address. To no avail. They knew exactly who he was. Harvey owned up.

MP and Guardsman accused

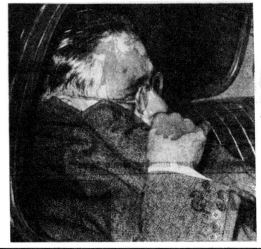

JUNIOR MINISTER ON 'OFFENCE IN PARK' CHARGES

Daily Express, 21 November 1958

The following morning the forty-four-year-old minister and the nineteen-year-old guardsman, Anthony Walter Plant, were charged with gross indecency and breaching the park's regulations by behaving in a way likely to offend against public decency. The case was adjourned. A 100-strong crowd was waiting outside the court. The minister made his escape in a taxi in the direction of Whitehall, but his two-minute court appearance, standing next to the slim, fair-haired soldier in blue dress uniform, made the front pages of the evening newspapers.

Harvey's local party pledged to stand by him, but the day after his court appearance he told the Prime Minister he intended to resign from Parliament. Though Macmillan, who desperately wanted to avoid a by-election, begged him to reconsider over the weekend, Harvey's mind was already made up.

When the case came to court the second time on 10 December, the gross indecency charge had been dropped. Counsel for Plant said he was young and naive, and 'as far as could be traced was not addicted in this way'. Returning from his fiancée's home in north London, he had only gone into the park with Harvey 'out of curiosity'. They were fined £5 each for breaching park regulations. Harvey paid Plant's fine. 'I felt it was the least I could do,' he said.

As he left the court he was mobbed by the press. Rather than run for cover he faced the music for ten minutes in the hope 'that if I got it all over there and then I was less likely to be plagued for interviews on the telephone . . . I felt no resentment because I knew that they were only doing their job and I wanted to make it as easy for them as I could.'

Harvey was resigned to being ostracized by former friends. 'The Conservative Party, quite understandably because of its outlook and make-up, did not want to know anything more about me.' Nor did any of his clubs. The Carlton Club accepted his resignation without comment. The Junior Carlton Club would allow him to keep his membership only if he did not set foot in it for two years. 'I thought this was rather an expensive indignity, so I declined to give the assurance and resigned.' The chairman of Pratt's showed mercy and urged him to stay. 'I knew, however, that there were a number of members who were less broad-minded.' He faced a further ordeal: dishonourable discharge from the Territorial Army despite his distinguished war record. It required the intervention of Hugh Fraser, a junior minister at the War Office, to spare him this fresh humiliation.

For more than two years he faced what he called 'purgatory. I went to several psychiatrists – the first treated me like a twit, as if I was simple-minded – and I drank a lot,' he told the *Daily Mirror* in 1972. After a period of total breakdown he became a Roman Catholic. He and his wife were divorced.

The disgraced Tory was persuaded to break his long silence by Lord Longford, the Roman Catholic Labour peer whose causes include Myra Hindley and who has argued consistently the evils of homosexuality. Harvey wrote his autobiography in 1971 and it was published by Longford's Sidgwick and Jackson publishing house. Lord Longford may have been disappointed that it shows more remorse at Harvey's folly than his homosexuality, and he later became honorary president of the Conservative Group for Homosexual Equality. From 1980 I saw him often, being parliamentary president myself. Ian wanted to help, but lacked confidence that his association with us was helpful, drank too much, and would issue half-hearted invitations to members of the group to accompany him home. Everybody liked him for his self-mocking humility, but his self-denigration seemed sad. He was a broken man, and looked it. He never came to terms with his fall from power, remarking once, 'I am the best politician the Tories haven't got.'

I wonder what happened to guardsman Plant? A book of inquiries into the fates of the forgotten halves of such scandals would be absorbing, but cruel.

Ian Harvey died in 1987. His immediate successor at the Foreign Office was one John Profumo.

THOMAS GALBRAITH – 1962

'Never catch a spy'

'We have arrested a spy who is a bugger and a minister is involved,' the Director of Public Prosecutions told the Attorney-General on the evening of 12 September 1962. 'Oh, that's bad news! Very bad news!' exclaimed Harold Macmillan, when told of the arrest at the Admiralty earlier that day. 'You know, you should never catch a spy. Discover him and then control him but never catch him. A spy causes far more trouble once he's caught.'

The Prime Minister was right. By the time the scandal had blown over, an obscure clerk, John Vassall, had been sent to prison; a junior minister had been forced out of office; a Cabinet minister had offered to resign; and – in a bombardment of press innuendo – Macmillan had retaliated and two journalists had been gaoled. Macmillan admits in his memoirs that the outcome 'infuriated Fleet Street, at every level of activity, and made the newspapers anxious to seek and exploit any possibility of counter-attack'. Fleet Street was already prepared for its revenge. Barely twelve months later a new name would enter the popular vocabulary: Profumo.

On 22 October 1962, John Vassall, a thirty-eight-year-old clerk in the Admiralty, was sentenced to eighteen years at the Old Bailey. The Cold War was at its hottest (the Cuban Missile Crisis broke the following week). So soon after the discovery of George Blake and the Portland spy ring, the *Daily Mail* was not alone in castigating the government for this 'latest woeful chapter in Britain's post-war catalogue of security failure'. The paper's hunt for Vassall's accomplices had already begun.

Vassall was a homosexual. When serving in the British Embassy in Moscow in the mid-1950s, he had starred in an orgy deftly stage-managed – and photographed – by the Soviet security services. Later, Vassall was helped in his decision to become a spy by a snapshot which showed him flourishing his underpants over his head in a Moscow hotel bedroom. The son of an Anglican clergyman, and a convert to Roman Catholicism, he commented in his *Autobiography of a Spy*: 'There I was, naked, grinning into the camera; naked, holding up a pair of men's briefs which must have been mine.'

The KGB's entrapment of Vassall paid off for them. Back in London he worked from 1957 until the autumn of 1959 as Assistant Private Secretary to Thomas Galbraith, Civil Lord of the Admiralty, and Conservative member for Glasgow Hillhead. Wellington and Oxford-educated and the son of the Tory peer, Lord Strathclyde, Galbraith had seemed a natural choice for the Admiralty after wartime service in the Mediterranean fleet.

Vassall's dutifulness towards the Civil Lord and his lady brought rewards. Galbraith would invite his underling to lunch and drinks in the family home in London. Vassall would make the long journey carrying secret documents to Barskimming, Galbraith's mansion in Ayrshire. Unknown to the minister, copies of the same documents were destined for the Kremlin.

After Vassall's arrest, there were rumours of a sexual liaison between the KGB spy and the forty-five-year-old minister. Unknown to the government, the tabloid *Sunday Pictorial* had paid £5,000 for Vassall's story. The treacherous clerk handed over to the newspaper handwritten letters and postcards from

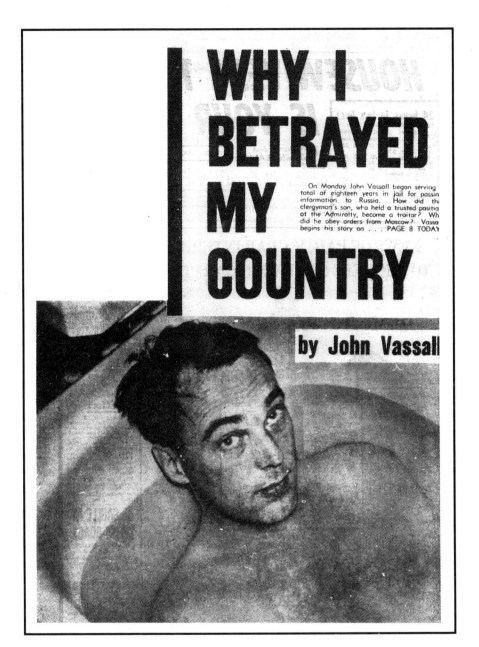

Sunday Pictorial, 28 October 1962

Galbraith and his wife. These surfaced two weeks after the key was turned on Vassall at Brixton Prison. While some of the letters merely dealt with mundane office matters, the most damaging were the ones written after Galbraith moved from the Admiralty to the Scottish Office in October 1959. Vassall was then working in the military branch and did not like it. He was determined to keep in touch with his former boss, and sent him fawning postcards from his expensive holidays abroad paid for by the proceeds of his spying.

The Annual Register for 1962 later remarked that the letters revealed 'nothing more damaging than the former Civil Lord's interest in his office carpets, crockery and paper clips. The most that could be said against Mr Galbraith was that he had suffered a socially pressing and plausible junior colleague a trifle too gladly.'

The press, meanwhile, was demanding to know why a spy, working at the heart of the government, had remained undetected for so long. Vassall was reviled by the press who, after his conviction, branded him 'a fawning mediocrity' and 'mother's boy'. The newspapers did not pull their punches: they reported that Vassall was known as 'Aunty' to junior clerks and typists, went shopping for women's underwear, and 'liked to spend the evening in the West End haunts of perverts'. They even unearthed friends from his old school, Monmouth, who were willing to turn the knife. One, Norman Stone (not the Oxford academic), described as a respectable country club owner, said: 'He was a sissy and a snob. No one who knew him then would be surprised to hear he is a homosexual.'

Newspapers asked a series of telling questions: how had Vassall charmed his way into the minister's inner circle? When it emerged that Vassall lived in an 'extravagantly furnished' Dolphin Square flat costing £10 a week on a salary of £15, they asked which minister or official had written the landlord a reference. The pressure grew on Galbraith when it emerged he had been a visitor at Vassall's luxury flat, a gaudy residence full of 'perfume bottles to an extent one would expect to find in a lady's accommodation', according to the *Pictorial*. Only after Galbraith's resignation did it emerge that the minister's visit had been a courtesy call following the death of Vassall's mother. He had been there for fifteen minutes, and had taken along his wife.

Once Vassall's trial was over, media speculation about the

minister grew. Galbraith, a steady infantryman in Macmillan's government, tried to restore his reputation. On 23 October, Galbraith went to print in the *Daily Mail* – the rival *Pictorial*'s secret cache of letters, meanwhile, being guarded night and day in a fortified office in Fleet Street. Galbraith wrote:

> Some people think he was a great buddy of mine, but in my six years as a departmental minister I have had over thirty officials in my house. I felt rather sorry for him – I felt he had a screw loose.
>
> Vassall would have coffee in the drawing-room while the bag was taken to my study, where I took out those things that needed urgent action. Sometimes he stayed to lunch.
>
> My relations with him were not different from those with other civil servants. The only thing that struck me as strange was his flat. But I believed he had been left money.

Galbraith's comments only made matters worse. It confirmed the suspicion widespread at Westminster and in the media that Vassall enjoyed unusually privileged access to the minister. The press seized on the contradictions in the article. If he had a 'screw loose', why was he permitted to carry secret documents around the country? The minister's comments merely fuelled the rumours of a sexual relationship between the two men. So much so that seven days later, on 1 November, Galbraith issued a statement through his lawyers declaring that he had not known Vassall was a homosexual. He stressed the point that Vassall had never stayed a single night at Galbraith's Scottish estate.

The media worked hard. Mrs Doris Murray, Vassall's cleaning lady, attracted their inquiries. She proved a sensational witness. In a taped interview with a journalist she insisted Galbraith had visited the Dolphin Square flat alone at least once. Dusting the ornaments on the mantelpiece, she saw the two men enter the bedroom together. They emerged fifteen minutes later. Vassall kept a framed photograph of his former ministerial master in the flat. Fortunately for the government some of these allegations were too racy for the fastidious 1960s press.

On Friday, 2 November, about a week and a half after Vassall's conviction, two Opposition frontbenchers, Patrick Gordon Walker and George Brown, demanded to know how Vassall's homosexuality and high spending had gone unnoticed for so long. Peter Thorneycroft, the Minister of Defence, later (to his amusement) Mrs Thatcher's first Chairman of the Conservative Party, blundered badly, lightly misreading public unease over the spate of spy scandals. 'It is very easy afterwards,' remarked Thorneycroft, 'when a man has put up his homosexual tendencies in defence, to say that you can identify them by just glancing at them. That is an illusion.' When asked about Vassall's expensive flat he replied with more candour than finesse: 'How many of us are living above our incomes in London squares?' There was an audible gasp of disbelief even from his own backbenchers. Thorneycroft claimed that the matter had been blown out of all proportion but he had himself unwittingly done some of the blowing. 'I really think some restraint ought to be exercised in public comment on these matters.'

The press became more determined than ever to arrange a ministerial funeral.

Days later, the *Sunday Pictorial* revealed its letters. Serializing Vassall's explicit life-story, illustrated by provocative photographs of the spy reclining semi-naked in bed, the newspaper primly proclaimed it had passed vital documents, which implicated a minister, to the government. The letters from Galbraith were handed to an internal inquiry looking at the security implications.

But the *Pictorial* struck a cruel blow at the government by sending an identical package to Hugh Gaitskell, the Leader of the Opposition, and his deputy George Brown. The following Tuesday, George Brown told the Commons that letters which he had just received 'indicated a degree of ministerial responsibility which goes far beyond the ordinary business of a minister'. There was consternation on the Tory benches when they realized Labour had been handed such explosive ammunition. Gaitskell calmly observed that he could not believe the Conservatives had not been passed documents by the press when they were in Opposition.

The next day, the *Daily Mail* led with 'Postcard to a Spy':

Amid the pile of correspondence is a postcard sent during a holiday abroad to Vassall by a leading figure. The same person wrote a letter to Vassall. His wife also sent a note of some length. The discovery of the picture postcard from abroad does not mean that there was any sexually improper relationship. It does indicate, the Opposition believes, a friendliness which one would not expect to exist between a clerk and a senior colleague.

What masters are English newspapers of the verbal wink! The 'leading figure' was not named. He did not have to be. Galbraith's fumbling attempts to clear his name had focused the spotlight even more keenly on his relationship with the homosexual spy. Later that day Sir Charles Cunningham, heading the internal inquiry, published the celebrated letters under the heading: 'The relationship between Vassall and those for whom he worked'. The decision to publish, sanctioned by Macmillan, meant the battle to keep the government clear of the Vassall affair had been lost. Galbraith had to go.

The following day the newspapers printed the letters, the *Daily Express* running them under the banner headline: 'My Dear Vassall'. Within hours Galbraith had resigned. The internal inquiry had found no evidence of any impropriety in the minister's relationship with his clerk, but, in his resignation letter to the Prime Minister, the minister conceded:

> It is apparent to me that my accustomed manner of dealing with officials and others who serve me has in the circumstances become an embarrassment to you and the government. For this reason alone I feel that my only proper course is to tender my resignation.

The resignation failed to stop a rot so widely enjoyed. The *Express* carried a new set of allegations: Lord Carrington, First Lord of the Admiralty and Galbraith's former ministerial boss, was accused of having known about the presence of another spy in his department when the Portland spy ring was exposed, a full eighteen months before Vassall's arrest.

Then a *Daily Sketch* journalist had dinner with Conservative MP Peter Tapsell. Even today, exactly what was said that night is the subject of much debate, but what is clear is that Macmillan was rocked by the report he received of the meeting. He went to the Commons on 14 November to announce the reasons why he had set up an independent tribunal into the affair. What Macmillan said was a sensation: 'One of the staff of the paper [the

Daily Sketch], had been told by a member of the police, or the security service, he was not sure which, that had Vassall not been arrested on 12 September it had been his intention to join Mr Galbraith in Italy and that Vassall then intended "to do a Pontecorvo" [a reference to the British nuclear physicist Bruno Pontecorvo who had defected to the Soviet Union in 1950]. That had the clear implication that my Hon. Friend either intended to defect to Russia or to assist Vassall to do so. It was also said that my Hon. Friend the former Civil Lord was believed to have spent holidays with Vassall before.'

Indeed, one postcard Vassall sent to Galbraith from Italy, which had been printed in the newspapers the previous week, was signed 'With memories of Italy', underlining the suspicion that they had enjoyed holidays together. Vassall, who was let out of prison to appear at the tribunal, denied this and insisted the message referred only to his own memories.

Macmillan, according to his memoirs, was also prompted to set up an independent tribunal by the press's behaviour. Their conduct was 'terrible, without any sense of responsibility. They want sensation.' Macmillan seems to have noticed this rather late. Lord Radcliffe, an eminent judge, presided over the hearing, only the fourth of its kind since the war. By agreeing to an independent examination of the security implications of the affair, the Prime Minister had yielded to pressure from the Opposition and the press, but even in the heat of scandal, Macmillan showed his guile. There was a sting in the tail. He cleverly included in Radcliffe's brief the powerful role played by the press. 'I have a feeling that the time has come for men of propriety and decency not to tolerate the growth of the spirit of Titus Oates and Senator McCarthy,' he told a packed Commons.

The Opposition smelt a rat. Macmillan had set up the tribunal, they warned, to save the government's reputation, rather than improve national security. What would happen if journalists failed to reveal their sources? Patrick Gordon Walker, Labour's Defence Spokesman, commented that Macmillan had made the prosecuting speech just before the whole matter went *sub judice*. Walker called the Prime Minister 'a very shrewd adroit politician'. Indeed he was. With the tribunal set up and the issue *sub judice*, a lid was effectively put on further speculation and rumour.

Radcliffe's tribunal, which took evidence in public and in

private for two months, had a moment of bitter farce when Mrs Murray, Vassall's charwoman, in her best clothes, was pressed about the time she had seen Galbraith disappear into the bedroom with the spy. Under the gaze of Lord Radcliffe she admitted she did not even know what Galbraith looked like. The tribunal's report was published on 25 April 1963 and exonerated Carrington and Galbraith. The First Lord of the Admiralty, Carrington, had been grossly slandered by the press, said the report, and Galbraith was cleared of any complicity in Vassall's espionage or his homosexual activities. The former Civil Lord of the Admiralty was 'not remiss in failing to suspect from his knowledge of Vassall that the latter was a security risk'.

However, after summoning several journalists in the first weeks of 1963, the tribunal was highly critical of the press. The seeds were sown for months of bitterness between the government and Fleet Street. Two journalists were sent to prison for refusing to reveal their sources: Brendan Mulholland of the *Daily Mail* preferred a six-month spell behind bars to disclosing, among other things, who had told him the spy was called 'Aunty' in his office. Reginald William Foster of the *Daily Sketch* was jailed for three months for refusing to reveal the source of his claim that Vassall bought women's clothing in the West End. Little of this was central to security, and disrespectful suspicion grew that the tribunal had been set up to punish the press.

Another journalist, Desmond Clough, also of the *Sketch*, narrowly escaped imprisonment for refusing to reveal the source of his claim that it was thanks to Vassall's spying that 'Russian trawler fleets managed to turn up with uncanny accuracy in the precise area and on the right date for secret Nato sea exercises' – an allegation the *Sketch* had printed the day after Vassall's conviction, 23 October. He was saved from prison when an Admiralty press officer came forward as his source.

Galbraith, who had kept public silence since his resignation, had been on the backbenches privately protesting his innocence. Exonerated by the tribunal, he gained undisclosed damages from Beaverbrook and Associated Newspapers. Although he was restored to the government in May 1963 as Parliamentary Secretary in the Department of Transport, a promotion from his previous job in the Scottish office, he never fulfilled his early potential. His marriage was dissolved in 1974. He remained a backbench MP, suffering from ill-health until his death in January 1982, a few weeks after receiving a knighthood. The Tory Establishment's loyalty to its own is remarkable.

Vassall served ten years for his spying, mostly at Maidstone prison in Kent. After his release in 1972 he went to a monastery to write his glutinous autobiography, published by Lord Longford's publishing house, Sidgwick and Jackson, in 1975. They lost track of him several years ago.

The journalists' appeal against imprisonment was rejected in the House of Lords on 6 March 1963. Resentment lingered on in Fleet Street, but the two jailed reporters were back behind their desks before – the whirligig of time bringing in its revenges early – their services were required to report the disgrace of Profumo, and the resignation of Macmillan.

JOHN PROFUMO – 1963

'The car needs oil in the gearbox, by the way'

> Oh what have you done, cried Christine,
> You've wrecked the whole party machine!
> To lie in the nude may be terribly rude,
> But to lie in the House is obscene.
>
> *Anon.*

As dusk fell on a warm Saturday evening at the beginning of the 1960s, Viscount Astor and his weekend guest, the Secretary of State for War John Profumo, both in dinner jackets, took a walk in the grounds of Astor's Cliveden estate. At the pool they found a beautiful nineteen-year-old woman swimming naked. Her male companion had hidden her swimsuit. Spotting a towel by the edge, she swam to it and wrapped it around herself in the water, then climbed from the pool to retrieve her costume. Playfully, Astor and Profumo intercepted her but the laughing teenager easily eluded them. As the other guests arrived from dinner the floodlights were switched on. The scene – two prominent middle-aged Tories caught, frolicking with a girl, in a sudden blinding light – could serve as a metaphor for the era.

According to the poet Philip Larkin, 1963 was the year sexual intercourse began. It was the year to which this incident led: the year in which Harold Macmillan's government faced a welter of accusations involving call-girls, Russian spies and society orgies; the year in which a senior judge thought himself obliged to ask an eminent doctor to examine the penis of a famous (and unnamed) politician.

Many have since seen the Profumo affair as a flagship scandal, emblematic of post-war moral decline. The press descended to new depths in its hunt for sensation but never lacked material. In a Commons speech Harold Wilson, Leader of the Opposition, depicted a government enmeshed in 'the London underworld of vice, dope, marijuana, blackmail, counter-blackmail, violence, and petty crime'. Squalid attempts at cover-up led to the trial at the Old Bailey of the socialite Stephen Ward. His subsequent suicide saw a government stoop – and fail – to save its skin. Five months later, Harold Macmillan resigned, exhausted and ill. Tarnished by the scandal, the succeeding administration, Sir Alec Douglas-Home's, fell the following year. Profumo had hastened the end of thirteen years of Conservative government. By finally lying to the House, he had committed what some branded the most heinous sin of all.

John Profumo (Jack to his friends) was born in 1915 of aristocratic Italian stock. Educated at Harrow and Oxford, he entered Parliament as Conservative member for Kettering in 1940, lost his seat in the Labour landslide five years later but was re-elected for Stratford-upon-Avon in 1950. Within two years he was a junior Transport minister. Profumo, whose family fortune was estimated at £9m, married the maturely handsome thirty-seven-year-old actress Valerie Hobson.

His circumstances seemed ideal: rich, clever, sociable, with a successful wife and (soon) a son, Profumo quickly rose to become

Secretary of State for War in 1960. A year later the Cabinet minister, now forty-six and tipped for the usual higher things, accepted (with his wife) a weekend invitation to Lord Astor's grandiose Cliveden estate in Buckinghamshire.

It was that Saturday night, 8 July 1961, that Profumo and Astor took their fateful stroll by the pool. The naked girl was called Christine Keeler, escorted by Stephen Ward, who had hidden her costume. Ward was a noted society osteopath who, in return for treating Lord Astor's back, had use of a cottage in the grounds of Cliveden. Profumo was mesmerized by his lady guest. Astor introduced Profumo to Ward.

Christine Keeler was living at Ward's London flat. Three years earlier, aged sixteen, the dark-haired and beautiful young woman had fled working-class life in Wraysbury, in search of the bright lights and perilous excesses of London. Working as a topless dancer in a Soho cabaret club, she had met Ward and a fellow showgirl, seventeen-year-old Mandy Rice-Davies, who had abandoned her Birmingham council estate for the lure of the capital.

On this particular weekend Keeler was Ward's guest. Astor now invited both to join his own house-party. Profumo took Keeler on a tour of the house. It degenerated into a chase through the bedrooms. Sex, the first element of the scandal, was now in delightful prospect. And so to the second element: espionage...

The next morning a presentable Soviet naval attaché, Colonel Eugene Ivanov, joined the party. Keeler told the *News of the World*: 'Now I liked Ivanov. He was a *man*. He was rugged with a hairy chest, strong and agile. But somehow when we decided to have a water piggy-back fight, it was Jack Profumo's shoulders I climbed on.' Profumo raced Astor and Ivanov across the pool, and won by breaking the rules and walking in the shallow end. 'That will teach you to trust a Minister of the Crown,' he told the others. By Sunday Profumo was planning to break rules of a more important kind. He had asked Keeler for her telephone number.

Ivanov, the balding minister's rival for Keeler's attentions, drove the flirtatious teenager back to London where she was staying with Ward at his Wimpole Mews flat. When they arrived they drank a bottle of vodka. According to Keeler, the burly Russian 'suddenly leant forward and kissed me. Before I knew what was happening, I was in his arms. He was a wonderful lover, so masculine. He left not long after and I felt a tremendous warmth about him: he was not the sort of man to do that sort of thing, and I could see he was sad to have weakened.' As she put it to the *News of the World* in spangled and penitential prose: 'We left serious discussion and I yielded to this wonderful huggy bear of a man. . .

John Profumo took only days to follow up his encounter with Keeler. Within a week he had arranged their first 'screw of convenience', as Keeler later called them. Their couplings took place at various venues – in Ward's flat; once in Profumo's Mini Minor; and once, while his wife was in Ireland, in his home. But she says: 'It had no more meaning than a hand-shake or a look across a crowded room.' Profumo showered her with gifts and money, to buy her mother a birthday present. Later this was described in Lord Denning's report as a polite way of paying for her services. I think that this is unfair. Profumo was smitten.

Keeler was not. Profumo had no idea he was sharing his mistress's bed with the Russian colonel. 'Unlike Jack, Ivanov was a party boy and loved to take me to the bright spots, wining and dining me. Jack never took me anywhere, except for drives all over London, and even then he was so anxious to be discreet that he used to borrow a big black car from Mr John Hare, the Minister of Labour.'

At this point MI5 intervened. Ward had been in contact with the security services since at least the beginning of June 1961 – a month before the Cliveden party. British Intelligence had singled out Ivanov as susceptible to Western temptations. As a high-ranking naval attaché at the Russian Embassy, Ivanov would have been a big catch if he had defected. A meeting between Ivanov and Ward was engineered by Sir Colin Coote, editor of the *Daily Telegraph*. Coote was a friend of both Ward and Sir Roger Hollis, head of MI5, later to be accused by Peter Wright of being the 'fifth man' in the notorious Soviet spy ring. They had lunch at the Garrick club.

Ward was a sensitive and intelligent man, a talented artist who had sketched members of the royal family, and, in a sardonic way, a social hanger-on. Whether or how far he lived off the earnings of the girls he introduced around, is uncertain. He was probably more of a friend than a lover to girls like Keeler; he enjoyed involvement with the rich and famous and liked to please them. He seemed to be drawn by the glamour of espionage. Having myself been asked by MI6 (and having agreed) to cultivate friendships with targeted Eastern European diplomats, I can understand the allure. Ward asked Ivanov to fix up for him artist's sittings with Soviet politicians.

MI5 wanted Ward to spring a 'honeytrap' on Ivanov, once he had fallen for Christine Keeler. Some observers have speculated that Ward was helping Soviet intelligence too, but there is no evidence for this. 'In the beginning, I was spying with Stephen Ward, delivering stuff to the Russian Embassy, but I didn't really know what I was doing,' Keeler alleged – to incredulity – in 1994.

MI5 learned about Profumo's month-long affair. Fearing it would compromise their honeytrap operation – and embarrass a Cabinet minister – Hollis warned the Cabinet Secretary, Sir Norman Brook, who called Profumo into his office on 9 August, to pass on the warning. The minister left and scribbled to his mistress the note which would later incriminate him.

> Darling,
>
> In great haste and because I can get no reply from your phone – alas something's blown up tomorrow night and I can't therefore make it. I'm terribly sorry especially as I leave the next day for various trips and then a holiday so won't be able to see you again until some time in September. Blast it. Please take great care of yourself and don't run away.
> Love J.
>
> PS I'm writing this 'cos I know you're off for the day tomorrow and I want you to know before you go if I still can't reach you by phone.

Profumo was infatuated. Despite the warning, he saw Keeler for another four months. It ended in December 1961, when Keeler refused to leave Ward's flat to let Profumo set her up in a discreet *pied-à-terre*. 'There was that amazing evening when Jack was round, and an army colonel showed up suddenly looking for Stephen. I had to introduce him to the War Minister. The colonel couldn't believe it. Jack nearly died,' was how Keeler described one close shave at Ward's flat.

MI5 began to realize that their honeytrap was unlikely to work. Ward's MI5 case-officer said: 'It is not easy to assess Ward's reliability but we believe he is probably not a man who would be actively disloyal, but that he is so under the influence of Ivanov that it would be most unwise to trust him.'

Profumo last saw Keeler in late 1961. The scandal blew up in early 1963. When it broke, Keeler was still living at Ward's flat, as was her friend Mandy Rice-Davies (after a brief affair with the notorious slum landlord Peter Rachman). After Profumo, Keeler had alternated between two West Indian lovers: Lucky Gordon, a jazz singer whom she had first met buying marijuana for Ward, and Johnny Edgecombe. The two black lovers fought over her in October 1962 in an all-night club in Wardour Street. Gordon's face was slashed. Keeler had briefly moved to Brentwood to live with Edgecombe, but before long she was back at Ward's flat in Wimpole Mews.

On 14 December 1962, the sound of gunshots shattered the silence in the quiet mews. Edgecombe, distraught that Keeler had left him, had tried to woo her back, but when she denied him entrance to Ward's flat he blasted the front door with bullets. The incident received minimal coverage in the press, though there had already been rumours about Keeler's involvement with Profumo. The police treated the shooting as attempted murder.

Cartoon by Cummings, 7 June 1963 (courtesy of *Daily Express*)

Ward was rattled and told Keeler to pack her bags. Keeler turned for help to one of Ward's patients, a solicitor, Michael Eddowes, who suspected that Ivanov and Ward were conspiring to compromise Profumo. Eddowes met Keeler and heard that Ward had asked her to find out from Profumo when the Germans were given atomic secrets.

A week later Keeler repeated the same story to another audience: Paul Mann, a journalist, and John Lewis, a Labour MP. Lewis met Keeler a week later and secretly tape-recorded a conversation in which she repeated many of her allegations. Lewis passed the information on to Colonel George Wigg, a poisonous Labour MP with a special interest in defence matters. Wigg had recently received a mysterious phone message: 'Forget the Vassall case; you want to look at Profumo.' He was also said to have a grudge against Profumo, who had bested him in the house.

The journalist Paul Mann persuaded Keeler to take her evidence to the press. She met a *Sunday Pictorial* reporter in late January, 1963, showing him the handwritten note from Profumo which she had astutely kept, and was offered £1,000 for her story: £200 in advance and £800 on publication. She repeated her story. The *Pictorial* was cautious – already in the dock before a parliamentary committee examining the role of the press in the Vassall affair (see p.134)

As negotiations with the paper continued, Ward tried to kill the story by tipping off the government. Profumo was persuaded to threaten to sue if anyone published. On 28 January Profumo, having failed to get MI5 to stop the story on security grounds, saw the Attorney-General, Sir John Hobson, and denied any affair with Keeler. He repeated the denial to the Solicitor-General, Sir Peter Rawlinson, and the Chief Whip, Martin Redmayne. Though sceptical, they were willing to accept the denial, to protect the government.

The newspaper insisted on securing Keeler's signature before they would publish. Ward put her under pressure not to sign and she agreed, but only after he had promised to compensate her for the lost newspaper fee – a figure 'five' was mentioned. When Ward's solicitor handed over £500 she was furious, having expected, she claimed, £5,000. Ward convinced the nervous *Pictorial* that her story was a pack of lies, and they dropped it. Keeler, enraged by Ward's desertion, made a series of accusations about her old friend to the police. One of them was procuring call girls for his rich clients.

Macmillan, his government already battered, was told the whole seedy story when he returned from a trip to Italy in February. He decided to do nothing. He wrote:

> Profumo had behaved foolishly and indiscreetly, but not wickedly. His wife... is very nice and sensible. Of course, all these people move in a selfish, theatrical, bohemian society, where no one really knows anyone and everyone is 'darling'. But Profumo does not seem to have realized that we have – in public life – to observe different standards from those prevalent today in many circles.

Does that mild and tolerant response seem naive, foolish or even enviable in the longer perspective?

On 8 March things started to happen: not in a Fleet Street rag, but in the obscure but authoritative weekly newsletter *Westminster Confidential*. Replacing a dull story about exchange rates the newsletter led, in prose dark with hint and half accusation, with a dramatic tale of sexual misdemeanour in high places...

> 'That is certain to bring down the Government,' a Tory MP wailed – 'and what will my wife say?' This combination of tragedy and tragi-comedy came from the efforts of this MP to check with a newspaperman on the story which had run like wildfire through Parliament. . .'

One of the choicest passages was from a letter signed 'Jack', on the stationery of the Secretary for War. The article went on:

> ...the allegation by this girl was that not only was this minister, who has a famous actress as his wife, her client, but also the Soviet military attaché, apparently a Colonel Ivanov. The famous actress wife, of course, would sue for divorce, the scandal ran. Who was using the girl to 'milk' whom of information – the War Secretary, or the Soviet military attaché? – ran in the minds of those primarily interested in security.

Profumo decided not to sue because, he said, the newsletter had a small circulation. On 10 March George Wigg, who had been secretly compiling a dossier on Profumo's relationship with Keeler, took it to Harold Wilson. But the new Labour leader advised caution. Wigg was persuaded to keep his powder dry. Another opportunity arose only days later.

On 14 March Johnny Edgecombe came up for trial at the Old Bailey charged with the attempted murder of Keeler during the shooting incident at Ward's flat. Yet the principal witness had disappeared. Rumours spread that Keeler had been got at. The following day the *Express* chanced its arm. Under the banner headline 'War Minister Shock' it claimed Profumo had offered his resignation for 'personal reasons'. Directly beneath was another article under the headline 'Vanished', and a picture of Keeler. The stories were not explicitly linked. Lord Denning, in his later report on the affair, wrote: 'The *Daily Express* told me that the juxtaposition of the two stories... was entirely coincidental and supplemented it with reasons. Accepting this to be so, it had nevertheless unfortunate results.'

On 19 March the case of the journalists jailed for refusing to reveal their sources to the Vassall tribunal was debated in the Commons. This was Wigg's chance (though barely 'in order' but safe from the laws of libel) to raise the allegations against Profumo:

> Here was a set of rumours that gained in strength, consumed men's reputations – might in fact have destroyed them – and which here infringed on the security of the State. But are we quite sure that the same thing is not happening again? There is not an hon Member in the House, not a journalist in the Press Gallery who, in the last few days, has not heard rumour upon rumour involving a member of the Government Front Bench. The Press has got as near as it could – it has shown itself willing to wound but afraid to strike. This all comes about because of the Vassall tribunal.
>
> In actual fact, these great Press Lords, these men who control great instruments of public opinion and power, do not have the guts to discharge the duty that they are now claiming for themselves. That being the case, I rightly use the Privilege of the House of Commons – that is what it is given

me for – to ask the Home Secretary who is the senior member of the Government on the Treasury Bench now, to go to the Dispatch Box – he knows the rumour to which I refer relates to Miss Christine Keeler and Miss Davies and a shooting by a West Indian – and, on behalf of the Government, categorically deny the truth of these rumours. On the other hand, if there is anything in them, I urge him to ask the Prime Minister to do what was not done in the Vassall case – set up a Select Committee so that these things can be dissipated, and the honour of the Minister concerned freed from the imputations and innuendoes that are being spread at the present time.

Wigg was supported in his demand by a leading Labour frontbencher, Richard Crossman – although at least one of their Labour colleagues, the eccentric, fox-hunting Reginald Paget, disagreed: 'What do these rumours amount to? They amount to the fact that a minister is said to be acquainted with an extremely pretty girl. As far as I am concerned, I should have thought that was a matter for congratulation rather than an inquiry.' Barbara Castle did not agree and raised the disappearance of Keeler. Henry Brooke, the Home Secretary, was outwardly dismissive:

I do not propose to comment on rumours which have been raised under the cloak of Privilege and safe from any action at law. The hon Member for Dudley (Wigg) and the hon Member for Blackburn (Castle) should seek other means of making these insinuations if they are prepared to substantiate them.

Privately the government was alarmed. That night Macmillan required Profumo to repeat to the Commons the following morning the denials he had made in private. After sunrise Profumo was summoned from his bed and quizzed again by the two law officers, Iain Macleod, Leader of the House, the Chief Whip and William Deedes, Minister without Portfolio (and future editor of the *Daily Telegraph*). Unrepentant, Profumo insisted he was innocent and that the word 'Darling', with which that as yet unpublished letter began, did not amount to an admission of adultery.

A couple of hours later, at 11 a.m. on Friday, 22 March, Profumo delivered his disastrous personal statement. Unusually for a Friday, the House was packed.

> I understand that in the debate on the Consolidated Fund Bill last night, under the protection of Parliamentary privilege the hon gentlemen, the Members for Dudley (Wigg) and for Coventry East (Crossman) and the hon lady, the Member for Blackburn (Castle), opposite, spoke of rumours connecting a Minister with a Miss Keeler and a recent trial at the Central Criminal Court. It was alleged that people in high places might have been responsible for concealing information concerning the disappearance of a witness and the perversion of justice. I understand that my name had been connected with the rumours about the disappearance of Miss Keeler. I would like to take this opportunity of making a personal statement about these matters. I last saw Miss Keeler in December 1961, and I have not seen her since. I have no idea where she is now. Any suggestion that I was in any way connected with or responsible for her absence from the trial at the Old Bailey is wholly and completely untrue. My wife and I first met Miss Keeler at a house party in July 1961 at Cliveden. Among a number of people there was Dr Stephen Ward, whom we already knew slightly, and Mr Ivanov, who was an attaché at the Russian Embassy. The only other occasion that my wife or I met Mr Ivanov was for a moment at the official reception for Major Gargarin at the Soviet Embassy. My wife and I had a standing invitation to visit Dr Ward. Between July and December 1961 I met Miss Keeler on about half a dozen occasions when I called to see him and his friends. Miss Keeler and I were on friendly terms. There was no impropriety whatsoever in my acquaintanceship with Miss Keeler. Mr Speaker, I have made this personal statement because of what was said in the House last evening by the three hon Members, and which, of course, was protected by privilege. I shall not hesitate to issue writs for libel and slander if scandalous allegations are made or repeated outside the House.

Even as Profumo was speaking the press were closing in on Christine Keeler, whom they found in Madrid a few days later.

Keeler, who was by now running scared from the powerful forces which had been unleashed against her, told the *Daily Express*:

> What Mr Profumo says is quite correct. I have not been in his company since December 1961. He was always very pleasant and on one occasion I met his wife, Valerie Hobson, at the swimming pool down at Cliveden. She was charming and we chatted for quite a while.

The indefatigable George Wigg never believed a word of Profumo's statement. The night before Keeler's denial on Monday, 25 March he appeared on the 'Panorama' television programme and bluntly stated that Ward and Ivanov were security risks. This outraged Ward who met Wigg the next day. Wigg left the private meeting convinced that Profumo was a liar. He reported the conversation to Wilson, who asked him to write a report of the meeting. An edited version was sent to Macmillan – who did not, however, see it for about two weeks. Meanwhile, Profumo had issued writs against *Il Tempo Illustrato* and *Paris Match*, both having published allegations that he and Keeler had been sexually involved.

Henry Brooke, the Home Secretary, held a meeting the following day with the head of MI5 to discuss Ward's explosive encounter with Wigg. It seems MI5 instructed the Commissioner of the Metropolitan Police to find evidence to bring any kind of criminal charges against Ward in a covert attempt to silence him. This was an arguably disgraceful move. As Philip Knightley and Caroline Kennedy, authors who have studied the affair in depth, point out, the police investigate crimes not individuals: to pursue someone to see what crime he might have committed is highly unusual.

> … yet the investigation of Ward's social and business activities was just such a 'fishing expedition' – as the wide variety of charges eventually brought against Ward confirms. It was as if someone had said, 'We want to prosecute Stephen Ward for a criminal offence. Go and find one that has a chance of sticking.'

The police began questioning Ward's friends and patients, many now frightened away from his clinic by the adverse publicity. On 23 April they stopped Keeler's friend Mandy Rice-Davies leaving for Spain where she was planning to marry her Spanish boyfriend. She was charged with possessing a false driving licence. The magistrates fixed bail at the exorbitant level of £2,000, prompting speculation that they were acting under pressure from above. The police told her that even if she managed to pay they had plenty of other potential charges to keep her in the country.

After Rice-Davies had spent ten days on remand in prison the two policemen on the case, Chief Inspector Herbert and Detective Sergeant Burrows, came, she says, to see her: 'Mandy, you don't like it here very much, do you? So you help us and we'll help you.'

She knew what she had to do: implicate Stephen Ward. She refused. Rice-Davies' case came up on 1 May , she was fined £42, and left for Spain. On her return she was arrested and charged with the theft of a TV set, a charge later dropped. Her passport was confiscated. For bail of £1,000 she was released on condition she reported to the police station on the same day Ward went to court in July. Tactics such as these persuaded her to testify.

Ward was beginning to despair. Friends were deserting. Lord Astor refused to let him keep the Cliveden cottage. On 7 May he went to see Tim Bligh, the Prime Minister's Parliamentary Private Secretary, and asked whether the investigation might be politically motivated:

> You see the facts as presented in Parliament were not strictly speaking just like that... I feel I should tell you the truth of what really happened... [Profumo] wrote Miss Keeler a series of letters... I don't know whether you have any feelings about this, whether there is anything you can do. I know myself here that there is a great deal of potentially extremely explosive material in what I have told you.

Bligh considered this attempted blackmail. He told Macmillan, who questioned Profumo again, but Profumo stuck to his story. An increasingly frantic Ward began reeling off letters to the Home Secretary, to his own MP, Sir Wavell Wakefield, and finally, on 20 May, to Harold Wilson, repeating his complaints about the police inquiry and his claim that Profumo had been lying. Brooke, the

Home Secretary, sent a terse reply: 'The Home Secretary has asked me to explain that the police, in making what enquiries they think proper, do not act under his direction.'

Wilson took it more seriously. He passed a copy of Ward's letter to the Prime Minister. On 29 May Macmillan and Wilson met. Macmillan agreed to set up an inquiry under Lord Dilhorne. The pressure was building up again; two Labour MPs put down questions to the Home Secretary about what information he had received from Ward.

On 4 June Profumo was recalled from holiday in Venice to appear before the Dilhorne inquiry. This time he told the truth. Unable to face cross-examination at the independent inquiry, he admitted to Macmillan's PPS and the Chief Whip that he had lied. He resigned the same day not only as a minister but as an MP. His letter of resignation, and Macmillan's reply, were published the following day:

Dear Prime Minister,

You will recollect that on 22 March, following certain allegations made in Parliament, I made a personal statement. At that time rumour had charged me with assisting in the disappearance of a witness and with being involved in some possible breach of security.

So serious were these charges that I allowed myself to think that my personal association with that witness, which had also been the subject of rumour, was, by comparison, of minor importance only. In my statement I said that there had been no impropriety in this association. To my very deep regret I have to admit that this was not true, and that I misled you, and my colleagues, and the House.

I ask you to understand that I did this to protect, as I thought, my wife and family, who were misled, as were my professional advisers.

I have come to realize that, by this deception, I have been guilty of a grave misdemeanour and despite the fact that there is no truth whatsoever in the other charges, I cannot remain a member of your Administration, nor of the House of Commons.

I cannot tell you of my deep remorse for the embarrassment I have caused you, to my colleagues in the

Government, to my constituents and to the Party which I have served for the past twenty-five years.

Yours sincerely,

Jack Profumo

Macmillan, ever the showman, responded by the implied rebuke that he had not even read Profumo's letter.

Dear Profumo,

The contents of your letter of 4 June have been communicated to me, and I have heard them with deep regret. This is a great tragedy for you, your family and your friends. Nevertheless, I am sure you will understand that in the circumstances I have no alternative but to advise the Queen to accept your resignation.

Yours very sincerely,

Harold Macmillan

It is now commonplace to observe that it was lying to the House which sealed the War Minister's fate. But had he been candid, would he have been likely to have survived? 'Lying to the House' was the simplest charge, of course, and colleagues would have found it an easier argument than entering the debate on public versus private life. But my own view is that Profumo was finished if found out, knew it, and – having nothing to lose – tried lying. This approach has not always failed in politics.

This time, though, it did. Profumo's career was over. But the scandal went into overdrive. Sensation was boosted by the fact that 5 June was not only the day on which Profumo's resignation was made public, but the first day in another trial: that of Keeler's other, West Indian boyfriend Lucky Gordon – charged with assaulting her outside the flat of a friend on 17 April. Keeler arrived at the trial in a chauffeur-driven Rolls-Royce.

The court case made wonderful copy. Papers could report what was said with impunity. Asked why she had sent the defendant £5 to pay a fine, Keeler replied: 'I would say Gordon was blackmailing me on this particular occasion.' A letter was then passed to the judge but remained unread in public. Gordon conducted his own case and made a series of allegations against

Ward. 'He is known as a crank and he is a crank. He gets his delight from seeing people get aggravated.' And he accused Keeler of having given him VD, provoking an outburst from her where she sat in the public gallery. Gordon's three-year sentence was quashed on appeal.

On 7 June Ward was interviewed by Desmond Wilcox on the TV programme 'This Week':

> The key point for me to clear my name was to indicate that I had not encouraged the relationship between Miss Keeler and Mr Profumo... I was disturbed about certain parts of it and, as tactfully as possible, I had informed the Security Service. I wanted to make it absolutely clear that I hadn't encouraged it and knowing that I had a friend in the Soviet Embassy, I think I was rightly disturbed about it.

The following day he was arrested on the charge of 'on diverse dates between January 1961 and June 1963 having knowingly lived wholly or in part on the earnings of prostitution at 17 Wimpole Mews W1'.

Profumo's resignation had made headlines around the world. This was 'the sordid side of London's high society'. Stories abounded, most famous of which was the tale of the mysterious 'man in the mask' who, it was said, frequently turned up at Ward's orgies. The story first surfaced on 8 June in the *Washington Star*, in an interview with Rice-Davies.

> At Scotland Yard's request Mandy cut short a continental holiday last month and came back to Britain. Newspapers said she was helping to uncover a top people's call-girl ring involving dozens of girls. Mandy herself said on June 1: 'I can say that probably a number of well-known people will be involved'. Mandy has talked of one gay little party she went to where the host who opened the door wore nothing but his socks. 'Then,' she said, 'there was a dinner party where a naked man wearing a mask waited on table like a slave. He had to have a mask because he was so well known.'

Who was the man in the mask? Rumour alternated between a Cabinet minister and a senior Royal. The story was first published in Britain by the *Express* on 21 June 1963. They quoted another guest:

> ...As the 'slave' handed (us) cocktail snacks the guests abused and reviled him. He was obviously enjoying it. I was told by the host that the man arrived first at the party. He undressed and put on a mask before the other guests arrived. The host revealed his true identity to me. I could hardly believe it. I left after a few minutes.

Three days later the *Mirror*'s front page read 'Prince Philip and the Profumo Scandal'. Under the headline was a denial of the 'foul rumour' linking the Queen's husband to the affair. The identity of the man in the mask still excites speculation today. Lord Denning later devoted a whole subsection of his report to this sub-plot:

> There is a great deal of evidence which satisfied me that there is a group of people who hold parties in private of a perverted nature. At some of these parties, the man who serves dinner is nearly naked except for a small square lace apron round his waist such as a waitress might wear. He wears a black mask over his head with slits for eye-holes. He cannot therefore be recognised by any of the guests. Some reports stop there and say that nothing evil takes place. It is done as a comic turn and no more. This may well be so at some of the parties. But at others I am satisfied that it is followed by perverted sex orgies: that the man in the mask is a 'slave' who is whipped: that guests undress and indulge in sexual intercourse one with the other: and indulge in other sexual activities of a vile and revolting nature.

Denning goes on, breathlessly:

> My only concern in my inquiry was to see whether any Minister or other person prominent in public life was present at these parties; for, if he were, he would, I should think, be exposing himself to blackmail.

And yet another whirlwind whipped along Fleet Street towards Westminster. This involved an alleged affair between a minister and a duchess: the Duchess of Argyll, involved in a famous divorce case. A Polaroid photograph of the naked Duchess engaged in a sexual act with a man was passed to the judge. The snapshot excluded the head, though only the head, of her aroused and enthusiastic lover. Rumours spread as to the identity of the mystery man: a Cabinet minister, it was said. Ward, the rumours added, had been involved in bribery to keep the MP's name out of the trial. Denning went to the unusual lengths of persuading the unnamed minister to submit himself to a medical examination

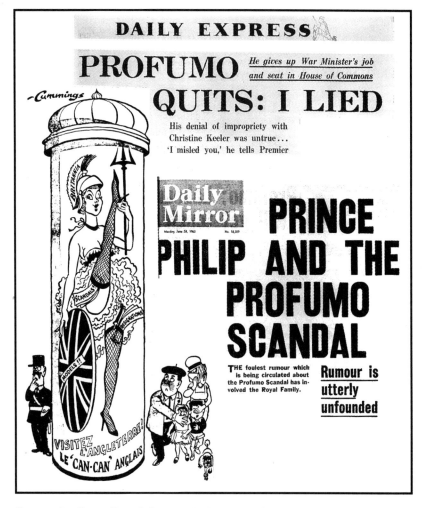

Cartoon by Cummings, 8 June 1963 (courtesy of *Daily Express*) with headlines from the *Daily Express*, 6 June 1963, and *Daily Mirror*, 24 June 1963

of his penis by a Harley Street consultant. Bernard Levin commented:

> ...Even in years so copiously provided with material on which madness could feel fat, there was one episode which stands out from the decade, and still stands out, as a monument to the willingness of man to suspend the operation of reason... how it came about, almost exactly two-thirds of the way through the twentieth century, and in a country as advanced as Britain, that a judge should have been obliged to ask a doctor to examine the penis of a politician, is something so extraordinary, and in many ways so significant, that it deserves examination as detailed as that which the Minister underwent.

Iain Crawford remarks in *The Profumo Affair* that 'the scandal had now reached the point at which almost anything could be said about anyone; provided it was sufficiently scabrous it was certain of wide circulation'. Mervyn Stockwood, the Bishop of Southwark, attacked both the newspapers and the news:

> Things have happened in Britain in recent weeks that have left an unpleasant smell – the smell of corruption in high places, of evil practices, and of a repudiation of the simple decencies and the basic values. The smell is so intensified in its unpleasantness by the squalid biographies in a particular section of the Sunday Press that thrives, no doubt with considerable financial gain, on sexual scandals. The time has come to clean the national stables.

Stockwood did not explain whether he wanted to suppress the sin, or the reports of it. The reverend prelate contrived both to have his cake of piety, and to eat it.

High on the list of commentators' questions was how Profumo managed to maintain the lie for so long. It had become apparent how long various members of the government had known about the letter, which was finally published on 9 June. Macmillan's knowledge of events made his own position awkward. Speculation began about his leadership. Ministers scrambled to distance themselves from any knowledge of their former friend's private

"Ladies and Gentlemen, Miss Chris—"

Cartoon by Giles, 11 June 1963 (courtesy of *Daily Express*)

diversions. Lord Hailsham, a likely contender for Macmillan's job, was vitriolic. On the BBC's 'Gallery' he said:

> It is intolerable for Mr Profumo in his position to have behaved in this way, and a tragedy that he should not have been found out – that he should have lied and lied and lied. Lied to his friends, lied to his solicitor and lied to the House of Commons.

Almost a lone voice, Sir Reginald Paget called that a 'virtuoso performance in the art of kicking a friend in the guts'. He added: 'When self-indulgence has reduced a man to the shape of Lord Hailsham, sexual continence involves no more than a sense of the ridiculous'.

Defensive at the charge of muck-raking, the press homed in on the security implications of the affair. The *Sunday Mirror* published as early as 9 June Rice-Davies's revelation that 'on more than one occasion – as Jack left Christine at the flat where she stayed, Eugene Ivanov, the handsome young Russian naval attaché, walked in. In fact it was something of a standing joke among us.'

Allegations that the government had treated questions about security too lightly emerged when, on 13 June, Michael Eddowes, the solicitor who had questioned Keeler after the shooting incident, issued a press statement claiming he had warned the Prime Minister. He had submitted his report on the security aspects of the affair to Special Branch as early as 29 March, but nothing had been done. It was through Eddowes that the alleged inquiry about when Germany had got the atom bomb first hit the news-stands. In her paid '*Confessions*' in the *News of the World* on 16 June, Keeler confirmed that someone, not Ivanov, had asked her to find this information out from Profumo.

On 11 June under the headline 'It *is* a Moral Issue', *The Times* commented:

Everyone has been so busy assuring the public that the affair is not one of morals, that it is time to assert that it is. Morals have been discounted too long. A judge may be justified in reminding a jury: 'This is not a court of morals'. The same exemption cannot be allowed in public opinion, without rot setting in and all standards suffering in the long run. The British are not by and large an immoral nation but through their pathetic fear of being called smug they make themselves out to be one . . .

. . . It remains strange that not a single member of the Government resigned when the affair broke in March and [Profumo] did not himself resign.

There is no hiding place from the tidal wave of overthrow and disaster.

Whether in the next few days some heads fall or none, damage has been done. It may be a caricature for the *Washington Post* to say that 'a picture of widespread decadence beneath the glitter of a large segment of stiff-lipped society is emerging'. But the essence of caricature is to exaggerate real traits.

There are plenty of earnest and serious men in the Conservative Party who know that all is not well. It is time they put first things first, stopped weighing electoral chances, and returned to the starker truths of an earlier day.

Popularity by affluence is about played out, especially when it rests on so insecure a basis. Even if the call had metaphorically to be for 'blood, sweat and tears', instead of to the fleshpots, they might be surprised by the result. The British are always at their best when they are braced.

When this dreadful prose was quoted at Lord Hailsham on the programme 'Gallery', he snapped back bitterly: '*The Times* is an anti-Conservative newspaper with an anti-Conservative editor.' On 17 June the affair was debated in the Commons. Harold Wilson piously attacked Macmillan's failure to act earlier.

This is a debate without precedent in the annals of this House. It arises from disclosures which have shocked the moral conscience of the nation. There is clear evidence of a sordid underworld network, the extent of which cannot yet be measured . . .

. . . After the Vassall case [the Prime Minister] felt that he could not stand another serious case involving a ministerial resignation, and he gambled desperately and hoped that nothing would ever come out. For political reasons he was gambling with national security.

Other attacks on Macmillan came from his own side of the House, most notably from Nigel Birch MP:

I must say that [Profumo] never struck me as a man at all like a cloistered monk; and Miss Keeler is a professional prostitute. There seems to me to be a basic improbability about the proposition that their relationship was purely platonic. What are whores about? [*turning to Macmillan*] What is to happen now? We cannot just have business as usual. I myself feel that the time will come very soon when my Right Honourable Friend ought to make way for a much younger colleague. I feel that ought to happen. I certainly will not quote at him the savage words of Cromwell, but perhaps some word of Browning might be appropriate:

. . . let him never come back to us!
There would be doubt, hesitation and pain.
Forced praise on our part – the glimmer of twilight,
Never glad confident morning again.

There was a delicacy to these razored words not likely to be found today.

Macmillan, though cruelly damaged by the affair, managed to survive. A three-line whip, and the prospect of a rout in any election, enabled the Prime Minister to limp on before resigning just ahead of the autumn Party Conference, Lord Hailsham resigning his peerage to throw his hat into the ring. More lasting was the damage to the public perception of the governing class and to the image of the Conservative Party. Perhaps some of the cynicism engendered remains to this day beneath the surface, waiting to be triggered by new scandal.

On 21 June, Macmillan announced that an inquiry would be conducted by Lord Denning. The Denning Report, published on 26 October 1963, was a best-seller, with 4,000 copies sold in the first hour. Many thought it a whitewash which laid the blame for the scandal largely at the feet of Ward. Denning has also been criticized because, in the words of Philip Knightley and Caroline Kennedy, 'he showed more interest in the sex and rumour part of the affair than in the security, which was his brief'. But then which is more interesting? 'Many of the witnesses said that he

Cartoon by Trog, 14 July 1963 (courtesy of *Private Eye)*

quizzed them on salacious and irrelevant details . . . sending the official stenographer out of the room when he thought that she might be embarrassed by the evidence.'

Denning's evidence remains unpublished, a Cabinet secret – obviously, for reasons of national security.

And in the end it was on Ward that the fury turned. Ward's eight-day trial at the Old Bailey in July attracted huge international media attention. A New Zealand newspaper was fined for indecency merely for reporting it. There were moments of pure farce. Court Number One erupted in laughter when Mandy Rice-Davies delivered the most quoted one-liner in English judicial history. It was put to her that Lord Astor denied friendship with her. 'Well, *he* would, wouldn't he?' she replied. Once, the judge mistakenly addressed her as Marilyn Monroe.

The judge, Sir Archie Pellow Marshall QC, delivered a 'hanging' direction. He told the jury of eleven men and one middle-aged woman that Ward had been deserted by his friends: 'There are many people of high estate and low who could have come forward and testified . . . One would have thought from the newspapers that this country has become a sink of iniquity. But you and I know that the even tenor of family life over the overwhelming majority of the population goes quietly and decently on.'

The judge's comments were too much for the ruined fifty-year-old osteopath to bear. On the night of 3 July, with the summing-up only half completed, Ward swallowed an overdose of sleeping draught. He went into a coma from which he never recovered. With Ward now unconscious at St Stephen's Hospital, and after four and a half hours' deliberation, the jury returned their verdict. Ward was found guilty on two charges of living on immoral earnings. Sentence was never passed. He died on 3 August.

Shortly before his overdose, Ward, having seen his character systematically torn apart, had turned to one of his few remaining friends, the *Express* reporter Tom Mangold, and said: 'This is a political revenge trial. Someone had to be sacrificed and that someone was me.' He killed himself in the Chelsea flat of a friend, Noel Howard-Jones. His note read:

Dear Noel,

        I am sorry I had to do this here! It is really more

than I can stand – the horror, day after day at the court and in the streets. It is not only fear, it is a wish not to let them get me. I would rather get myself. I do hope I have not let people down too much. I tried to do my stuff but after Marshall's summing-up, I've given up all hope. The car needs oil in the gearbox, by the way. Be happy in it. Incidentally, it was surprisingly easy and required no guts. I am sorry to disappoint the vultures.

I only hope this has done the job. Delay resuscitation as long as possible.

The *News of the World* commented, with posthumous valour, that Ward was 'a cornered rat' with 'a fiendish smile', 'utterly depraved' with dirty hands 'now with ugly little marks on them'. 'Now he is dead,' wrote the journalist Peter Earle, 'I'm not surprised. I had known for a long time that he was a coward.'

Profumo disappeared from political life and threw himself into charity work for which he was given a CBE in 1975. He remains independently wealthy, and married to Valerie Hobson.

Shortly after the Ward trial, Keeler, who had failed to attend Lucky Gordon's trial, was jailed for six months for contempt of court. She now has two sons from two marriages, both annulled, and lives in South London. She survives on the proceeds of her 1989 autobiography, *Scandal*, which was made into a film. I understand that John Profumo saw the film incognito.

Mandy Rice-Davies has not spoken to Keeler for thirty years. She has written a string of novels, acted in films, opened two nightclubs in Israel, and is on her second marriage: to the millionaire businessman Ken Foreman. When I met her recently she said I was the first Tory politician she had ever met, winked, then giggled.

George Wigg remained an MP until 1967, when he was made a life peer. He became chairman of the Horse Race Betting Levy Board, and later president of the Betting Office Licensees' Association. He pleaded guilty to charges arising from kerb-crawling in Soho, in pursuit of prostitutes. He died in 1983.

There were six mourners at Ward's funeral and only two wreaths. One was from his family. The other had contained 100 white carnations and was from Kenneth Tynan, John Osborne, Annie Ross, Dominick Elwes, Arnold Wesker, Joe Orton and

Penelope Gilliat. The card on it read: 'To Stephen Ward, Victim of Hypocrisy.' You cannot apologize to the dead and nobody in British public life seems to apologize anyway, but there are people alive today (not Profumo) who wronged Stephen Ward badly. Some indication of remorse would have been refreshing.

I sent Mr Profumo this account of the events, in draft, in case there were anything incorrect or unfair. He replied on 29 June 1995:

> . . . Since 1963 there have been unceasing publications, both written and spoken, relating to what you refer to in your letter as 'the Keeler interlude'. The majority of these have increasingly contained deeply distressing inaccuracies, so I have resolved to refrain from any sort of personal comment, and I propose to continue thus.
>
> I hope – indeed I believe – you will understand and acquit me of discourtesy.

Indeed I do. Writing recently for *The Times*, I described the night a good-looking young Bulgarian diplomat tried to seduce me when I was twenty-five-year old Foreign Office official in 1976. As I went on to become a Tory MP, the story might have been interesting. Fortunately he had dreadful breath. Upon the smallest things destinies can turn.

REGINALD MAUDLING – 1972

A Civilized Man, a Whiff of Greed

It is to Reggie Maudling that we owe the Commons Register of Members' Interests, which was set up during one of the nation's habitual moral panics about 'sleaze waves'. This one, involving allegations over the business activities of Maudling and two other MPs, began in the early 70s.

Reginald Maudling was Home Secretary in 1972 when – appearing to set an unusual standard for honourable conduct in ministers – he suddenly resigned. The Prime Minister, Edward Heath, had begged him to remain in the government while Scotland Yard mounted an investigation into allegations of corruption against one of the Home Secretary's former business associates, John Poulson. But as the overall head of the Metropolitan Police, Maudling insisted on going. The *Daily Express* wrote in July 1972: 'His resignation as Home Secretary was a gesture without parallel in recent politics.'

As events unfolded, the resignation began to look less surprising. It took five years to resolve the affair and though Maudling escaped criminal charges, he did not escape censure. By that time anyway, with Labour in power, it was too late. He died eighteen months later, never unambiguously implicated in any wrongdoing, never wholly exonerated. A faint whiff – if not of corruption – of greed, hung about his name. It still does.

This was a pity. Maudling was an unusually civilized and intelligent politician, and life could have turned out very differently. After Merchant Taylors' School and Merton College, Oxford, a spell at the Bar, and active service with the RAF, Maudling became one of R. A. Butler's 'backroom boys' at Conservative Central Office after the war. In 1950 he entered Parliament for Chipping Barnet. He was a Cabinet minister and Privy Councillor within five years and a forty-five-year-old Chancellor of the Exchequer in 1962.

With Labour winning the 1964 election and Edward Heath securing the Tory leadership, Maudling decided to concentrate on his business interests – or, as he put it, 'a little pot of gold'. His own hopes for the leadership of his party had been dashed and a certain disillusion set in. In 1965 he took a consultancy from the well-known Labour supporter and Wilson hanger-on, Eric Miller, Chairman of Peachey Property Corporation. Keen to avoid paying income tax, the former Chancellor of the Exchequer waived his £5,000 annual remuneration. Instead, Peachey bought the freehold of his country house and rented it back to him for £2 a week. In October 1977 Miller, whose financial affairs were under investigation, would shoot himself on the patio of his South Kensington home.

But Maudling grew richer. Already a Lloyd's Name, he accumulated several directorships, putting his annual income beyond £20,000 – four times a ministerial salary. He had a house in Hertfordshire and a Regency home in Chester Square, Belgravia. He wanted more. In his 1978 memoirs he remarked that politicians 'cannot reasonably be expected to neglect their interests and those of their families'. In particular he sought a position for his eldest son, Martin, who had recently graduated from Oxford. His involvements with Dunlop and Kleinwort Benson were lucrative but unspectacular. Maudling's downfall was his move into the booming property market.

In 1966 the Yorkshire architect John Poulson, by then vividly active in town hall corruption, walked into Maudling's life. Poulson had secured the services of the backbench Labour MP Albert Roberts, but wanted a political heavyweight to front the overseas branch of Poulson's new company, International Technical and Construction Services. Maudling fitted the bill.

Poulson's strategy worked. With Maudling's help he snapped up a lucrative contract from the Maltese government for a hospital on the island of Gozo. A former Chancellor does not come cheaply. Poulson made an £8,000 annual covenant (worth £27,000, a tidy sum in those days) to Mrs Beryl Maudling's favourite theatre project in East Grinstead, the Adèle Genée. He also made Martin Maudling a director of one of his companies; and the Maudling family acquired shares in the Poulson empire.

With Maudling, Poulson had struck gold. He decided to share his political ambassador with one of his friends. The Tory MP went to work for the corrupt (as it later emerged) Real Estate Fund of America, headed by the thirty-nine-year-old American financier Jerry Hoffman. Maudling persuaded at least two foreign banks to invest in Hoffman's venture. He waived his fee in return for 250,000 shares in the company. Maudling wisely severed this involvement in July 1969. The following year the company crashed with debts of £4 million. Hoffman was sent to jail for two years by an Illinois court.

When the Tories came to power in 1970, the new Prime Minister, Edward Heath, made Maudling Home Secretary. He immediately resigned all his remaining directorships. But the storm was gathering. Poulson was in deep financial trouble. He had over-extended, and neglected to pay his taxes. In 1972 the sixty-two-year-old architect filed for bankruptcy. At the sensational hearing which followed, Poulson revealed, among much else, the existence of his £8,000 covenant to Mrs Maudling's pet theatre.

Maudling went straight to the Prime Minister. In a long intimate conversation at 10 Downing Street on the evening of Monday, 17 July 1972, he warned his leader that if the police asked for an inquiry into Poulson's bankruptcy he would have to resign. He could not contemplate the embarrassment of the police having to question their political master.

His fears were realized the following day. The Attorney-General Sir Peter Rawlinson's report arrived at 12.30 p.m. on both Heath's and Maudling's desks. Events followed the course the two men had agreed the previous evening. The Home Secretary wrote his resignation letter over lunch. After twenty years on the frontbench, he said: 'I think I can reasonably claim a respite from the burdens of responsibility and the glare of publicity, which inevitably surrounds a Minister and, inexcusably, engulfs the private life even of his family.' But there was no mention of the fact that Maudling and members of his family owned shares in Poulson's companies or that his son Martin was a director of one.

Heath, in a rare public outburst of warmth, replied: 'I profoundly regret your going now and I hope that it will not be long before you are able to resume your position in the public life of this country.'

THE Sun

My dear
Ted ... the
resignation
letter
—Page Two

The man
who could
have been
Premier
—Pages 4 and 5

WARD WITH THE PEOPLE 3p   Wednesday, July 19, 1972

-THE TRAGEDY-
OF MAUDLING

Reggie's 'I quit' is a disaster for Heath and the Government

'I can reasonably claim a respite from the burdens of responsibility and from the glare of publicity which surrounds a Minister, and inexcusably engulfs the private lives even of his family'

Sun, 19 July 1972

When Maudling's resignation was disclosed to an astonished Commons, even political foes such as Labour's former Home Secretary James Callaghan, and the Liberal leader Jeremy Thorpe, reflected the confident view of most MPs: that Maudling would be cleared of any improper conduct. *The Times* was perhaps closer to the mark. The paper's editorial warned: 'A leading political figure who goes into business puts the stamp of his reputation on those with whom he associates, and he owes a particular obligation to satisfy himself that he is dealing with sound business.'

The first arrests arising from the Poulson investigation were made in June 1973. The following March, Poulson himself was convicted of corruption and gaoled for seven years.

Two other MPs had also been involved with Poulson. John Cordle, the Tory MP for Bournemouth East, and Albert Roberts, the Labour MP for Normanton, had helped the discredited property developer gain business in West Africa, Spain and Portugal. Neither was ever charged, but the feeling that they should have been more open in their business dealings, and the hint that Maudling in particular should have known what sort of a man he was collaborating with – and that he possibly did know – hung in the air. Allegations of sleaze led the new Labour government to set up the voluntary Register of Members' Interests when they came to power that year, 1974.

In October 1976 the DPP announced an end to any further prosecutions. With the criminal investigation over, the *Observer*, among other voices, asked what action would be taken against Maudling and the two other MPs who had helped Poulson. James Callaghan, now Prime Minister, offered an inquiry to look at procedure for the future rather than past events. The outcry, particularly from his own backbenchers, caused a climb-down within twenty-four hours. A select committee of ten MPs was established. It would examine the role of Maudling and the other MPs in the Poulson collapse.

Its report, published on 15 July 1977, unanimously accused Maudling and Roberts of conduct 'inconsistent with the standards which the House is entitled to expect from its members' by not declaring an interest. It alleged that Maudling's resignation letter had been 'lacking in frankness' when it said his only payment had been Poulson's charitable covenant to the East

Grinstead theatre and failed to mention his shares in Poulson companies, and the fact that his son was a director of one firm.

John Cordle came off worse. A damning piece of evidence against the Bournemouth MP was a letter he had written to Poulson after the architect had complained about the MP's work rate. Stung by the criticism, the Tory backbencher had penned a detailed reply. The picture he presented of his energetic efforts to earn his consultancy fee (£5,628 over six years) made sour reading. The committee felt Cordle's conduct amounted to 'a contempt of the House'. Having served as an MP for nineteen years, he resigned on 22 July before the report was even debated. He said he wanted to avoid an 'acrimonious and divisive debate'. Cordle had been, according to Poulson, not 'even a minnow'.

The Select Committee report was debated in the Commons on 26 July 1977. Both Maudling and Roberts, who survived as an MP until 1983, spoke in their own defence before leaving the Chamber, as custom dictated. In a highly charged debate, Edward Heath, now an influential backbencher, stoutly defended his former Cabinet colleague. He chose to criticize the committee instead, for suggesting that Maudling had misled him in his resignation letter.

The House Leader, Michael Foot, warned MPs not to succumb to a 'liberal form of lynch-law . . . Of all mobs the most objectionable is the sanctimonious.' The Commons voted 230 to 207 to adopt the inoffensive motion to 'take note' of the report. By a majority of 320 they rejected a move to expel Maudling from the Commons and by a margin of 227 to suspend him for six months without pay.

For someone who had plainly acted, at best, very foolishly, and in the opinion of some, corruptly, Reginald Maudling still commanded much affection and respect. This was due, I am told, to his high reputation as a moderate, thinking Conservative and a pleasant, intelligent colleague, 'clubbable', and bright. Looking older than his sixty years, he told reporters after the vote: 'It must be the end of the matter . . . for God's sake, after five years.' It was. He died eighteen months later.

I remember him, his career almost over when mine at the Conservative Research Department was just beginning. He seemed bored, lacklustre and tired, and all out of tune with the new Thatcherite certainties gripping a party preparing for government. But he also seemed wise: thoughtful and undogmatic in his discourse and in his political responses. It is not unusual, I observe, to find that men, who have been touched both by power and also by some kind of public disgrace, show towards the end a sort of frankness, an impatience with certitude, and a weary humanity. We can lose by forgoing their services.

A colleague remembers a telling moment not far from the close of Maudling's life. The portly and discredited figure was on his feet in a debate about the ailing British car industry, complaining that 'it takes a German worker one day and a half to build a car, whereas it takes his British equivalent more than three days . . .' Maudling was interrupted by a growl from the Labour MP Dennis Skinner: 'An' 'ow long would it tek *you*, fats?'

LORD LAMBTON and LORD JELLICOE – 1973

'Surely all men patronize whores?'

Within three days in May 1973 Edward Heath's government lost two ministers, both implicated in call-girl scandals. In forty-eight hours Lord Lambton went from ministerial cars and red boxes at the Ministry of Defence, to questions about drugs at Scotland Yard. Lord Jellicoe, one of the best-liked members of the Cabinet, stood down after being linked with a Scotland Yard inquiry into a 'top people's vice ring'.

Antony Claud Frederick, Viscount Lambton was elected MP for Berwick-on-Tweed in 1950. When his father, the 5th Earl of Durham, died in 1970, he disclaimed the title to remain in the Commons. He was given ministerial responsibility for the Royal Air Force.

In the early summer of 1972 Lambton was making regular use of a high-class call-girl service. His favourite was the twenty-six-year-old Norma Russell. What the popular newspapers were to call their torrid encounters took place at her Maida Vale flat. Other prostitutes often accompanied Norma to satisfy the minister's lively tastes. Marijuana lent an added exoticism to the scene. At first Lambton covered his tracks by using a bogus identity, 'Mr Lucas', but he became careless, and dispensed with precaution. So careless did he become that one evening he paid by personal cheque. Miss Russell seemed unlikely to shop him. 'I vote for the Tories. They are my best clients,' she later said.

In November 1972 Norma married Colin Levy, a twenty-eight-year-old heavy drinker with a criminal record for dishonesty. The marriage stayed on an even keel until March 1973 when, after a domestic dispute, Colin Levy went abroad. His wife told the police he had gone on a drugs-buying run. She also let slip that one of her clients was Lambton. The police pounced when Levy returned, though they found no drugs. Levy, however, implicated Lambton in drugs and prostitution. The police passed the information on to the Serious Crime Squad which was investigating a high-class London vice ring. They in turn passed the information on to MI5, who told the Home Secretary. Edward Heath was informed. The Prime Minister, aware of Macmillan's failings only ten years earlier, ordered MI5 and the police to co-operate in securing any evidence.

Meanwhile, Colin Levy was planning to cash in on his wife's connections. Levy and an accomplice hid cine-equipment and a microphone (the latter up a teddy bear's nose) in his wife's bedroom to capture the minister *in flagrante delicto*. On 5 May they offered the film show to the *News of the World* for £30,000. The pictures were not good enough so the newspaper installed its own equipment in the flat. On 9 May Levy used a tape recorder to capture a conversation about drugs between Lambton and Norma.

The following day, a *News of the World* photographer hid in the wardrobe behind a two-way mirror and took pictures of the minister cavorting on the bed with Norma and a black prostitute. Inexplicably, the newspaper shelved the story and returned the evidence to Levy. He tried and failed to sell it to the German magazine *Stern*. The *Sunday People* was next on his list. Levy demanded £45,000. The *Sunday People* offered £750, with a further £5,250 if they published the story. Reluctantly, Levy agreed. The newspaper gave the material straight to the police.

Norma Levy then embarked on the course which was to prove fatal to Lambton. She told her story to the well-connected wife of the man who ran the upmarket London nightclub 'Eve', where Norma plied her trade. The woman contacted James Prior, the Leader of the House of Commons, through a mutual friend who happened to be an old business acquaintance of the minister's. They met Robert Armstrong, a senior civil servant (later to become Cabinet Secretary), in the incongruously dignified surroundings of the Privy Council Office.

Prior doubted 'if the room had ever witnessed a more bizarre yet intriguing story'. His discoveries were conveyed to the Prime Minister. On 22 May, hours after Prior had emerged from the Privy Council room, Lambton resigned from the government and Parliament. His statement was frank and devoid of self-pity. 'This is the sordid story,' he wrote:

> There has been no security risk and no blackmail and never at any time have I spoken of any aspect of my late job. All that has happened is that some sneak pimp has seen an opportunity of making money by the sale of the story and secret photographs to the papers at home and abroad. My own feelings may be imagined but I have no excuses whatsoever to make. I behaved with incredible stupidity.

Lambton was later to comment that he couldn't think 'what all the fuss is about; surely all men patronize whores?'

The following day, 'a day of sensation' (*Daily Mirror*), it was revealed that Scotland Yard was investigating a 'top people's vice ring'. Within hours of Lambton's resignation statement, the Attorney-General announced that the former minister was to be investigated for drugs offences.

Senior Scotland Yard officers carried out summonses for the possession of cannabis and amphetamines. Lambton, in a second statement that night, said: 'The police appeared to believe I was a heroin addict and asked to inspect the veins on my arms and legs. I consented. They were unmarked.' The press latched on to the fact that the minister stripped to his distinctive red flannel underwear. They searched his house. 'I willingly complied and showed them at

Daily Mirror, 24 May 1973

once a small parcel of soft drugs that I had confiscated from a friend many months ago. They also found barbiturate pills which I have had, on and off, on prescription for fifteen years. If I had any sense of guilt I had ample time to hide the pills. I made no attempt to do so.' He later pleaded guilty to two charges of possessing cannabis and amphetamines. He was fined £300.

But the Yard's inquiries into the vice ring had uncovered the name of another senior member of the government. The name on the secret dossier which had been handed to the Home Secretary, Robert Carr, was George Patrick John Rushworth, the 2nd Earl Jellicoe, DSO, MC, godson of King George V. Since 1970 Jellicoe had been Leader of the House of Lords. It was alleged that on five or six occasions in the past year he had used call-girls from two agencies which advertised in the *Evening Standard*.

Jellicoe, twice married, took the prostitutes for dinner. After the mints came sex in his London flat. The day after Lambton's resignation the Prime Minister, Edward Heath, had asked Jellicoe if he knew anything about the case; the truthful reply had been No. But Jellicoe, a Cambridge man, felt honour-bound to return to the Prime Minister the next day to tender his resignation. The PM accepted – mainly because he could not now truthfully deny knowledge of Jellicoe's indiscretions.

It was one of the few examples of unextracted honesty in the story of modern political scandal. It is also an odd reflection on Edward Heath, who in his later years radiates a mellow and indulgent 'seen it all before' mood, that he reacted as he did. It is unlikely that the oddly tolerant Margaret Thatcher – for all her reputation for 'Victorian values' – would have asked for Jellicoe's resignation. But we have to remember that the Profumo affair had been traumatic for the political class of the day. The country and its media were perhaps experiencing a wave of moral edginess not dissimilar to that which grips us in the mid-1990s.

On Jellicoe's revelations, Lambton commented: 'The way things are going it will soon be clear that Heath is the only member of the government who doesn't do it.' Lambton also gave a startling television interview to Robin Day. He admitted to taking drugs, a habit he had picked up in Singapore, but he added: 'Taking opium in China is different to taking it in Berwick-on-Tweed.'

Lambton, married to his wife Belinda for thirty years, was the father of five; Jellicoe had a distinguished war record and had been awarded the Croix de Guerre. There was some public sympathy for both, especially Jellicoe. The *Daily Express* commented:

> In this modern so-called permissive age a splendid [parliamentarian] and junior minister have been cast into the wilderness . . . Can we really afford to discard men of talent, wit and patriotism because their personal lives fall short of blameless perfection?

Edward Heath was forced to set up an inquiry. The Diplock report, delivered within two months, expressed satisfaction that there had been no compromise of security in either case. If Jellicoe hadn't resigned, said the report, he would have been allowed clearance for secret material. The same was not true of Lambton. The committee concluded:

> We do not suggest that Lord Lambton would consciously commit indiscretions when in his normal state of mind; but we think that there would be a real risk that he might do so in a mood of irresponsibility induced by drugs. . .

Ten years later, Lord Lambton was to return to the theme of double standards for politicians and the public. Commenting on the Cecil Parkinson scandal he remarked: 'I felt very sorry for

Parkinson. I felt sorry for him because he had full attention on him and I know what that's like. But to tell you the truth, I couldn't quite see what he had done.'

Lambton ducked out of the public eye for many years, retiring to a peaceful villa in Sienna in Italy. He wrote a string of novels.

His daughter appeared as 'Miss Whiplash' in the 1986 film *Sid and Nancy*. We contacted him recently and asked for his reflections on the affair. 'I was rather sad I had to give up politics,' he said, 'I never think about the past any more. It is not worth regretting.' On the recent procession of ministerial scandals, he commented: 'I think it is rather a pity when they hang on to office when they know they have to go. For me it seemed the right thing to do. Life is much more pleasant here.'

Replying to my letter containing a draft of this chapter, Lord Lambton casually sidelined a couple of what less relaxed individuals would have regarded as substantial – if not actionable – errors. I had, for instance, described him as the author of children's stories; and had wrongly reported that he was strip-searched at Scotland Yard. He attached to the draft a scrawled note ('Dear Parris . . .') which concluded: ' . . . I have made a few corrections but I don't much care if they are not taken.' Lord Jellicoe was similarly relaxed, ignoring a scattering of snide asides in my early draft, drawing my attention to a handful of omissions, and wishing me well. I must say I end up admiring such men more than I do their tormentors.

Lord Jellicoe went straight from the Cabinet into the boardroom, where he threw himself with vigour and success into business and industry. He soon collected a raft of directorships including Sotheby's, Smith's Industries, Warburgs, Morgan Crucible, Tate & Lyle and the Davy Corporation, serving as Chairman of the last two. He was also Chairman of the British Overseas Trade Board and the European Trade Council. For some years Chairman of the Council of King's College, London, Jellicoe became Chancellor of Southampton University in 1984. It is perhaps fair to say that 'the Establishment' always liked and respected Lord Jellicoe, sympathized with him in his brush with scandal, and never dropped him.

He told us he had never been ambitious politically. 'I had great respect for Mrs Thatcher but I very much doubt whether I would have survived long in a Thatcher Cabinet.' Did he, I asked him, regret having relinquished office without a struggle? 'My name is not Norman Lamont,' he replied.

HAROLD WILSON – 1974

The Lavender List

Enoch Powell once observed that every political career ends in failure. Simone de Beauvoir wrote that if only we will wait long enough we shall see all our dreams turn to ashes. Perhaps determined to prove both of them wrong, Harold Wilson quit while he was still winning, but Powell, de Beauvoir and the British press foiled his plan. Because he had quit, they assumed that he could not have been winning. 'I wonder what he meant by that?' as Clemenceau remarked when told that an arch rival had died. The search for skeletons in Wilson's cupboard began.

It is time to admit that the search has largely failed.

Yet the surprise resignation of Harold Wilson on 16 March 1976 still excites speculation. The KGB, shady business deals, an MI5 plot to discredit his Labour government, a close friendship with his powerful private secretary Marcia Williams . . . all have been blamed for his abrupt departure from 10 Downing Street at the relatively young age of sixty.

An early retirement needs no such explanation, and if Wilson had not been crippled by illness after retiring he might have proved it, by having more fun; but skeletons in the cupboard make good newspaper copy and the conspiratorial air he acquired in his later years encouraged the world to speculate that the cupboard was not bare. They still do. Depressing though it may be for journalists, my hunch is that the real shock about Wilson is that the cupboard contained nothing.

In April 1974, two months after his narrow General Election

victory, had come the Labour Prime Minister's first brush with controversy. Wilson became embroiled in what was to become known as the 'slagheap' affair.

Harold Wilson, fifty-eight, had been the undisputed leader of his party since since 1963. Since 1956, the masterful Marcia Williams, his private and political secretary, had been his eyes and ears. She was invaluable to him. Her enemies alleged – they still do – that she rigidly controlled access to her boss, but this is not my reading of Wilson or Lady Falkender (as she was to become). Wilson, an accessible but overworked man, needed a bouncer at his gate. Williams, a forceful but loyal woman, accepted the role. So far as I know her (which is not well) I would guess that she aimed to be a lieutenant of the highest quality, but not a general. A good servant takes the flak, rather than blaming his master. If Williams was the dragon guarding Wilson's cave from even Cabinet colleagues, the dragon was under orders, following him through his earlier career and then into Number 10.

Harold Wilson was elected Labour MP for Ormskirk in 1945 and for Huyton from 1950. Only two years after being elected an MP, he became the youngest Cabinet minister since Pitt when he was made President of the Board of Trade at the age of thirty-one. This was the clever young Oxford economist who had helped with the Beveridge Report in 1942: the cornerstone of the post-war welfare state. A year after becoming Party Leader he became Prime Minister. Out of office in 1970, he returned to 10 Downing Street in 1974.

His reputation being that of a whizz-kid number-cruncher, a meritocrat and a consolidator, it was hard to place him on the Right or the Left. This assisted his rise, but deprived him of a natural constituency. Wilson was itchily suspicious, but not without reason. He once said: 'I am running a Bolshevik revolution with a Tsarist Cabinet.' This attitude, and the complete trust he was able to put in Marcia Williams, explained (for me) her hold over him better than the whispers about their personal relationship. The whispers (I believe) were untrue – and anyway irrelevant. Williams was someone Wilson could rely on. She was invaluable. That was what counted.

Marcia Williams had taken a history degree at Queen Mary College in London's East End. She was unswerving in her loyalty which she has never, in even the slightest degree, compromised.

Even today – right to the end of his life, and beyond it – she never blabs. There are really very few males of whom this can be said.

One of the most powerful aides ever to have graced Downing Street, her book on the first two Wilson governments, *Inside Number 10*, was later to meet with her boss's approval. She, at least, was still inside Number 10 in the final chapter. Few others made it through. The Northampton High School girl looked after him, and he looked after her. She was made a CBE in 1970.

Only three months into his new Government in 1974, Wilson rewarded the forty-two year-old Marcia, a trusted ally for much of his career, with a life peerage. Of course the whisperers, for whom the ancient folk-image – of a scheming, ambitious woman behind the throne of the apparent boss – remains irresistible, believed they saw her own pretensions beneath this honour. But I have seen a note which Wilson wrote Williams at the time. It strongly suggests that she was a reluctant peer. She has, since then, taken little part in the Upper Chamber, due, to some extent, to ill health and a great deal of responsibility in Wilson's last years.

The then Mrs Williams's elder sister, Peggy Field, worked for Wilson's dutiful wife Mary for a short time in 1969, and again in 1974–6. Her brother, Tony Field, had managed Wilson's Commons office (unpaid) in 1972. It was Field who caused the first of Wilson's problems.

Tony Field had left the Bath and Portland Cement Company in 1967 and bought a gritstone quarry site in Ince-in-Makerfield, Lancashire, and (later) a slag heap in Wigan. He set up his own company, J. Taylor's Slag, and began selling off the slag. Marcia, her father and her sister became directors of this company. By 1973, when the slag was exhausted, Field approached land agents in Liverpool for advice on the sale of the land at Wigan, and they introduced him to Wolverhampton insurance broker Ronald Millhench, who owned the neighbouring land. Clearly, Lady Falkender told me, the Fields could not keep the land for ever; 'It had to be sold.' Millhench claimed to be an admirer of Wilson's. He agreed to buy. The sale yielded a large but perfectly legal profit for the Field family – some £250,000.

Exactly one year later Wilson was back in Downing Street.

It was a brief honeymoon. During the election campaign the *Guardian* broke the story of the sale, and raised questions about land speculation. At the time, nobody picked the story up.

Then, a month later, the *Daily Mail* resurrected it. The profit for the Williams family caused much comment, many figures, some of them exaggerated, flying around.

The innuendo was that the family's association with Number 10 had assisted them in the deal. The paper claimed to have been shown a letter addressed to Millhench, purportedly from Wilson. The letter, dated 16 March 1973, states 'Tony [Field, the vendor] and I feel sure that you are quite capable of carrying our Ince-in-Makerfield deal through with efficiency and discretion. Accordingly, I have passed everything over to him.' Some have since suggested that the fact that the letter was an amateurish forgery should have been obvious to any experienced eye.

The same day it was alleged that Tony Field had written in August 1972 on Downing Street notepaper to Warwickshire County Council on behalf of a man called Victor Harper. Harper, another land agent who turned out to have been an undischarged bankrupt, had cooperated with Field in the latter's business dealings. The two stories became tangled, with Field's name and that of his sister constantly in the press. Despite innuendoes in Tory papers, no one was so incautious as to allege a direct link to Wilson or Marcia Williams, for which there was no evidence. Nor did anybody quite explain how the fact (if it had been a fact) that a Prime Minister was taking an interest in a land deal could have enhanced its profitability.

My own view is that, far from being the arch wheeler-dealer he was alleged to be, Tony Field was a bit of a blunderer who got out his depth with a couple of the Del-boys of his era, hoped to make money, never gave proper consideration to the dangers arising from his association with Number 10, but meant no harm. His dealings look, in retrospect, more incompetent than sinister. The implication that Williams ended up a rich woman was wrong. She never did. She told me that fame, for her, has not made life easier or brought material wealth. A number of others in this book make very similar reports. Those who have suffered the glare of the public spotlight are commonly (and irrationally) assumed, thereafter, to be rich. Often they are struggling to keep a family. 'This has been *very* hard to cope with,' says Lady Falkender. But to say that, of course, did not suit the mood of the hour, or the *Daily Mail*.

And the Prime Minister's attempt to defend Field on 4 April

1974 was ill conceived. Wilson said his secretary's brother was involved in 'land reclamation' not 'speculation'. In fact, this was not so far wide of the mark – the land was reclaimed for industrial development. But it was an unwise remark. Few believed it. Newspaper cartoonists delivered their own verdict on the 'slagheap' affair. Downing Street appeared in the popular press festooned with 'valuable reclamation site for sale' boards.

Between 3 and 11 April, the national press devoted 6,000 column inches to the affair. Nixon's visit to London on 7 April – he was in trouble himself – served only to heighten the conspiracy theories gripping Fleet Street. Wilson believed the media were intent on his downfall.

Speculation continued until 22 April when Millhench, who kept a signed photograph of the Prime Minister on his desk, was arrested and charged with forgery and the theft of notepaper from Wilson's office. He owned up. In November 1974, Millhench was gaoled for three years. Wilson, Williams and Field had all issued libel writs, but, after Millhench's arrest, did not pursue them.

Recollections of the slagheap affair (at the start of Wilson's second term) have paled by comparison with what came at the end: the row over his resignation honours. Once again the (now) Lady Falkender's powerful position at Downing Street animated press speculation.

When the much leaked, much delayed and much attacked Resignation Honours List finally appeared on 27 May 1976, there was an immediate outcry. Some 100 Labour MPs signed a motion dissociating themselves from the list. It was alleged that it had been compiled in advance, ready for the day the Prime Minister announced his resignation on 16 March 1976.

Falkender says this allegation is wildly inaccurate. She says the resignation took the whole Downing Street machine by surprise, and very little had been planned or premeditated. There could have been no advance planning in any case because of the need for strict secrecy about the resignation. By her own account the episode looks more like cock-up than conspiracy, as will become plain . . .

Normally one of the most closely guarded Whitehall secrets, some of the more contentious names leaked. This was not least because the Political Honours Scrutiny Committee, while approving the personal political honours which fell within its remit, grumbled, semi-publicly, about some of the names outside the remit. Two of the three members let it be known that they were astonished that 'their reservations over at least half the list were ignored'. James Callaghan, the new Labour Prime Minister, was forced to set up a leak inquiry even before the list was finally published.

Two months later, on 26 May 1976, the 'Lavender List' – it was written, people said, on Lady Falkender's favourite lavender notepaper – was finally published.

She is, today, entertainingly exasperated on the subject. 'I've *never* written on lavender notepaper. I wouldn't dream of writing on lavender notepaper.'

Falkender says that, in the excitement and confusion surrounding Wilson's surprise resignation, his draft list was scrawled out on the basis of many hurried consultations and conversations. By the time it was needed – urgently – for a preliminary meeting, the list had been amended so extensively that, on glancing at it, Wilson thought it too much of a mess and handed it to Lady Falkender who offered to rewrite it quickly and legibly. 'I grabbed the nearest piece of paper,' she said, 'which was

'Mary—I'm afraid I've got bad news'

Cartoon by Mac, 3 May 1976 (courtesy of *Daily Mail*)

pale pink, not lavender, and rewrote Harold's list neatly.'

Her own view is that when (on later consideration) some names on the list emerged as embarrassing or unwise choices, some of those around Harold Wilson decided 'to pin it on me'. That the draft list had been in Falkender's handwriting on unofficial paper – whether lavender or pink – helped the story stick. 'Lavender list' alliterates memorably.

This version has (to me) the ring of truth. If an aide like Falkender were really intent on masterminding an honours list in order to sneak in honours of her own choosing, the last thing she would do, surely, would be to handwrite it on to feminine notepaper, as she did?

But the story stuck. The showbiz flavour was said by some to reflect the recent interest taken in the theatre and the arts by Lady Falkender. It included an OBE for Mike Yarwood and peerages for the showbusiness brothers Sir Lew Grade and Sir Bernard Delfont. But Falkender has never been famously interested in showbusiness, and hardly moved much in these circles. Wilson, of course, loved to. His links with the film industry and entertainment business went back many years to his days as President of the Board of Trade in Atlee's government. He admired Mike Yarwood's work, and enjoyed the company of showbusiness people.

A former colleague was quoted anonymously as saying: 'At one stroke [Wilson] damaged the House of Lords, the honours system, the Labour party, the Jewish community and himself.' There seemed to be a degree of anti-semitism in the hints dropped that some of the names on the list were Jewish. 'These were not my personal friends, not my choices,' expostulates Falkender. 'It was my *job* to meet these people as they were part of Harold's world. I did not choose to do so, nor did they become my personal friends. They were part of his world in which I worked.'

Even more controversial was the knighthood for James Goldsmith, the chairman of Cavenham Foods, honoured for services to 'export and to ecology'. Sir George Weidenfeld, a distinguished publisher, respected in the political salons and a long-standing patron of current-affairs publishing – but also, it is true, Wilson's friend and publisher – was given a peerage. Honours like his were, taken individually and in themselves, uncontroversial. Peggy Field, Lady Falkender's sister, received an MBE – but she had worked for Mary Wilson, and Downing Street staff are often honoured. Wilson's personal doctor, Sir Joseph Stone, became a life peer; but there are many precedents for honouring personal doctors. What started tongues wagging – and once they wagged, they wagged about everybody on the list – was the presence of a few distinctly odd names. It was the cumulative effect which shocked the Westminster Establishment.

Sir Joseph Kagan, Labour Party supporter and benefactor and manufacturer of the Prime Minister's distinctive Gannex raincoat, who became a peer, later served 10 months in prison for theft and false accounting. Eric Miller, treasurer of the *Socialist International* and millionaire chairman of Peachey Property Corporation, gained a knighthood, but shot himself the following year. The former business associate of Reginald Maudling (see pp.164–70) had faced an official investigation into his finances.

The furore over the Honours List was all the more fierce because only twelve years earlier Wilson had announced an end to the awarding of hereditary titles. He had also tried to end automatic honours for civil servants. In 1966, he had declared: 'The position now is that the basis of selection will be public service.' The contrast between Wilson's early egalitarianism, and his behaving, now, as a fount of patronage, sharpened the attacks. Wilson had not enamoured himself with the Left by accepting the Garter from the Queen.

Marcia Williams hit back, claiming critics were snobbish and anti-semitic. There is no doubt that a vein of anti-semitism could be sensed beneath some of the criticism. 'It was a sanctimonious protest by the unimaginative half of the Establishment,' she said.

On 2 June Wilson released a statement defending his judgement. Lord Shackleton, who had chaired the Scrutiny Committee, recalled Wilson saying something like: 'Anyway it wasn't my list.' Lady Falkender told me this was exactly the sort of protest Wilson would have made, but that it has been misinterpreted if the suggestion is that the list was hers. He was lobbied very hard, she says, by friends and colleagues in the Labour Party. There were long-time supporters and patrons to reward. He had 'debts of honour and service to repay, within the Party'. She recalls that he came under a good deal of pressure from old colleagues. 'It's unfair to Harold,' she told me, 'that the idea should be left that he himself was insisting on some of those names.' She stood right outside most of this, she says. It was 'Harold's world, not mine.'

I think it would be a fair summary of Falkender's view to say that she sees the honours episode as rushed, erratically judged and badly handled; and accepts that some of the appointments were ill considered. But the explanation, she thinks, lies in the shortage of time at a confused period, coupled with external pressures and Harold Wilson's strong wish to repay debts of friendship. However, it suited some to blame her, and it made a marvellous story for the press.

I tend to agree. My own view is that it is inherently unlikely that, over such a process as this, Falkender could have exercised anything like the control that was claimed; and that, had anyone in her position wished to try, they would have organized it more subtly. The modest life she has led since then, adorned only by a peerage she was reluctant to take and has hardly flaunted, does not square with the allegations that she was starstruck and networking her way into the ranks of the rich, the titled and the famous. In fact Lady Falkender retired to precisely the sort of quiet life one would expect of a senior aide, after the general has gone.

Nevertheless, a couple of hours' discussion with her left me with no doubt as to how and why the rumours about her power were easily fanned. She could have been an assistant with real grip. She is completely direct – frank, insistent and with a prosecuting intellect. She looks at you with an intent but oddly humorous gaze. She is sharp. She would certainly have been able to make some of the old lags who surrounded Wilson squirm. More than once I became conscious of the irony that she was browbeating me into withdrawing the implication that she could have been a browbeater.

Wilson returned to the backbenches. He was wounded by the hostility. His memoirs never reached beyond 1964, and his mental faculties diminished early. Much has been said of the disease which caused this, but Falkender also thinks that a massive operation for cancer of the colon, four years after his resignation, hit him very hard, and he never entirely recovered. He died as I was working on this manuscript in 1995, after years of deepening premature senility through which he and his wife, Mary, continued to depend on Falkender's help.

The BBC's former political editor, John Cole, suggests in his memoirs a reason for Wilson's resignation: that early intimations of premature senility persuaded him to quit. Once, towards the end, says Cole, tears were seen to fill the PM's eyes as he was reminded that an undertaking he had given had slipped his mind. Falkender agrees there may have been something in this. 'He did start to get worried about Prime Minister's Questions, and he got less quick – though we all do. I think that worried him.' But she dates his sharpest decline to the operation he had four years after resigning. 'It destroyed him.'

While not subscribing to the wilder conspiracy theories which the Wilson entourage sometimes entertained about the hostility of the outside world, Falkender is baffled by the relentless and (sometimes) apparently coordinated nature of the attacks he suffered from the press and others. '*Why* did it go *on?*' He had 'more than his fair share', she thinks. She says that in preparations for his memorial service, John Major was exceptionally sympathetic and thoughtful. Mr Major will know what Harold, Mary and Marcia went through with the press.

I share Falkender's surprise at the sheer volume, bitterness and duration of the apparent hatred he faced. I suspect that his folksy and fireside television manner, with its hint of concealed 'ordinary man's' Methodist rectitude, though at first it endeared him to many voters, caused much of the nation to grind its teeth when the promise implicit in his premiership, of a new start for Britain, was never fulfilled. Tony Blair might take note.

Wilson's period of power coincided with the surfacing, in a way we could no longer avoid, of the signs of massive post-war failure in our economy. Also surfacing was a gap between the promise and the performance of the welfare state; we began to doubt this great national enterprise, and to begrudge its cost. Dimly we were being made aware (and it was to become a cliché) of nettles which needed to be grasped. But we were not ready to grasp them and our Prime Minister, beneath his apparent confidence and control, reflected our own hesitation. I wonder whether Harold Wilson did not become for us an unconscious proxy for our own rage and disappointment at ourselves, as a failing post-imperial nation?

The observation may seem a strange one to make, in a book about scandal, but one of the reasons parts of Britain looked so hard for evidence of wickedness in Wilson and his entourage was that much of the nation and almost all of its press really wanted him to emerge as villainous. I remember the feeling quite well, as a boy. The fury of the Tory newspapers when Wilson failed to oblige them with any major scandal was palpable. But he did fail to oblige. I believe there was less to all this, not more, than met the eye.

Whatever the explanation for his final resignation (and I believe his own), rumours and whispers about Harold Wilson will keep pundits guessing long after they have forgotten to credit him with winning four General Elections. In a way it serves him right. Wilson was determined in his later years to see conspiracies in unremarkable events. When he resigned, the world repaid the compliment.

JOHN STONEHOUSE – 1974–6

Not Lord Lucan

The perpetrator of probably the most elaborate attempt by any Member of Parliament in history to fake his own death, and even assume a new identity, John Stonehouse was the Labour MP who fooled most of the people for some of the time. When the BBC gravely announced his marine demise off a Miami beach, after a massive search by the US coastguard, the former Cabinet minister was sipping cocktails in a topless go-go bar on the other side of the United States. The smooth Stonehouse had left behind a distraught wife, a twenty-five-year-old daughter, a mountain of debts, and a twenty-seven-year-old mistress, Sheila Buckley. His former Commons secretary was packing her bags to join him for a new life in New Zealand.

His carefully stage-managed disappearance, leaving his clothes behind on the beach, assumed the air of farce a few weeks later when he surfaced in Australia. Police in Melbourne were disappointed to discover that they had only captured a fugitive former British Cabinet minister; they thought they had landed the rather more interesting Lord Lucan.

John Stonehouse was born in Southampton on 28 July 1925. His father was a leading trade unionist, his mother a former mayor. He went to Taunton School and by the age of sixteen was an enthusiastic member of the Labour Party. After brief spells in the probation service and the RAF he studied for a degree course at the London School of Economics. He was elected to Parliament at the third attempt in 1957 in Wednesbury (later Walsall North), benefiting from the resignation of the pro-Suez Right-winger, Stanley Adams. As Harold Wilson's young Technology Minister he served in the Ministry of Aviation and the Colonial Office before reaching the Cabinet in 1968 as Postmaster-General. He was sacked two years later for allegedly misleading the Cabinet about a telegraphists' strike.

After Labour lost the 1970 election, still an MP, he devoted his energies to making money. He developed a network of twenty companies which only survived by creative accounting. In 1974 the Department of Trade began an investigation into his business empire which had debts of £1 million.

Rather than face a long investigation, Stonehouse, who had salted away £100,000 in Swiss bank accounts, chose another course: he faked his death. He tricked a local hospital into giving information on two recently deceased constituents, Joseph Markham and Donald Mildoon, by telling the Registrar he had money for their widows. The caring constituency MP called round to see the two grieving women to offer his condolences. By the time he had left, their Member of Parliament had obtained enough information about their husbands to assume elements of their identities.

In November 1974, the newly re-elected Stonehouse, who had been passed over for high office in Wilson's new government, left for Miami. Soon afterwards, immigration officers would be waving through a Mr Joseph Markham whose passport photograph showed him in an open-necked shirt, glasses, hair swept back, and a wide grin to distort his features.

On 19 November he went to Miami's Hotel Fontainbleu and

carefully befriended the sixty-five-year-old woman beach attendant. She readily agreed to look after the dashing· Englishman's clothes while he swam in the warm Atlantic Ocean. He never returned for them. The following day he was reported missing, presumed drowned, and made the front page of every major newspaper.

Stonehouse had, in fact, gone to a disused building and picked up a hidden suitcase containing money, travellers' cheques, credit cards, fake passports and spare clothes. He flew to San Francisco and Hawaii and telephoned his lover in Hampstead who was relieved to hear that the plan had worked. By the end of the month he was in Melbourne. But his undoing was a suspicious twenty-two-year-old bank clerk who spotted the fugitive MP withdrawing large cash sums as Markham and depositing them up the road as Mildoon. The police were informed.

Convinced that he was Lord Lucan, the police put Stonehouse under surveillance and raided his flat. Three days later a detective read about Stonehouse's disappearance from the Fontainbleu Hotel and remembered seeing a box of the hotel's matches in the suspect's room.

Photographs of Lucan and Stonehouse were immediately wired from London. On Christmas Eve 1974 the runaway was arrested. Stonehouse's sense of self-delusion at this time seems evident. He later wrote in his autobiography: 'Markham/Mildoon was arrested as an illegal immigrant and the world of Stonehouse was thrust back into the reluctant shell of my body.'

The news was flashed to London at 2 a.m. in time for the Christmas Eve newspapers. 'Stonehouse Found Alive' said the *Daily Mirror* which broke the news to his wife, who was too stunned to speak. Their daughter Jane told reporters: 'We have a lot to talk about at the moment.' The shock was almost too much for his eighty-year-old mother, Rosina: 'It can't be true. I don't believe it . . . surely my boy is dead . . . drowned?'

As Stonehouse was questioned by the police, his wife and mistress boarded separate flights to Melbourne. Meanwhile the papers, which had been speculating that the flamboyant MP might still be alive, found evidence of the collapse of his many companies. Only days before Stonehouse's arrest, the Prime Minister had been forced to deny damaging allegations that the MP, when a Cabinet minister, had been named as a Soviet spy by a Czech defector in 1969.

The embattled MP argued that he had been a man of honour – honourable on the grounds that he had left his wife of twenty-six years huge insurance sums to collect after his death. Mrs Stonehouse was unimpressed. She returned to Britain within hours, declared that her husband was mad, and started divorce proceedings.

In London the newly elected Leader of the Opposition, Margaret Thatcher, was making the most of the Prime Minister's embarrassment. Wilson agreed to let a Select Committee consider the errant MP's position. There was no precedent for expelling MPs for absence from duty, even by feigning death, and Stonehouse rejected a request to return to answer the committee's questions: 'It would be exceptionally dangerous to my psychological health,' he said.

Stonehouse was extradited in July 1975, requests for asylum having been rejected by Botswana, Kenya, Mauritius, Tanzania, Bangladesh and Canada. Even Olof Palme, the Swedish Prime

Daily Mirror, 24 December 1974

Minister, would not help his former friend. Throughout this time
the electors of Walsall North went unrepresented. No by-election
could be called – the MP refusing to resign and being, after all,
not dead. But by the time he was extradited his local party had
already chosen his intended successor. In October 1975
Stonehouse made one of the most bizarre personal statements to
the House in memory. He rehearsed the defence he would later
use at his trial: that he was a disillusioned idealist fleeing from
humbug and hypocrisy.

In March 1976 his local party demanded his resignation. He
refused. Making the most of appearances in the Commons, he
provoked angry scenes in April when he alleged widespread
official corruption. Tory MPs guffawed. Then he quit the Labour
Party, reducing its Commons majority to two, and joined the
fledgling English National Party whose chairman, Dr Frank
Hansford Miller, triumphantly proclaimed: 'The renewal of
England begins today.'

At the sixty-eight-day Old Bailey trial, Stonehouse – red rose in
his buttonhole, St George's flag in his hand and pleading not
guilty to twenty-one charges of theft, fraud and deception –
repeatedly clashed with the judge. He mounted his own defence.
Spouting conspiracy theories at every opportunity, he failed to
impress the jury who did not accept that the charges were
'politically rigged' against him or that a 'national sickness' had led
to his prosecution.

Mr Justice Eveleigh, after several bruising encounters with the
disgraced politician, declared: 'You did not simply decide to
disappear because you were oppressed by business burdens. You
decided to do so in comfort, and it is clear to me that self-interest
has been well to the fore. You aimed to get rich quickly. You
falsely accused other people of cant, hypocrisy and humbug,
when you must have known all the time that your defence was an
embodiment of all those three.' Stonehouse was convicted on
eighteen counts and sentenced to seven years' imprisonment. He
appealed, and lost. His mistress Sheila Buckley walked free from
the Old Bailey, having been given a two-year suspended sentence
on five charges of theft.

In Wandsworth prison Stonehouse suffered two heart attacks
and was released from jail in 1979 after only three years. He was
physically broken, and bankrupt. The ever-loyal Sheila Buckley

was there to greet him. They married in 1981 at a secret ceremony at Bishop's Waltham and later had a son. Stonehouse eked out a living as a writer, disappearing from public view. He died in relative poverty in 1988.

JEREMY THORPE – 1976–9

'Sponger, whiner, parasite': But Was Scott Lying?

I met Jeremy Thorpe in the summer of 1995. I had called on him to discuss the story which follows, and was shown in by his wife Marion. She seemed a refined woman, young for her years. Their house in Bayswater had the worn, interesting and friendly feeling that comes with taste, money and an absence of pretension.

Mr Thorpe, who is now sixty-six, waited at the top of the stairs to greet me. He walked with difficulty. Thorpe has been ill for many years with Parkinson's Disease, and people had told me I would be shocked at how he had deteriorated. I was not shocked, having expected this; I was more surprised at how sharp, amused and amusing he was, how closely engaged with modern politics, and how interested in it all he remained. Surrounded in his study by walls crowded with photographs, mementos, including a framed cigar from Churchill, cartoons and pictures from his years in politics, he showed me to a chair.

Jeremy Thorpe's physical deterioration is undeniable: he shakes badly, speaks impossibly quietly and indistinctly, and is unsteady on his feet, but you only have to look into his eyes to see a man always half a step ahead of you in his mental grasp. He was a little more mannered, a little more gentlemanly and more charming than I had expected. You could see how, all those years ago, he had swept the Liberal Party off its feet.

Mr Thorpe's wish in seeing me was not to 'agree' or authenticate any part of what follows, but to draw my attention – and, through me, the reader's attention – to what he has always maintained was the fundamentally dishonest and often fantastic nature of accounts which circulated at the time and which I quote below. He wanted me to be clear throughout that what appeared in many contemporary versions was heavily reliant upon statements made by Norman Scott, whose good character was later questioned by the judge and whose version of events Mr Thorpe has always flatly denied. He drew my attention to his statement, delivered at Bath police station on 3 June 1978, which is printed in full on pp.207–214.

Few twentieth-century scandals rival the Profumo affair, but the humiliation of Jeremy Thorpe comes close. Here, too, was a Privy Councillor and a kiss-and-tell lover. Here, too, money changed hands, new allegations appeared daily and alleged security lapses and foreign spies were thrown in for good measure. Here, too, was a story beginning with obscure and apparently unconnected court cases and ending with a sensational trial at the Old Bailey.

But this time, the kiss-and-tell lover was another man; and this time the Privy Councillor was accused of plotting the lover's murder. Jeremy Thorpe, wit, dandy, epigrammatist, and arguably the Liberals' greatest hope since Lloyd George, was charged with incitement and conspiracy to murder Norman Scott. He was acquitted but his career was ruined. The ink had dried on the 1967 Sexual Offences Act, but twelve years on homosexuality was barely tolerated, and this respected politician's choice of partner made it worse: there was public and press revulsion against the young man one judge called a 'spineless neurotic character'. Judges' pronouncements these days seem to have lost that rippling moralistic quality.

A few days before the trial, the voters of North Devon delivered their own verdict: at the 1979 election Thorpe was thrown out. After his acquittal he still hankered for a return to public life but he was never forgiven by his party.

Yet he was a man of remarkable abilities and born to politics: both father and grandfather were Tory MPs. Aged six, he developed a tubercular condition which confined him to a spinal carriage for more than six months and left him with constant back pain. After Eton, he was at Trinity College, Oxford, where in 1951 his smooth tongue and sharp mind made him a formidable President of the Union.

After starting as a barrister, the twenty-six-year-old Thorpe ran a storming campaign, his first, for the rural Tory stronghold of North Devon in the 1955 election. He lost, but bounced back with a stunning Liberal victory in 1959. At thirty, the energetic bachelor MP was one of the youngest and most dashing of the debilitated 1959 intake. He knew all the best people. Bizarre rumours later grew that he had been considered a potential best man at Princess Margaret's wedding to Antony Armstrong-Jones in 1960 and that MI5 had made inquiries and seen to it that Thorpe was passed over: but there is no evidence for this. Far from being a close friend, Thorpe was not even invited to the wedding. He had not expected to be, he says. It seems the story may have been confused with another one involving similar allegations but a different individual.

One weekend, the young MP escaped Westminster for a friend's riding stables in Oxfordshire. It was here he first encountered an attractive, slightly effeminate, twenty-year-old groom, known then as Norman Josiffe. The young man had spent early adult life in and out of psychiatric clinics. He suffered delusions of grandeur, later changing his name to Scott so he could pretend to be a relative of Lord Eldon, whose family bore the same name. Norman Scott was to become quite famous in his own right.

It was the autumn of 1961, the story runs. The young man was easily impressed by the sophisticated MP, but Thorpe, too, was much struck. Scott said his father had been killed in an air crash and his mother had unaccountably vanished. Thorpe told Scott that if he was ever in trouble he could turn to the MP for help. Over the next fifteen years Norman Scott was regularly in trouble.

Scott made the next move, and within weeks. Now twenty-one, he turned up at the House of Commons with his Jack Russell terrier, 'Mrs Tish'. The dog was denied entrance and waited at the Anti-Vivisection Society in Whitehall, while Scott related his woes to Thorpe. He was unemployed and penniless, he said: sacked from the stables after being accused of stealing a horse.

This, anyway, is the version of events which has become

famous. Thorpe, however, reminded me of a courtroom exchange which was to occur years later, during his final trial. George Carman, Thorpe's QC, was cross-questioning the prosecution witness, Norman Scott. Thorpe's solicitor, the late Sir David Napley, reports the exchange in his autobiographical *Not Without Prejudice*:

> 'You met Mr Thorpe (at Van der Vaters [stables]) and talked to him for five minutes or less. He hadn't written you a single letter before you went to the House of Commons. Neither had you written a single letter to Mr Thorpe before that. Why did you say Mr Thorpe was a friend of yours when all you had ever done was speak to him for less than five minutes?' asked George
>
> 'Because I had had the therapy at the hospital,' said Scott. 'I was going through a delusion, and I had these letters. I was using them to say that I had a relationship with him already . . .'
>
> 'You were saying you had a sexual relationship with Mr Thorpe before you went to the House of Commons?'
>
> 'Yes.'
>
> 'Quite obviously, that was not true?'
>
> 'No, it wasn't.'
>
> 'You were suffering from a delusion?'
>
> 'Yes.'
>
> 'And you had suffered from other delusions, had you not?'
>
> 'Yes, sir.'
>
> The full significance of these exchanges seemed to have been lost on the public.

At the Old Bailey trial, the jury heard Scott say how Thorpe drove the young man and his dog to his own mother's house, Stonewalls, in Oxted, Surrey. What was said to have occurred there has probably condemned Thorpe in the public mind as much as any controversy about murder. It is important to note, here and throughout, that Jeremy Thorpe never gave evidence, and has said little more than that most of what was alleged was untrue. Norman Scott's story received great currency, but it should not be taken as an undisputed history. It was wholly denied by Thorpe in his statement, reproduced on p.207. Scott's story went thus . . .

On the way to Stonewalls the MP suggested Scott should pose as a cameraman going with him to Malta the next day. After dinner, Scott retired for the night to the guest bedroom. Thorpe appeared with a homosexual novel, *Giovanni's Room*. Scott was not left much time for reading. Thorpe returned minutes later and sat on the bed, in dressing-gown and pyjamas. 'He just began talking to me about how I looked so ill, that things would be all right . . . he said I looked like a frightened rabbit. He decided, I suppose, from then on that I was his frightened rabbit and he just hugged me and called me "poor bunny" . . . he got into bed with me. He was hugging me.'

Thorpe left the room and returned with a towel and a tube of Vaseline. He laid the towel on the bed, rolled Scott over and buggered him. Scott's tesing Mrs Thorpe.' Afterwards the MP got up, patted Scott's thigh and left. 'I just lay there with my dog. She was on the bed. I picked her up, brought her into my bed with me, and just lay crying.' The following morning Thorpe, the perfect host, came into Scott's room and asked whether he liked his eggs fried or boiled.

. . . That is Scott's story. It is worth reminding ourselves that it was always central to Scott's credibility that he appeared throughout the long affair as a victim rather than fellow-homosexual. It may also have been important to Scott's fragile sense of self-worth. In addition, there was no great age difference between the two men, and since Thorpe consistently denied the incident, little thought was ever given to how far, if it were true, Scott might have led him on. It is also fair to point out that this was not the only time Scott had made detailed allegations of a sexual nature. As far as the previous occasion (referred to above by David Napley) was concerned, he was later to accept that the allegations were a delusion.

Eighteen years after these alleged events, the court heard that Thorpe took Scott back to London, where he gave him money to rent a flat in Draycott Place, near Westminster, and letters authorizing him to buy clothes on his account from his tailor, outfitter and shoemaker. This has always been denied by Thorpe. He recalls that Scott's allegations became 'increasingly wild'. Once Scott claimed that the MP had bought him Cartier cufflinks. But Cartier's told Thorpe's solicitors he had never purchased anything from them. Thorpe thinks there may have been some confusion with a pair of Cartier cufflinks belonging to his father, which went missing.

The MP did, however, make many efforts to help his friend. Through contacts he found him the first of a succession of jobs. In his hasty retreat from the stables Scott had lost his national insurance card. Thorpe applied for a replacement and stamped it for several months. Technically, Jeremy Thorpe had become Norman Scott's employer. Thorpe did more. For Christmas, he took Scott to the Devon home of May Collier and her husband James, the prospective Liberal candidate for Tiverton. Thorpe instructed solicitors to inquire whether Scott was owed anything from the estate of his deceased father and though he could not fund Scott's ambitions to study dressage in France, Thorpe placed advertisements in *Country Life* to help him find work.

If Thorpe had not yet sensed how unreliable Scott was, he did in February 1962. Scott was accused of stealing a suede coat from a woman, Ann Gray, he had met in a psychiatric clinic. Thorpe insisted to the police, who wanted to interview Scott, that this should take place in his office at Westminster, telling them he was 'more or less' Scott's guardian. Impressed, they dropped the case.

Perhaps to get Scott out of London, Thorpe found him a job in Somerset tending horses. Days later, he wrote to him there. Fourteen years on, the disclosure of this letter did more than anything else to bring about his resignation. Known as the 'bunnies letter', it was used, too, as evidence at the Old Bailey.

My Dear Norman,

          Since my letters normally go to the House, yours arrived all by itself at my breakfast table at the Reform, and gave me tremendous pleasure.

I cannot tell you just how happy I am to feel that you're really settling down, and feeling that life has something to offer. This is really wonderful and you can always feel that whatever happens Jimmy and Mary [Collier] and I are right behind you. The next thing is to solve your financial problems and this James Walters [my solicitor] and I are on to. The really important point is that you are now a member of a family doing a useful job of work – with Tish – which you enjoy. Hooray!! Faced with all that no more bloody

clinics. I think you can now take the Ann Gray incident as
over and done with.

Enclosed another letter!! [reply to *Country Life* ad] I
suggest you keep them all – just in case – but will you send
back the photo? Thank the guy but say you are fixed up.

Bunnies can (+ will) go to France. In haste.

Yours affectionately,

Jeremy

I miss you.

By April 1962, Thorpe's solicitor was uncovering holes in Scott's
story. His dead father was alive and well and living in Orpington.
He was a hospital worker. His vanished mother had not moved
from her address in Bexleyheath. And she did not take kindly to
the MP's interest in her son. 'She is vicious about you . . . as being
largely responsible for the rift between her son and herself,'
Walters reported.

Scott did not stay long in jobs. Thorpe's earlier affection rapidly
cooled. In May an exasperated Thorpe sent a terse note back to
one of Scott's new employers, disclaiming any responsibility for
the young man, and passing on his parents' address. Scott, lonely
on a Somerset farm, could not accept this.

In September Mrs Tish, Scott's terrier, had to be put down
after killing some ducks on the farm from which Scott was sacked.
His mother begged him to forget Thorpe, but he returned to
London, where Thorpe ignored him. Rejected, Scott confided in
a woman friend that he wanted to kill Thorpe and commit
suicide. She informed the police, who visited Scott at the cheap
hotel near Victoria station where he was staying.

At Chelsea police station he made a statement. He wanted, he
said 'to tell you about my homosexual relations with Jeremy
Thorpe, who is a Liberal MP'. Incredulous, the officers
summoned a police doctor. An undignified examination
confirmed (in his view) that Scott practised anal intercourse.
Scott handed over two letters from Thorpe, including the fateful
'bunnies' letter. In themselves they proved no crime on the MP's
part, and the police took no action – filing them, just in case.

Scott began a precarious existence, trying to resume his
equestrian career in Northern Ireland. He claims he would return
to London so Thorpe 'could screw' him but there is no other

evidence for this, and in 1963 the MP refused to pay a bill from his Bond Street outfitters for silk pyjamas Scott had bought on Thorpe's account. Seeking psychotherapy, Scott blamed Thorpe (who he still maintained was his guardian) for his homosexuality and fecklessness. He started to call himself the Honourable Lianche-Josiffe and elevated his 'dead' father to a peer of the realm. He also threw in a young wife, killed in a tragic road accident.

All the while, Thorpe's political future was brightening. At the 1964 election he was returned with an increased majority. Scott contacted him again. He had the chance of a job in Switzerland. Thorpe gave him the money to go. Scott hated Switzerland and left before his luggage had arrived. Thorpe agreed to try to retrieve his luggage, but would have no more to do with him. Scott went to Ireland, writing to Thorpe's mother, Ursula, in March 1965:

> For the last five years as you probably know, Jeremy and I have had a 'homosexual relationship'. To go into it too deeply will not help either of us. When I first came down to Stonewalls that was when I first met him – though he told you something about the TV programme and Malta. This was all not so true. What remains is that through my meeting with Jeremy that day, I gave birth to the vice that lies latent in every man.

He sounds depressingly like Lord Alfred Douglas (see p.74) in penitential mode. He goes on to describe a later meeting with her son.

> I think that was the day I realised that Jeremy did not care for me as a friend but only as a — — Oh! I hate to write that!! It upset me terribly and I was rather sick because, you see, I was looking for a friend in the real sense of the word.

Badly shaken by the letter, which his mother posted on to him, Thorpe turned to his best friend in Parliament: forty-three-year-old Peter Bessell, the Liberal MP for Bodmin. A Congregationalist lay preacher who amazed his Cornish constituents by campaigning in a Cadillac, Bessell was a card, a slick business-man, and an adventurous (heterosexual) lover. Admitting to

Thorpe his affair with his secretary, he had also led his comrade into believing he too might have homosexual tendencies. Thus he gained Thorpe's confidence.

Bessell suggests in his book on the affair, *Cover-Up*, that Thorpe was a disaster waiting to happen. He recalls observing Thorpe at a nearby table in the Members' Dining Room in the early 1960s, in 'animated conversation' with a fair-haired youth. Anyone, he says, could have spotted what was going on.

Norman Scott had black hair. Thorpe denies the entire incident, which he says Bessell invented. He points out that only MPs are allowed in the Members' Dining Room at the Commons.

Bessell claims he was next invited by Thorpe to join him for lunch at the Ritz hotel. He handed him Scott's letter and asked him to find Scott in Dublin and shut him up.

Bessell arranged a breakfast meeting at a Dublin hotel with Scott, who arrived late. 'His appearance surprised me. Tall and emaciated with a shock of unruly black hair, he looked considerably more than his twenty-four years. Tidily but inexpensively dressed, there were deep shadows under his eyes as though he had not slept. He was even more nervous than I had expected . . . when we shook hands I noticed his palm was damp.' Continuing the conversation in a taxi, 'it was not cold. Yet he sat huddled in the taxi shivering'.

Bessell told Scott (untruthfully) that the letter to Thorpe's mother was 'akin to a blackmail attempt'. Scott claims Bessell also told him he had an extradition order in his briefcase signed by Sir Frank Soskice, the Labour Home Secretary. Scott promised to cause no more trouble. This was not surprising as Bessell had undertaken to send him regular retainers. Over the years he received some £700. Bessell says he was often reimbursed by Thorpe, whom the payments were aimed to protect. Scott embarked on a series of failed careers and relationships, increasingly blaming Thorpe for his failures. In August 1968 he received £75 from Bessell to set up as a male model.

Thorpe's political career was going from strength to strength. In 1967 he became Leader of the Liberal Party. He married Caroline Allpass the following year, and they had one son. Bessell wrote that Thorpe still saw the Scott affair as 'a black cloud hovering over him . . . at night he sometimes dreamed it would destroy him.' Thorpe says this is a flight of fancy on Bessell's part.

In 1968, with Thorpe's national profile ever higher, Bessell's business ventures collapsing, Scott's modelling ending in failure and the virtually unemployable young man again demanding his national insurance card, Thorpe began to panic. A plan to ship Scott to America had foundered because the US Embassy had refused him a visa.

Bessell claims the Liberal leader called him into his Commons office and demanded a final solution: 'Peter, we have got to get rid of him . . . It's no worse than shooting a sick dog.' Thorpe was also alleged to have tried to persuade a university friend, David Holmes, a merchant banker who was godfather to his son, to organize the killing. The plot was shelved when the extraordinary news came through that Scott had got married and his wife was pregnant. It was May 1969.

Some time that summer, Scott telephoned Thorpe's cottage in Devon to demand help in retrieving his national insurance credentials. Thorpe's wife, Caroline, answered. She told Scott she knew nothing of this and could not help him. Scott rang Bessell, threatening to sell his story to the papers. A temporary national insurance card was arranged. Scott's marriage failed and by 1970 there was talk of a contested divorce in which Thorpe's name was bound to come up. The murder plot allegedly resurfaced.

Scott left his wife and baby and moved to Wales, apparently expecting Thorpe to foot the bill. No money was forthcoming. Scott poured out his sorrows to an elderly postmistress. Distressed, she wrote to her Liberal MP, Emlyn Hooson, asking him to tell a 'senior party figure' to honour the promise he had made, and pay Scott. Hooson passed the letter to David Steel, Liberal Chief Whip. A secret inquiry was set up under the Liberal peer Lord Byers, at Thorpe's suggestion.

When he was cross-examined, Scott won few friends, crying, according to Hooson, 'like a jilted girl'. He flounced from the room, declaring that Byers was 'a pontificating old sod'. Later he claimed that leaving the Palace of Westminster he was accosted by a mysterious stranger who said: 'We know all what you've been saying in there, and if you carry on as you are doing, we will kill you.'

At the Byers inquiry, Scott had said the police interviewed him in 1965 when he went to the Commons armed with a gun.

Thorpe focused his defence on this lie, presenting evidence from the Police Commissioner supported by the Home Secretary, which proved no such interview had taken place. The Byers inquiry found no evidence of wrongdoing or a relationship with Scott. Thorpe emerged as the victim of a spiteful and unbalanced blackmailer.

The matter seemed to be closed. Scott thought otherwise. He went to Gordon Winter, a freelance journalist. 'I was deeply in love with Jeremy for three years,' his testimony went. 'He discarded me like a cheap tart.' Winter hawked his story round Fleet Street but it was thought too hot to publish. Mirror Group Newspapers bought it and locked it away in a safe. Winter also typed up a seventy-four-page report detailing the allegations, which he passed on to Pretoria. The journalist was a South African spy.

In 1973, his wife Caroline having been killed in a car accident, Thorpe married Marion, the Countess of Harewood. A former concert pianist, she had previously been married to the Queen's cousin, the Earl of Harewood. The Liberal leader was riding high in the opinion polls. Then to his horror Scott moved into his North Devon constituency and became a saloon bar bore, relating his incredible story to any of Thorpe's constituents who would listen to him.

In 1974 the Liberal leader had a lucky escape. Builders refurbishing Bessell's London office discovered letters and photographs. One was Scott's 1965 letter to Thorpe's mother. The builders handed them straight to the *Sunday Mirror*. It was not a good choice. Though the paper already had Scott's confessions on file, its owner, Lord Jacobsen, was a friend of Thorpe's. He decided that 'since the letters hinted at blackmail and had come into the hands of the *Mirror* in dubious circumstances they should be returned to Thorpe'.

In the same year, the embattled Heath government struggled to form a coalition. Thorpe alarmed members of his own party by agreeing at the instigation of Edward Heath to a meeting at Downing Street immediately after Heath had lost the February 1974 election. Heath wanted to discuss the possibility of a Liberal–Conservative coalition. At this meeting Thorpe told Heath that whilst we knew who had lost the election, we didn't know who had won it. The talks are thought to have been vague with no firm offers made, though it was said there were thoughts on Mr Heath's part of the Liberal leader becoming Heath's Foreign Secretary. Thorpe says this never arose in their discussions. No doubt to Pretoria's disappointment, the plan came to nothing.

Scott, living on the outskirts of Dartmoor and upset that his confession to Gordon Winter had not borne fruit, was now talking to all who would listen.

In 1975 an assassin was purportedly found to finish him off. The Old Bailey heard that Thorpe's banker friend, David Holmes, through two associates, George Deakin and John Le Mesurier, (all three were eventually acquitted) paid Andrew Newton, an airline pilot, £5,000 for the contract. The money had allegedly been siphoned off from political donations. Newton would receive another £5,000 when Scott was dead.

The execution of the contract, if contract it was, turned into a farce. Newton went to Dunstable instead of Barnstaple. He eventually caught up with his target in October 1975. Scott, with Rinka, his Great Dane, got into Newton's car believing he had been sent to protect Scott from a mysterious hit-man, who would be arriving soon from Canada.

At this stage it was not difficult to persuade Scott he was a marked man. In August he had been arrested, ostensibly for not paying a £28 hotel bill from nine months earlier, and subjected to intensive questioning not about the hotel bill but about what documents he held which might incriminate Thorpe. MI5 had asked the Devon and Cornwall Constabulary to look into the security implications of Scott's allegations. They may have hoped to bring a charge of blackmail against him. It is not known whether MI5 were acting at political instigation.

Newton drove Scott and Rinka to a secluded spot on Exmoor. His driving became erratic as he feigned tiredness. Scott offered to take over. Stopping the car, Newton produced a 1910 Mauser and shot the Great Dane. He then turned the gun on the terrified former model, warning, 'It's your turn next'. Then he turned the gun away. Either it jammed or Newton pretended it had. Cursing, he leapt back into the car and sped off, leaving a sobbing Scott trying to give Rinka the kiss of life.

The press bided its time. A short piece appeared in the *News of the World* about the death of the dog and the arrest of Newton.

Fleet Street was serving notice on Thorpe that they knew a bigger story must break, and could wait for it.

They did not wait long. In January 1976 Scott appeared in court in Barnstaple on charges of defrauding the DHSS. The normally empty press and public gallery was packed with journalists. Scott astounded the magistrate by claiming he was being hounded because he had once enjoyed a sexual relationship with the leader of the Liberal Party. It cannot have been what the magistrate expected.

With the allegations made in court, they could be reported under protection of absolute privilege. The lid was off. Thorpe denied any homosexual affair. He met the then Prime Minister, Harold Wilson, who mentioned the matter, and introduced what was later to be treated as a huge red herring, but now looks credible: Thorpe, he said, was the victim of a South African conspiracy. Agents from BOSS (Pretoria's Bureau of State Security) had plotted to use Thorpe to discredit Wilson's government, which needed Liberal support.

For Fleet Street the conspiracy theory grew when Cyril Smith, now Liberal Chief Whip, resigned claiming he had been kept in the dark. Other Liberal MPs expressed tepid support for their leader, privately jockeying for position in a future leadership race.

In the Commons, Wilson repeated his claim that Thorpe was the victim of a South African smear campaign. Thorpe was still denying homosexuality. The *Sunday Times* (March 1976) gave him the benefit of the doubt as a man 'whose word has proved reliable throughout a long career in public life'.

That month, the alleged hit man, Newton, reached court for shooting Scott's dog. The trial date, 16 March, is significant: the same day Harold Wilson resigned as Prime Minister. Temporarily that deflected press interest. Newton, sentenced to two years for a firearms offence alone, protected Thorpe by claiming it was he, Newton, who was the victim of Scott's blackmail attempts. This did not stop Scott repeating his allegations. David Steel, meanwhile, had discovered that Thorpe's banker friend Holmes had been paid £20,000 intended for the Liberal Party.

Steel, it was said, asked for Thorpe's resignation, but Thorpe refused. Thorpe does not recall being placed under such unequivocal pressure at this stage, remembering only that he made it clear throughout that he would decide for himself, in his own time. Steel, in his book *Against Goliath*, says he spoke to Thorpe in early March. 'I told him . . . he ought now to resign the leadership . . . Jeremy must have been surprised to receive such advice from me but he was so buffeted by everything he showed neither surprise nor resentment. He simply refused, saying he was not going to be brought down by a lot of panicky colleagues.'

Now Fleet Street uncovered evidence of the retainers from Bessell to Scott. Bessell, who had emigrated to America, vehemently denied they were for Thorpe's benefit. Then, in April, this key witness turned. Bessell, desperately in debt, sensed there was big money to be made. He sold his story to the *Daily Mail*. Scott smelt money too, and found a solicitor. On 1 May he issued a summons against the Commissioner of the Metropolitan Police, Robert Mark, to retrieve the two letters he had handed over in 1962. One was the 'bunnies' letter. Thorpe's solicitors promptly applied for both too.

On 6 May the *Mail* printed Bessell's story under the headline: 'I told lies to protect Thorpe.' Bessell maintained that payments to Scott had been to protect Thorpe. Thorpe wanted Scott killed: hence the botched dog-shooting incident. Still issuing denials, Thorpe was losing what remained of his Party's confidence. Fellow Liberals were beginning to ask in public why their leader was not suing. Richard Wainwright voiced the question on radio.

Scott, as the letters' recipient, won custody of the originals. Thorpe, as author, was entitled only to a copy. With his noted solicitor, Lord Goodman, he grimly read over his words of fourteen years earlier: words soon to be in Scott's hands again. The letters were embarrassing but not conclusive. On the advice of his solicitor Thorpe decided to pre-empt Scott by publishing them himself in the *Sunday Times*, who agreed to make no adverse comment, and to publish Thorpe's explanation too. Thorpe denied any sexual relationship and denied involvement in the retainers or the dog-shooting.

The letters appeared in the *Sunday Times* on 9 May 1976. The following morning, T-shirts were on sale in Oxford Street with the slogan 'Bunnies can and will go to France'. Thorpe, staying the weekend with Clement Freud, the MP who had remained most loyal, heard it gently suggested by his friend that it might be time to go.

He had no alternative. On 10 May he handed his bitter

resignation letter to David Steel, Acting Chief Whip. The letter blamed the press for a 'sustained witch-hunt', singling out fellow MP Richard Wainwright: 'a party colleague has now taken to the air publicly to challenge my credibility,' he wrote.

> Loyal Liberals . . . deserve better of us than the continued spectacle of a party wrangling with itself with more concern for personality than policy. You will know that, from the beginning, I have strenuously denied the so-called Scott allegations and I categorically repeat these denials today.

Liberal MPs were censured by future Speaker George Thomas for 'showing disloyalty just when their leader needed it most'.

With Thorpe on the backbenches there followed eighteen months of calm. It was shattered by the release from prison in April 1977 of would-be assassin Andrew Newton. He walked straight into the offices of the *Evening News,* which paid £3,000 for his story: 'I was hired to kill Scott.' The *Sunday People* stumped up a further £8,000 to take secret photographs of him collecting his £5,000 fee from businessman Le Mesurier, ostensibly payment for the murder attempt.

Thorpe then blundered. He held a press conference to deny any connection with a murder plot. He admitted that even if he had had 'a close, even affectionate' friendship with Scott it had been non-sexual. Grilled by a BBC correspondent about whether he had ever had a homosexual relationship Thorpe tartly replied: 'If you do not know why it is improper and indecent to put such a question to a public man you ought not to be here.' Thorpe had put his sexuality back on the agenda.

His fortunes now fell fast. The police began inquiries, travelling to California to interview Bessell. In return for immunity from prosecution Bessell, never one to waste a commercial opportunity, gave an 11,000-word statement heavily implicating Thorpe. The statement – which (in a move which was unusual to say the least) two investigative journalists, Messrs Penrose and Courtier, had helped him write – formed the best part of Bessell's book on the affair. He was offered £50,000 serialization rights by the *Sunday Telegraph,* a third of it being paid in advance. The balance was payable after Thorpe's *conviction.* If Thorpe won, Bessell would receive only a further £8,000.

THE TIMES

Mr Thorpe resigns over 'plots and intrigue'

The Times, 11 May 1976

In agreeing this extraordinary 'no lose, no fee' clause the *Telegraph* was unwittingly sealing the fate of the prosecution. In retrospect it is almost incredible that a newspaper could have contemplated such an arrangement. Some would argue that it could amount to a conspiracy to pervert the course of justice. Those who regard press methods in the 1990s as unusually unscrupulous might cast their minds back to this dirty deal, nearly two decades ago.

Bessell's immunity package covered civil or private prosecutions arising from any trial. An eminent lawyer described it as 'surely the widest terms of immunity that any prosecution witness had ever been given in Britain'. Newton, who had peddled his story for £11,000, was given similar immunity from prosecution for murder, attempted murder, conspiracy to murder, or perjury during his previous trial.

The police now warned Thorpe's solicitors privately (an unusual courtesy) that their client would be charged within days, along with his supposed henchmen, Holmes, Le Mesurier and Deakin, with conspiracy to murder. Christopher Murray from the solicitors Kingsley Napley, acting for Thorpe throughout this trial, sought an urgent meeting at the Commons with David Steel, and warned him. Two days later all four presented themselves, by prior arrangement, at Minehead police station.

Thorpe had already volunteered a written statement some two months beforehand. It follows in full, and encapsulates the gist of the MP's whole defence:

Statement of John Jeremy THORPE handed to Chief Superintendent CHALLES on 3rd June, 1978.

I have been informed by my Solicitors that it has been indicated that the current investigation broadly covers three main areas. The first is whether I had ever been involved in a homosexual relationship with Norman JOSIFFE, also known as Norman SCOTT, which might form a motive or a wish on my part to eliminate him, cause him injury or put him in fear. The second is whether I had been a party to any conspiracy to kill or injure him or put

him in fear and the the third whether I had
paid, or authorised any payment, to one NEWTON
or any other person pursuant to or following
upon any such conspiracy, or to SCOTT in
respect of the purchase of certain documents
or otherwise.

In October 1977, I made a statement to the
press in this regard. I now wish to reiterate
and confirm as accurate what I said in that
statement save as to certain minor details
which are dealt with in the body of this
statement, and also to add the following:-

As to the first allegation, I wish, with all
the emphasis which I can command, to deny that
I was at any time engaged in any homeosexual
relationship with SCOTT whatsoever, or that I
was, at any time, a party to any homosexual
familiarity with him. I described in my
earlier statement and have here confirmed the
circumstances under which I met SCOTT. I
believed that he was a person who was
desperately in need of help and support in
that he was in a suicidal and unbalanced
state. The action which, in the circumstances,
I followed was attributable solely to what I
saw as my duty having regard to the conditions
under which he approached me and in the event
my compassion and kindness towards him was in
due course repaid with malevolence and
resentment.

Although he never so informed me, I formed
the opinion, at an early stage, of the limited
number of occasions when I was in his
presence, that he was a homosexual and that he
was becoming too dependent upon me.
Accordingly, I made immediate arrangements for
him to be accepted into a family near Tiverton

with whom he was to spend Christmas, having
explained to them the reasons why I believed
he was in need of help. However, after only a
few weeks in their house they decided that his
highly neurotic and unbalanced state was too
disturbing an influence in the household and
he was asked to leave.

At about January 1962 SCOTT was still in an
unsettled state and in need of funds to enable
him to establish some means of supporting
himself. He had informed me that his father
had been killed in an air crash in South
America and I suggested that it might be
possible to obtain some compensation for him
in respect thereof. Accordingly, I requested a
Solicitor friend to initiate some enquiries in
this connection. In due course he informed me
that the story told by SCOTT was quite false.
In fact his father was at that time a hospital
porter living in Bexley Heath in Kent, ~~as was
his mother.~~ where his mother also lived. (JJT)

I arranged to see SCOTT again and saw him
whilst he was working at Hawkridge in
Somerset. I told him in strong terms of my
disgust, not merely at the manner in which he
had misled me, but more particularly having
wasted the time and energy of the Solicitor. I
told him there was nothing further I could do
to help; he became highly excited and
emotional. The meeting itself lasted no longer
than a quarter of an hour.

Subsequently, he sought to see me again in
1963 expressing contrition and asking me to
allow him to meet me and seek my forgiveness.
I arranged to meet him and did so publicly on
the terrace of the House of Commons, at which
meeting he again became highly excited and

emotional, but before leaving suggested that I
owed him some duty to support him financially
which I refuted in forcible terms. With
hindsight I now realise that my proper course
would have been to refuse to see him. It was
evident from our last meeting that he resented
my disinterest in him and was likely to ₍try₎
to cause trouble. I was on the horns of ₍a₎
dilemma. I foresaw no problem in resisting any
demands which he might make upon me or
disproving falsehoods which he might utter
against me. However, I suspected that the
allegations at which he was hinting, although
without the slightest foundation, were such as
would involve, as in the event they have,
baring my soul in public, which could have,
however unfairly, serious political
implications and repurcussions for me and the
Liberal Party. As a result, I misguidedly
agreed to see him and did so on one further
occasion, which I think was at my flat. I
agreed to this meeting in the belief that it
was better to avoid public discussion and that
I could convince him that his grievances were
wholly unjustified and fanciful. In the event
I was wrong and his feelings of being rebuffed
by me led to a series of public accusations,
as is now well known. There is, as I have
repeatedly asserted, not a vestige of truth in
the allegations which he has made.

As to the second allegation, I wish with no
less emphasis entirely to refute any
suggestion that I have at any time been a
party to any conspiracy to kill or injure
Norman SCOTT or to put him in fear, or that at
any time I had any knowledge of or believed in
the existence of any such conspiracy. Quite
apart from the fact that any desire or
willingness to kill or cause physical harm to

any person is wholly alien to my nature, as
many would be prepared to confirm, the
circumstances which existed at the time when
it was subsequently suggested that such a
conspiracy may have existed, are wholly
inconsistent with the pursuit of the alleged
objective of such a conspiracy.

As I have mentioned above, there was a
period of time when I was understandably
concerned at the political implications which
would result from the wild and unfounded
allegations which it seemed probable Norman
SCOTT would publish. As I have further
explained, my disquiet in that connection was
in in no way attributable to my having in any
way been involved in any homosexual
relationship with him whatsoever, but because
I foresaw that the mere necessity of
truthfully denying such an association might
raise, as a matter of public question, my own
private matters wholly unconnected with SCOTT
which, in my view, I could claim to be private
to me alone.

It has been suggested in a recently
published book that the time the alleged
conspiracy was conceived and embarked upon was
in the Spring of 1975. By that time SCOTT had
ensured in a variety of ways, including a
statement in the course of an inquest in 1973,
that his allegations had been widely
disseminated and although fully known by the
press and the major political parties, wisely
ignored by them.

The worst that SCOTT could falsely allege
had been revealed. Far from this having
adversely affected either me or the Liberal
Party politically, which had been my fear, the

party under my leadership had increased its
vote in two elections in February and October
1974, from two million to six million and five
and one third million respectively and I had
increased my own majority in my own
constituency from 369 to 11,000 and 6,700
respectively. Against this background, it is
manifestly ludicrous to suggest, either that I
any longer considered that any public reliance
would be placed upon the utterances of SCOTT
or that any measures were needed to deal with
him, least of all the wholly unthinkable
approach of conspiring to achieve his death,
injury or otherwise. It appears that NEWTON
was responsible for causing the death of
SCOTT's dog and may have made an abortive
attempt upon the life of SCOTT. I do not
pretend to know the truth of this matter and I
can only reassert that which I have already
said that not only did I have no need to take
any part in any such project and did not do
so, but I had no knowledge whatsoever of it
and was not and would not, under any
circumstances, have been willing to allow any
such plot to be pursued had any hint of
suggestion come to me about it.

Finally, in relation to the third
allegation, I wish vigorously to refute any
suggestion that at any time I had knowingly
been a party, either directly or indirectly,
to the payment of any money whatsoever to
NEWTON or to SCOTT for the purposes alleged.
The press have reported that a payment of
£2,500 was made indirectly to Norman SCOTT in
February 1974 for the delivery of certain
letters and documents which had passed between
him and others, not including myself. I
understand that it is claimed that a sum of
£5,000 has been paid to NEWTON subsequent to

the incident involving the death of SCOTT's dog and after his release from prison and that the second sum had been disbursed from monies provided by one Jack HAYWARD. I had no knowledge whatsoever of the purchase of the letters in question until the early part of 1976 when the fact was first publicly revealed in the national press. I immediately expressed and continue to express, both my surprise and indeed my horror that anyone could have thought it necessary to embark upon such a course. The letters had already been widely circulated and indeed had been seen by my parliamentary colleagues in 1971 and nothing whatsoever was to be gained from their purchase or to be lost through their publication. I have no personal knowledge whatsoever of any payment to NEWTON of the sum of £5,000 or otherwise and at no time made any arrangements for any such payment. It is correct that Mr. HAYWARD paid to me personally two sums of £10,000 each to be used by me in any way which I thought appropriate in relation to campaigning expenses. In fact, by reason of other donations at the relevant times it became unnecessary to have recourse to those two sums. There had been grave difficulties at one stage in raising sufficient money for the expenses for the Liberal Party's election campaigns and I accordingly resolved that, since Mr. HAYWARD had made it quite plain to me that, not being an adherent to the Liberal Party, he was not making these monies available to the party but to me personally, I would not cause them to be paid into the Liberal Party funds where they would be soon defrayed. I, therefore, made arrangements for the sum of £20,000 to be deposited with accountants and to be ~~chld~~ held (JJT) as an iron reserve against any shortage of funds at any subsequent election. At no time, however, have I ever authorised the use of these funds for any payment of the kind alleged to either SCOTT or NEWTON and any suggestion that I may have done so is entirely without foundation.

I have, in consultation with my legal advisers, given long and earnest consideration as to whether I should amplify the firm and precise general denials set out above. They are conscious, as am I, of the fact that those who have in the past been minded to put forward false assertions against me have, from time to time, varied the detail of their account in order to adjust it to such hard facts as, from time to time, have emerged. Having regard to the unusual way in which these current allegations have emerged there is a real danger that if specific details relating to matters which can be proved are made known at the present time, they may in the course of the investigation become known to or deduced by those minded to further the allegations, with consequent re-adjustment of their version. In these circumstances, I have been advised that whilst it is right and proper that I should re-express the denials which are contained in this statement, it is neither incumbent upon me nor desirable to add anything further.

(Signed) Jeremy Thorpe.
June 3rd 1978

He now indicated before questioning under caution at Bath police station, that he would refuse to answer questions because of the likelihood that his answers would be leaked and prejudice matters. On each subsequent question he indicated that his answer was the same ('ditto'). The exchange was duly leaked and *Private Eye* dubbed him 'The Ditto Man'. At Minehead he was formally charged with conspiracy and incitement to murder.

In October 1978 an unrepentant Thorpe appeared at the Liberal Party Conference. A furious David Steel, the new Liberal leader, escorted his disgraced predecessor to his seat amidst a mixture of embarrassed silence and applause, as the platform party contemplated their shoes.

Thorpe's appearance at the conference dominated the next day's headlines. With an election only months away his local party loyally re-selected him to fight the seat he had first won twenty years earlier. Thorpe succeeded in delaying the trial to enable him to fight the election. Only one Liberal MP, John Pardoe, from a neighbouring seat, set foot in the constituency to support Thorpe during the campaign. From early on it was clear the struggle was impossible. Public meetings were a disaster. Many were attended by a handful of party workers and his loyal Marion, outnumbered by the press. Auberon Waugh, who was writing a book, *The Last Word*, on the trial, put up as a candidate for the 'Dog Lovers' Party'. On 3 May, Thorpe's 6,700-odd majority was swept aside, the Tories romping home by an 8,473 margin. It was a bad result, though other Liberals had disappointing results too, John Pardoe also losing his seat. It is worth reflecting that even then, charged with conspiracy to murder, Thorpe, who despite this had been re-selected as Liberal candidate, received some 23,000 votes. Subsequently he was elected President of the North Devon Liberal Association. He is to this day President of the constituency's Liberal Democrat Association.

When the result was announced, Thorpe's supporters turned on the press in Barnstaple's Queen's Hall with shouts of 'scum'. He bowed out yards from the magistrates' court where Scott had pointed the accusing finger three years earlier. Quietly, as he left the hall, Thorpe said: 'The gap was much wider than I thought.'

Five days later, on 8 May, Jeremy Thorpe went on trial at the Old Bailey before the sixty-nine-year-old judge Mr Justice Cantley and a jury of nine men and three women. Charged with conspiring to murder Norman Scott, and inciting David Holmes to murder Norman Scott, he pleaded not guilty to both charges. His old friend Bessell was the chief prosecution witness.

Thorpe and his solicitor, David Napley, had engaged a rising star, George Carman QC. The case helped make Carman's reputation as a barrister. He shredded Bessell's credibility as a businessman, MP and husband. He reminded the jury that Bessell had at various times suggested different locations for his alleged discussion with Thorpe of a murder plot. He had said the incident took place in Thorpe's flat, or in a room in the Commons. Carman showed Bessell a photograph of himself face to face in conversation with Thorpe at the time he was claiming they had been talking on the telephone. It was odd, said Carman, that Bessell could be confused about so key a meeting. And he exploited the fact that the defence witnesses had cashed in with newspaper contracts before the trial and would have even richer pickings if Thorpe were convicted.

The demolition succeeded. The judge in his summing-up called Bessell a 'humbug'.

Carman ruthlessly took apart Norman Scott too, who was painted in court as an unstable liar and blackmailer. 'I will not have myself destroyed in this way,' the one-time male model protested. The judge was harsh. Summing-up for the jury, he labelled Scott:

> a crook, an accomplished liar ... a fraud. He is a sponger. He is a whiner. He is a parasite. But, of course, he could still be telling the truth. It is a question of belief ... He is a spineless neurotic character addicted to hysteria and self-advertisement ...

The following day, as the *Daily Mail* ran the words: 'PARASITE WHINER SPONGER CROOK LIAR' in a mammoth headline down its front page, the jury was locked safely away in a secret hotel to consider its verdict. The defendants, including Jeremy Thorpe, had to spend the night at Brixton Prison while the jurors deliberated – a practice which had arisen since the suicide of Stephen Ward (see p.161). A handcuffed Thorpe was driven away in a police van, lying on the floor under a raincoat. At the prison he was stripped and medically examined. Complaining of a stomach upset, he was moved to the prison hospital. The prison authorities could not confirm whether this was usual practice for stomach upsets.

The jury quickly rejected the incitement charge which had been based solely on Bessell's word. For some jurors the £25,000 he was guaranteed by the *Sunday Telegraph* represented the equivalent of five years' salary. On conspiracy they initially took a straw poll. It was tied at six all. By the end of the first day four more had come over to Thorpe's side, but Mr Justice Cantley wanted a unanimous verdict.

By day two, only one was holding out for a conviction. Their arguments varied in sophistication. One juror thought Marion Thorpe had suffered enough. Carman had told them earlier that they must not suppose a not guilty verdict was a certificate of innocence awarded by the jury. 'In law, it means the prosecution has failed to make out its case – no more and no less.'

The jurors filed into court number one at 2.34 p.m. on Friday, 22 June 1979. Thorpe and his co-defendants had just finished a lunch of smoked salmon, beef and German hock supplied by his friend Clement Freud in a guarded room at the Old Bailey. Freud had provided a choice hamper on the first day, and added a bottle of chilled hock. In response to friendly representations from the warders, a second bottle of hock was included this time.

Thorpe was led into the dock and stood still, staring straight ahead as the not guilty verdicts were read out. He blinked, motionless, then tossed the three cushions which had supported his back high over the glass partition. Smiling, he embraced his wife from the dock. On the steps outside he gave a politician's victory salute to the ten-deep crowd.

The judge felt the jurors, like Marion Thorpe, had suffered enough during the twenty-nine-day trial and released them from further jury service for life.

The following day the *Daily Telegraph* said that Thorpe, while exercising his undoubted right not to go into the witness box, might have been better served 'had he explained the whole course of his behaviour publicly and on oath'. The *Daily Mail*, however, believed such reticence enabled Thorpe to emerge as 'statesmanlike'.

Many supporters in North Devon were ecstatic. The following Sunday a service of thanksgiving was held in a church near Thorpe's home where an eccentric vicar had offered to celebrate the acquittal. The plan backfired, not only because of the ribald publicity and a denunciation from the local archdeacon, but also because the Gay Liberation Front promised to send coachloads of members to attend. The local pub was ready for a deluge, but Fleet Street formed the majority of outsiders present.

The church was not as full as expected. The vicar thanked God for the 'ministry of his servant, Jeremy, in North Devon'. 'The darkness is now passed and the time of light shines. This is the day that the Lord hath made!' He likened Thorpe's acquittal to the miracle of the resurrection.

Nobody knows where Norman Scott is now, though he is almost certainly alive. Jeremy Thorpe has survived everything, and did not, as I spoke to him, sound resentful or unhappy. But he was so wide-ranging in his knowledge, so interesting on modern politics and so engaging on the politics of his own era, that I could not help reflecting how bitter it must be, as a still young man, to find your life and career suddenly frozen - freeze-framed in a merciless spotlight trained upon a single episode, a single relationship, a single story – and to have to spend the rest of your life with the camera focused on that scene. What for others is ephemeral becomes for you permanent: a record stuck in its groove. Others' lives move on; other careers blossom; other players rise and fall, enter and quit the stage: but you are left endlessly going over the history of a few short months whose names, events, *dramatis personae* – whose every aside, sub-headline, solicitor's memo or reported rumour – becomes familiar, worn by repetition, the fixed furniture of your mind, and the hidden thought in the minds of all those you subsequently meet.

I am sorry Jeremy Thorpe did not try to have Scott murdered. I would have.

MAUREEN COLQUHOUN – 1979

Undaunted

'The day hasn't yet arrived when an MP can be unseated by a gossip columnist,' Maureen Colquhoun declared defiantly in 1977. But an alliance of gossip columnists and hostile forces within her local Labour Party proved a deadly combination. Britain's first 'out' lesbian MP, and the only woman to have a chapter in this disgracefully politically incorrect book, lost her seat at the 1979 General Election. It is interesting to note that some of the lonely crusades she initiated, and which wrecked her career, are now quite fashionable. I always thought she was rather brave, but many contemporaries thought her ridiculous and some found her threatening. Where all agree is that she was imprudent. In her five years as MP for Northampton North, Colquhoun had waged a feminist war from within what remains essentially an exclusive gentlemen's London club: the House of Commons.

Maureen Colquhoun arrived at Westminster after the February 1974 election nonchalantly carrying a 'Shop at the Co-Op' plastic carrier bag instead of a briefcase: a portent of things to come. Forty-five and still living with her husband Keith, a journalist to whom she had been married for twenty-five years, she had three grown-up children. She had won her marginal seat with a majority of 1,538.

The following year, the Tribunite MP left her husband for another journalist. This time it was a woman: Babs Todd, a British Council officer who was also a director of *Sappho*, a magazine for lesbians. At first this move was known mainly to friends. But Colquhoun was an irrepressibly open politician: fierce in her beliefs, impatient to advertise them, and loath to compromise. Like Margaret Thatcher, she was not a woman to build bridges with those who opposed her. Unlike Thatcher, she never took care to keep in with her natural allies: in Colquhoun's case, the Left. Step by step, she was to antagonize Right, Left and

Centre. There was something admirable about Colquhoun's utter disregard for protecting her own back.

In February 1976 Colquhoun asked the Speaker, George Thomas, to refer to her as either 'Maureen Colquhoun' or 'Ms Colquhoun'. At the time this appeared a wildly defiant request. No Honourable Lady had ever made it before. The Speaker was flummoxed. He wrote back: 'In the interests of the House, I think I must continue to use some form of prefix, but I will endeavour to slur it in such a way as to reduce, if not entirely eliminate, the audible distinction between "Mrs" and "Miss".' The press publicity was predictable.

Even Labour MPs – many of them – were scornful. Political correctness had not yet reached Westminster. Colquhoun was making a stand in an era in which the page seven topless model in the *Star* was still called the 'Starbird'. Newspapers turned on her and she was dubbed 'Trendy Ms Colquhoun' and 'Thoroughly Modern Maureen'. 'When a Ms Is As Good As a Male,' giggled one paper.

Colquhoun had drawn attention to herself. More circumspect parliamentarians, stung by the reaction, would have lain low for a while. The following month, in March 1976, Colquhoun held a housewarming party with her new partner Babs Todd at their East London home. By less than straightforward means, Nigel Dempster got hold of one of the invitations which on 15 April he cheerily described in his widely read *Daily Mail* column as picturing 'two entwined females' labelled Maureen and Babs. Their home was immediately besieged by reporters.

Ms Colquhoun protested to the Press Complaints Council. Dempster appeared before the PCC, trumpeting the public's 'right to know'. The PCC sided with the MP and ruled that the *Mail* had harassed her and her partner. *The Times* commented on 8 December 1976: 'The methods used to obtain information from her were a gross intrusion into privacy, and harassment of a serious kind.' But the paper added that her private life was relevant as she had taken a public stance on feminist issues. Reports of her decision to leave her husband and move in with Ms Todd were in the public interest, the newspaper argued.

Timider folk would have avoided controversy for a while. Colquhoun, however, was now campaigning on issues such as abortion, the decriminalisation of cannabis and prostitution. She earned the epithet 'loony feminist'. She was ridiculed for demanding that the word 'female' be removed from rail tickets.

Just when a period of silence was most called for, Ms Colquhoun moved to hammer into her parliamentary coffin perhaps (after her open homosexuality) the most significant nail of all. Her local Labour Party, especially its Left-wingers, were convulsed when Colquhoun, who had a high immigrant population in her constituency, appeared to side with Enoch Powell in the controversy over his 'Rivers of Blood' speech. 'I am rapidly concluding,' she said, 'that Mr Powell, whom I had always believed to be a racialist before I went into the House of Commons, is not one.' Labour was in government at the time and this attack appeared to side with the Tory Right. Labour members, she charged, had closed their ears to what Powell had to say 'and I think sometimes they ought to listen'. She attacked her colleagues for demonizing Powell rather than addressing the issues. 'The real bogeymen are in the Labour Party, who use soft words and put no money into solving the problems of poor blacks and poor whites in inner cities,' she said later.

Time started running out for this volcanic dyke when in December 1976 she punched a car-park attendant in a fracas over a complimentary parking ticket. The middle-aged MP – a 'cheery butch battleaxe', commented one journalist, of her photograph – confronted the attendant when he slammed the parking barrier down on her car as she tried to leave. 'He was totally insulting. . . I bonked him one' (words have changed their meaning). 'And he also hit me, which he later denied,' Colquhoun wrote later in her memoirs, *A Woman in the House*.

It did not take the press long. On 5 December the *Sunday People* published the story on its front page under the headline: 'Woman MP socked me.' They ran a photograph of the attendant holding what would have been the wrong side of his allegedly damaged face.

The inevitable dreary succession of Tory councillors in Northampton offered to pay the car-park attendant's legal fees if he sued. In the Commons chamber, Tory MPs clutched their faces in mock pain when they saw her enter, or rise to speak. Colquhoun was inundated with letters from sympathetic Northampton car owners who had encountered the allegedly belligerent parking attendant before.

Anything Nigel Dempster could do Northampton North Labour Party could do better. In the days when local Labour Party witch-hunts were widespread, their MP had invoked the wrath of certain members who accused her of being 'too middle-class' and snubbing the general management committee. Colquhoun then threatened legal action against anyone making unsubstantiated allegations, but a small group concentrated in one ward was already plotting to unseat her.

She complained in the national press, 'The Park ward seems to have taken over this constituency.' It proposed a motion that 'in view of her recent statements and public behaviour, Mrs [*sic*] Colquhoun is no longer acceptable as the representative in Parliament of Northampton North Constituency Labour Party, which therefore states its intention not to adopt her as the candidate at the next General Election.' In the *Guardian* she vowed to fight the 'bent rule-book infiltrators' from the ward.

In September 1977, after a fierce battle ('I have been dealt a mortal blow,' she told the press), Colquhoun was de-selected. Accused by local party members of an obsession with 'trivial' concerns such as women's rights, she was reproached for her spat with the car-park attendant, the Powell remarks, and her widely mocked campaign for all train passengers to travel first class. After she was de-selected by twenty-three votes to eighteen she admitted to reporters what had been plain for years, but what she had avoided admitting in terms which would have made an easy tabloid headline: that she was a lesbian. The local party chairman denied they had dumped her because of this. He said: 'Her sexual behaviour is not the issue.' Opposition to her had arisen around 'a lot of small things which amounted to larger things when added up'.

But the world knew better. The previous month, her local party secretary, Mr Pat Garrett, told the *Daily Express*: 'This matter hasn't been raised officially but the publicity did upset people and certain party workers felt that it might lose votes.' Weeks later Norman Ashby, party chairman, came clean to the *Sunday Telegraph*: 'Maureen got in on the supermarket vote as a solid wife and mother. This business blackened her image irredeemably.'

At Westminster Colquhoun's lesbianism embarrassed rather than angered MPs. 'I found a lot of support within the House. But it came mainly from heterosexual MPs – not the homosexual ones, for the obvious reasons that they felt threatened by my frankness. Men can now be real friends knowing I'm an absolute lost cause,' she later said. Undaunted – every chapter in her story begins 'Undaunted'! – she returned to her causes with a vengeance, introducing bills to protect prostitutes from victimization and to install more women on to public bodies. Both failed.

Her marriage to Keith, who with rare good sense has always refused to respond to journalists' questions about the matter, was dissolved in 1980. Colquhoun altered her *Who's Who* entry to include Babs alongside her husband: an amendment which broke new ground, perturbing the publication's editors.

A group of feminists now set up the Colquhoun Action Committee to challenge her de-selection. The National Executive Committee held an inquiry. She won. She was reinstated: the second MP ever to be reinstated by Labour's NEC, after Bessie Braddock. It was all in vain. She lost the 1979 General Election to Tony Marlow, a staunch supporter of the leader (Margaret Thatcher) whom Colquhoun described as a 'man with tits'. There must be something about the water in Northampton North: Marlow fast became an equally colourful and independent member, boasting a mistress, numerous children, and an extraordinary range of opinions, from the anti-European Right, to the authoritarian, to the libertarian.

Although Ms Colquhoun will go down as the lesbian who lost Labour Northampton North, the swing against her was smaller than that suffered by plenty of other MPs who lost their seats. She was not bitter. She wrote: 'I felt no sense of loss. Just a sense of relief. I was glad to be rid of Northampton and that the electorate had freed me of my Northampton Labour Party opponents for ever.' She went on to become information officer with Gingerbread, the charity for single parents. She did not retire from politics and became a councillor in her home borough of Hackney in 1982.

The rows continued. A long-running dispute between the council and the unions NALGO and NUPE led to Colquhoun, the vice-chairperson of the Housing Committee, being locked out of a local housing office. It did not stop residents turning up for her regular surgery and the former MP was forced to offer interviews in the snow-covered street.

She remained a Hackney councillor until 1990. By 1984

Colquhoun had given up hopes of returning to Westminster as an MP. Colquhoun, who now has six grandchildren, went back instead as a researcher for a Labour MP. She still works at Westminster today on a part-time basis: she has worked with two MPs and in recent years has been arranging parliamentary seminars on the way the House works. The rest of the time she spends in her Lake District home with her partner Babs. She describes their relationship, now of twenty years, as 'more respectable than most heterosexual ones'.

She recalls that when she was being pilloried over her sexuality, she found support in some unexpected quarters – and not from expected quarters. She never got the support she hoped for from the Left. One or two women MPs, she told me, were remarkably cool. Only one MP wrote a kind note: Jeremy Thorpe. 'Jeremy told me it was times like these that you knew who your friends were. I was very touched as he was himself in great trouble.'

JAMES DUNN – 1980

A Sleeping Pill and an Unusual Shopping Spree

Some Labour ministers took the 1979 election defeat harder than others. Only two months after losing his chauffeur-driven ministerial car, James Dunn was caught red-handed on a shoplifting expedition only 500 yards from the Commons.

On 27 July, Dunn, who had been a junior Northern Ireland minister in James Callaghan's government, went into the Army & Navy store – the MPs' nearest department store – in Victoria Street. He stuffed two ties, two armbands and a sweatshirt, worth £15.13, into a plastic carrier bag and left by the front door. Two store detectives set off in hot pursuit. They saw the fifty-three-year-old MP for Kirkdale, Liverpool, slip into a stationer's and remove a map worth 60p. When they apprehended him Dunn asked his captors, 'Can I have a quiet chat, and I will tell you all about it?' Unimpressed, the store detectives turned the hapless MP over to the police.

The case came to court on 12 May 1980. Dunn, an MP for fifteen years, told the Inner London Crown Court that he had panicked when he saw the store detectives staring at him. He said: 'I immediately associated one of them with some of the men I had had to deal with in Northern Ireland.' The 'father of four' admitted taking the goods, but pleaded not guilty to theft, his defence being based on his claimed state of mind at the time of the incident. He told the court that flying to Ulster, sometimes twice in one day, had exhausted him. Often he spent less than an hour and a half in a week at his homes in Liverpool and London.

He had suffered a heart attack in 1978 and was also on anti-depressants. The evening before the offence he had attended a late-night debate. He had drunk five half-pints of beer in a Commons bar. A sleeping tablet had given him a fitful night's sleep. The following morning, when he went on his illicit shopping expedition, he could not, he said, remember precisely what happened.

That this last claim at least may indeed have been the case, the judge found herself inclined to accept. The errant MP, she agreed, was 'acting entirely out of character, which was attributable to [his] appalling state of health'. The jury found Dunn guilty, and the judge conditionally discharged him for a year, and ordered him to pay £100 costs.

Dunn defected to the SDP in 1981 but lost his seat in the 1983 General Election. He died two years later. If he had been a Tory, and if the year had been 1995 instead of 1979, we should have accounted the episode evidence of a 'growing wave of sleaze'. As it was, however, the affair was little noted, quickly over, and seen for what it was: a small, isolated, personal tragedy.

ALLAN ROBERTS – 1981

'Nein, it is Rover!'

A seedy gay nightclub in Berlin's red light district. Whips. Men in SS uniforms. Studded dog collars. Torture chambers. The Labour MP, the late Allan Roberts. I always liked him. Allan had a terrific sense of fun.

The Left-wing bachelor had a track record for living it up. In 1978, the year before his election, neighbours had demanded his eviction after a string of outrageous parties at his aptly named Shady Lane home in Manchester. In February 1981 the ginger-haired former social worker struck again.

Roberts's antics in Berlin's Buddy Club made the front pages after a *Private Eye* investigation. The *News of the World* reported that the MP for Bootle had donned a studded dog collar for the late night visit and had been whipped so severely he had required hospital treatment.

Roberts wisely refused to talk to the *News of the World*, but admitted he had been involved in a 'drunken spree' at the club. He explained to his constituency association that he was so inebriated he had fallen over, had a slight accident, and required one stitch. But *Private Eye* tracked down the doctor who had administered emergency medical treatment to the MP. 'I declined to administer any sutures as the swelling was so great that additional damage could have been caused,' he said. Roberts had discharged himself the next day without paying the £110 bill.

Questioned later, Roberts went on the offensive, denying any involvement in bondage. As to the unpaid hospital bill, he told his local party: 'I thought there was an arrangement between the NHS and Germany.' The bill had, in the end, had been paid by Charles Irving, then the Tory MP for Cheltenham, who happened to be in Berlin himself on official business. Charles, who died in 1995, was the kindest of men and escapes our attention in this book.

The *News of the World* hit back the following week. It printed a signed statement from one of the MP's six companions at the club, detailing the night's events. A man wearing an SS uniform had asked Roberts, a leading supporter of CND, his name. He was not satisfied with the answer, Allan. '*Nein*,' he barked, 'it is Rover.' He then attached a dog lead to the studded dog collar already in place around the MP's neck. He dragged the MP for Bootle around the floor and, egged on by dozens of other baying S&M enthusiasts, repeatedly whipped Roberts, who (the testimony continued), bleeding from the wounds, screamed: 'That was beautiful, baby.'

Private Eye alleged that the painful weekend in Berlin had been organized by the 'Motorcycle Leather Club'. The club was an 'Interpoof' organization which had branches throughout Europe. The magazine probed some of Allan's other social outings. It regaled its readers with a party at the American Embassy in London from which the MP and some of his friends were ejected. One of them stood on a bar and denounced Ronald Reagan for being anti-gay.

Private Eye also recalled a speech Roberts had given to Manchester City Council. For once the flamboyant MP eschewed his usual arm-waving technique and kept his right hand planted firmly in his jacket pocket. The reason became clear at the end when a particularly excited supporter ran up to shake his hand. Dragging the MP's right hand free, his jaw dropped. A set of handcuffs was dangling from Roberts's wrist. During his swift exit his only audible words were 'f—ing key . . .'

The press, who tried and failed to 'out' Roberts (Allan never admitted to being gay, let alone a masochist) resorted to attacking his Left-wing views. In 1981 he was dubbed 'Afghan Roberts' when he described the newly installed Soviet regime in Afghanistan as the 'lesser evil' after a controversial fact-finding visit to Kabul with two other Labour MPs, including Ron Brown (see pp.267–73), in 1981. He opposed what he called Neil Kinnock's 'witch-hunt' against the Militant Tendency and supported the Left-wing Eric Heffer in his leadership bid.

In 1984, Roberts was awarded libel damages against the *News of the World* and *Private Eye* over allegations that he was being investigated by the police for sexual offences. He invested the money in a constituency office and a share in a London East End pub.

Despite the constant stream of bad publicity, Roberts received a unanimous vote of confidence from his local party. When he died after a long battle against illness in March 1990, he commanded a 24,447 majority – one of the biggest in the Commons.

The adverse press attention never damaged his parliamentary career and he went on to become a respected member of Labour's frontbench Environment team. Politically he remained an outspoken defender of gay rights.

I attended music-hall nights at his pub more than once. Allan was jolly company, funny, bright, and a generous host. In his flat afterwards there would sometimes be marijuana, sometimes just alcohol. Allan would make an odd addition to Tony Blair's new Labour Party. There was an unmistakably degenerate strand in his personality and a wild side to his life, but he was kind to men and women he could help, sponsor, shelter or give part-time work to. He burned the candle riotously at both ends, and finally burned himself out.

NICHOLAS FAIRBAIRN – 1982

'Everything which is not dull becomes scandalous'

So protested the late Sir Nicholas Fairbairn. Sir Nicholas was certainly never dull. The press were fascinated by him – and Bernard Levin was unapologetic: '. . . when the lamp-posts outside a man's home are thick with the bodies of ladies mad for his love, or at the very least for his double-breasted waistcoats, he must expect more than a passing interest in the matter to be shown, if only by the envious.'

Fairbairn not only expected attention, but sought it. His

daughter Charlotte has described to the *Daily Mail* some of the clothes he created for himself: 'A see-through negligée top, with a huge black cross beneath it, and white flared trousers'. He was, she adds 'stubbornly fond of a waistcoat made up from the skins of two antelopes'. At his house in Roupell Street, panels had been painted showing Lord Whitelaw as a bullfrog, Lady Thatcher as a heron and Lord St John of Fawsley as a toad climbing up a slippery pole.

He was also an inveterate lecher, who once remarked, 'What is a skirt but an open gateway?' Being chauffeured to his daughter's wedding he talked loudly to her of gonorrhea. 'Charlotte was familiar with the range of her father's interests, the driver less so. "He was trying hard not to listen, but he obviously heard. He ended up taking the wrong route and we were late to church."'

Judged by the recent spate of ministerial resignations, Fairbairn, once Scotland's Solicitor-General, got off lightly. Few ministers would expect to survive today if their teenage daughter was reported to have discovered their divorced Dad's lover hanging from a lamp-post outside the family's London home. The bizarre stunt claimed in newspaper reports may never have happened quite like this, but there was undoubtedly a suicide bid, in 1981: a cry for help from the forty-seven-year-old Fairbairn's thirty-four-year-old lover.

Mrs Thatcher, however Victorian her own values, was unmoved by the ensuing scandal. It was a 'private matter' (though it dominated the front pages for days) between 'two single people'. She had no intention of intervening.

Fairbairn discovered weeks later that MPs were less forgiving when he, as a minister, dared to breach one of Parliament's hallowed rules. Scotland's most powerful law officer spoke to a newspaper about a controversial rape case before he told Parliament. This time there was no forgiveness and he was forced to resign.

MP for the vast and beautiful constituency of Kinross and West Perthshire, Fairbairn dwelt in a castle. He entered Parliament in 1974. An able if erratic speaker, an often brilliant advocate, and at home with the hangers and floggers (though neither himself) on the Right of the party but never with the Mother Grundies, he got on well with Mrs Thatcher, who overlooked his flippancy. Fairbairn's *Who's Who* 'hobbies' changed each year. One entry

read: 'drawing ships, confounding whips and scuttling drips';
another: 'debunking bishops, serving Queens' (real ones; he
loathed homosexuality) 'restoring castles, entertaining knights
and befriending pawns'. An earlier entry said 'making love, ends
meet, people laugh'. He did.

The Chief Whip had known about the 'lamp-post' allegations
(some reports said iron railings, others an overdose of aspirins)
within hours of the suicide bid in the early hours of 26 October
1981. He chose not to burden Mrs Thatcher with the news until
it was just about to break, two days before Christmas. There was
a clamour for Fairbairn's resignation. It was the topic of
conversation at Christmas lunches throughout the land, though
perhaps not at Chequers.

Pursued by the press, the spurned lover, a former House of
Commons secretary, denied hanging from anything – saying she
'wouldn't even have had the energy to climb up a lamp-post'. The
love affair, she claimed, had started in 1974 when the colourful
laird of Fordell Castle in Fife was still married to his first wife, the
Honourable Elizabeth Mackay. Fairbairn had wooed her, she said,
with red roses, passionate love letters and proposals of marriage.

The Scottish Solicitor-General pulled up the drawbridge on his
castle to wait for reporters to leave. They didn't. So he emerged,
arrayed in a blue and white dressing gown, to tell the press it had
been a happy relationship. But it was the lady, not he, who was the
ardent suitor. She had demanded his hand in marriage, not the
other way round.

He labelled the press 'vicious, priggish and pseudo-priggish'
(an elegant distinction) but reserved most venom for Colonel
Michael Mates (see pp.304–8), the MP for Petersfield, who had
been accused by some MPs of being the 'fourth-form sneak' who
tipped off the press. There is no evidence for this.

The lady survived her suicide attempt and Fairbairn survived
the lady. It was then that he pushed his luck too far. There was an
outcry when he tried to justify the decision not to prosecute three
Glasgow youths for rape. The mistake was to make his case (that
there was insufficient evidence) in the *Glasgow Daily Record* the
day before he was due to make a statement to the Commons.

As well as a discourtesy to the Commons – a hanging offence
among MPs – his comments prejudiced any possible private
prosecution. Such was the outrage that an emotional apology in

RAPE ROW LAW CHIEF IS SACKED

MRS THATCHER sacked her flamboyant Scottish law officer Nicholas Fairbairn last night.

Daily Mail, 22 January 1982

the House was not enough. He resigned the next day. Having
stuck by her errant minister thus far, Mrs Thatcher summoned
him to 10 Downing Street. One report claimed Fairbairn was
handed a copy of his resignation letter and a pen, and told: 'Sign
this.' Fairbairn showed loyalty, claiming afterwards that she was
'probably the warmest and kindest human being that those who
have met her have ever encountered'.

Nicky Fairbairn was one of the most gifted Queen's Counsel of
his generation. His style was flamboyant. He designed for himself
the extraordinary tartan trousers and waistcoats he wore at the
Commons. He was seldom out of the limelight for long. In
October 1982 he was cited in the divorce case of Alasdair
MacInnes, an investment consultant. He had enjoyed an affair
with MacInnes's wife, Suzanne, whom he affectionately called
Sambo and married the next year. But the headlines 'Top Tory
stole my wife' infuriated him.

The following month he delivered a coruscating attack in *The
Times* on what he saw as the hypocritical moral crusades of the
press:

> Scandal may be good copy, but it adds nothing to the
> integrity of our institutions. I do not think they were any
> worse, indeed I think they were probably much better, when
> those who ruled us were known and seen to have healthy
> sexual liaisons with many mistresses and lovers.

Acknowledging his well-wishers earlier that year, Fairbairn
thanked one of the great train robbers for a gift he had sent.

I knew him, though not well, for a decade and the incident is
typical. He could rarely resist putting two fingers up to the
conventional tut-tutters, and the trait endeared him to many, and
enraged a few. During the Commons debate on salmonella in
eggs (Mrs Edwina Currie, a junior Health minister at the time,
had started a national alarm – a false alarm, some believed –
about the bacteria) Fairbairn reminded Mrs Currie that she had
once been an egg and added that members on both sides of the
House regretted its fertilization.

His opinions were unspeakable, his behaviour objectionable,
and he drank far, far too much. A former Chief Whip remarked
to me that a whip's test of the viability of a ministerial

appointment was 'whether, when the chap's in the *wrong*, other chaps, who know he's in the wrong, can still be found to defend him in the House. When Nicky was in the wrong, other chaps stayed away.'

But he took punches on the chin, seldom whined and never sued. And even near the end there were moments when his wit could wither an opponent, his logic slice an argument, or his rhetoric soar. Speaking of her father, Charlotte remarked: 'There was nothing to stop Papa. It was almost as if he did it deliberately. He had a self-destructive element, which became apparent when his creative side was frustrated.'

He is dead now. It appears he cut his daughters out of his will in a death-bed codicil signed in shaking hand, 'F of F' (Fairbairn of Fordell). He died in February 1995, his liver having given up the unequal struggle. Close to death he took the opportunity to denounce his would-be successor, the Tory candidate John Godfrey, a London-based banker: 'He's a clone. I don't think he knows anything about Perthshire or Scotland. He is totally irrelevant.' Mr Godfrey lost the election. The *Daily Mail* later reported that Fairbairn had fathered a son, whose existence had been kept secret, nine years before his death.

There are few in the Commons – but, to be fair, there *are* a few – who do not think the place poorer for the loss.

CECIL PARKINSON – 1983

'Is there no flaw?'

'In some ways, he seems too good to be true,' it was said in *The Times* of Cecil Parkinson in October 1981. The remark was without irony. 'Tall, handsome, charming and likeable . . . the perfect constituency MP, intelligent without being intellectual,

self-made, brilliantly supported by a politically-committed wife –
is there, one wonders, no flaw?'

There was. The fifty-year-old Chairman of the Conservative
Party had a thirty-four-year-old mistress, Sara Keays, who was to
become pregnant. The story which follows relies heavily upon her
own account. The (now) Lord Parkinson has written little about
the affair, and does not comment on it; but I know he would have
his own perspective on the story.

Fixed now in the public mind is the focal chapter of that story,
though much had gone before and much was to follow. I shall
sketch out that chapter to remind the reader, then return to begin
at the beginning. The chapter started in June 1983, as the Tories
won a General Election, and ended in October, as Parkinson was
all but torpedoed off the Conference platform.

'Golden boy' is a cliché, but apt, for the political persona was a
cliché. Very much the golden boy of early 1980s Tory politics,
Cecil Parkinson had organized Margaret Thatcher's 1983
General Election landslide. As Mrs Thatcher and her Party
Chairman waved to their ecstatic supporters from an upstairs
window at Conservative Central Office, no one would have
guessed anything was wrong. But only hours earlier, on 9 June, as
the country went to the polls, Parkinson had made a startling
confession.

Thatcher, already convinced that victory was in the bag, had
just offered her favourite minister any Cabinet job he wanted in
her next government. The Foreign Office was Parkinson's for the
asking. His reply was the last thing she expected. Parkinson,
married for twenty-seven years, with three grown-up daughters,
admitted to having a 'serious personal problem'. He said: 'I'm not
sure I should be in your Cabinet at all.' Mrs Thatcher listened in
unaccustomed silence as Parkinson explained that Sara Keays, his
Commons secretary since 1971, was carrying his child.

In his autobiography, Parkinson wrote: 'Mrs Thatcher was
immensely sympathetic, not at all censorious.' She agreed to his
becoming Trade and Industry Secretary. As to the baby, 'she said
she was sure that as sensible people we could sort it out'. She
could not have been more wrong.

Even as they spoke, Colonel Hastings Keays, soon to be a
proud grandfather, fired the first salvo in a guerrilla war which
was to end with Parkinson's dramatic capitulation at 2.00 a.m. on

14 October 1983 at the Tory Party Conference.

Parkinson left Blackpool with his loyal and formidable wife, Ann, by his side, only hours before Mrs Thatcher was due to address the party faithful and bask in the glory of June's election victory. The theme of her speech was to be 'rejoice'. Press photographs of the Parkinsons returning to London identified their companion as a detective. In fact it was a young man – Parkinson's special adviser – whom few would have recognized at the time: Michael Portillo, not yet an MP.

Parkinson, a self-made millionaire, had been forced to pay a bitter price by Keays for at least twice breaking his promise to marry her. On Friday, 14 October, *The Times* published a sensational statement from the jilted Keays. She said that when she had broken the news of the baby to Parkinson he had asked her to end her pregnancy. 'I was not aware that political expediency was sufficient grounds for an abortion,' she told *The Times* . . .

Permit me to break this narrative for a moment. Time and again a responsible narrator must remind the reader that he is hearing only one person's account of the story: that of Sara Keays. We hardly have Parkinson's. Imagine how many different accounts could be offered, all true, but each from a different perspective, of a discussion between a man and a woman about the possibility of an abortion.

Nor must Parkinson's silence be interpreted as implying that he has nothing to say. In conversations not only with him, but with a number of others mentioned in this book, I have so often encountered the view (variously expressed) that 'least said soonest mended'. It is felt that where one has been guilty there is more to be lost than gained through joining a debate about just how guilty one has been; or which accusations are wholly and which only partly true. British MPs have a genuine dislike of what looks like special pleading: they have to put up with so much of it from others.

There is also an emotional horror of returning in one's mind to a period of anger and shame. Many of those I have interviewed for this book approach their recollections in a way which is almost pathologically post-traumatic.

. . . But to return to our story, and begin at the beginning.

Cecil Parkinson had travelled far from a humble start as the son of a Lancashire railwayman. He was born in 1931 and educated at the Royal Lancaster Grammar School and Emmanuel College, Cambridge. He met his wife, the independently wealthy Ann Jarvis, in 1955, they married the following year, and at the same time he joined the Conservative Party. Earlier, he had inclined to the political Left.

He qualified as a chartered accountant in 1959 and went on to become a director of several companies in the 1960s and 70s. He founded Parkinson Hart Securities in 1967. By now a millionaire, he owned homes in Hertfordshire, Pimlico and Cornwall. He entered Parliament in 1970 as MP for Enfield West, moving to nearby Hertsmere after boundary changes.

One year later, on 2 June 1971, the twenty-three-year-old Sara Keays walked into the thirty-nine-year-old MP's life when she became a Commons secretary. Keays claims the affair began soon after: 'It was not a mere "dalliance", a "sad and silly blunder", but a long-standing, genuine love affair.'

In March 1974, according to her widely publicized book on the affair, *A Matter of Judgement*, serialized in the *Daily Mirror* and described, rather surprisingly, in a review by the late Lord Goodman as 'this unpleasant and unnecessary book', Keays had started to work for Parkinson. She says she tried to quit the job but that Parkinson refused to let her. This, she wrote, marked a fundamental change in their relationship. She said they were very much in love, and spent more and more time together.

Parkinson enjoyed a rapid rise within both party and government. After a period as junior Trade minister, he became Party Chairman in 1981, joining the Cabinet. His closeness to the Prime Minister earned him a place in her War Cabinet during the Falklands conflict.

Parkinson and his mistress separated when Keays went to Brussels to work for Roy Jenkins in July 1979. When she returned briefly to London on 27 October they met up, according to her book. He proposed, she says. She accepted. Yet there was no ring, nor wedding date. Parkinson, outwardly still happily married to Ann, explained to Keays (she wrote) that timing was everything. He could not afford, at just this point, to jeopardize his soaring political career.

At the end of 1980, Ann Parkinson became seriously ill, and went into hospital for surgery. One of their daughters, Mary, got into difficulties with drugs. This was no time to leave his wife and family. But he and Keays did not stop seeing each other when she came back to work in the Commons. In January 1981, his car was stolen from outside her mews house in Southwark. Disaster was only narrowly averted. His two distinctive red ministerial boxes were in the car. Although the car was returned, Parkinson had to tell the Home Secretary, William Whitelaw, of its inconvenient position. According to Keays, Whitelaw replied: 'There but for the grace of God go a great many of us.'

Those who read or hear Keays's descriptions of their affair will form an insistent impression that Parkinson was the pursuer: an impression based, not least, on her reports that he was repeatedly promising to marry her. This impression, of one individual as victim and the other as huntsman, is really quite central to the moral perspective of the picture which has arisen in many minds. It is overwhelmingly based on Keays's account.

In September 1981, Parkinson was a surprise choice as Party Chairman. He fast proved a highly effective salesman for his party. A year later he was faced, as Chairman, with a cruel dilemma: how cruel, few can have known.

Keays had political ambitions of her own. She had stood

THE TORY MINISTER AND THE EX-SECRETARY

"IT'S A FULL CABINET MEETING SIR"

Cartoon by Jak, *Daily Express*, 8 October 1983 (courtesy of *Daily Mail*)

unsuccessfully as a candidate in Southwark council elections. She came close in October 1982 to securing the Conservative nomination to fight the seat of Bermondsey at the General Election. Then the Tory selection process for Bermondsey had to be repeated when the sitting member, Bob Mellish, died. A by-election was called, and the candidate who had beaten Keays for the seat resigned, unable to fight a by-election.

It fell to Conservative Central Office to advise Bermondsey Tories whether to select their runner-up – Keays – as candidate, or to re-open the selection. As Party Chairman, Parkinson's judgement was critical. He decided that in the new circumstances Bermondsey should re-select. They did, choosing a young man called Robert Hughes (see p.319). We may surmise that Parkinson would be damned if he did act to 'install' Keays in Bermondsey, and damned if he didn't. She may have felt that Parkinson had scuppered her chances. He may have felt that he was rescuing her from a wretched campaign. We remember what befell another candidate in that by-election, Peter Tatchell.

Yet their affair drifted on until May 1983, when she became pregnant. She told him on 21 May. A June General Election was looming. In her book she said that Parkinson, in calling for an abortion, threatened never to see her again if she had the baby. 'I was appalled. So that was how he really felt. His talk of marriage had been a sham. He did not love me and probably had ceased to love me a long time ago.'

Keays turned for support to her family in Marksbury near Bath. It was agreed to deliver an ultimatum to Parkinson. Her father, the Colonel, intervened. Throughout this affair the Colonel was a colourful figure, his interventions as dramatic as they were unexpected. He now sent a letter by courier to the Prime Minister. How Mrs Thatcher took this extraordinary missive we do not know. Keays says that Parkinson telephoned her on election day; she wanted him to marry her; he told her (she says) that he had now discussed the affair with the Prime Minister, who was offering him the Cabinet post of Trade and Industry Secretary, in addition to his Party Chairmanship role.

On 11 June, two days after the election, Colonel Keays received a telephone call from Parkinson. He assured him 'he intended to do the right thing by Sara and that he intended to look after her and the child'. Colonel Keays was unenthusiastic about this statement.

On 5 August Parkinson went on holiday to the Bahamas, after paying £5,000 into his pregnant mistress's bank account. The press had by now got hold of the story. On 23 August *Daily Mirror* reporters chased the five-months-pregnant secretary through London demanding to know if Parkinson was the father. So hot was the pursuit that Keays and the reporters were involved in a minor collision.

Parkinson, with time to reflect in the Bahamian sunshine, resolved to stay with Ann. On his return Keays says he telephoned her and in a heated conversation accused her of trying to blackmail him into marriage. They agreed that all further dealings should be conducted through solicitors.

Keays demanded that Parkinson tell the Prime Minister of what Keays said was his change of heart about marriage. On 2 September, Colonel Keays wrote to Mrs Thatcher and warned her 'that a public scandal must be regarded as imminent'.

The countdown to the biggest parliamentary scandal to trouble Mrs Thatcher's reign had begun. At this stage (after the election victory but before the Party Conference) the election-night conversation between Parkinson and Mrs Thatcher had not leaked out. But there had been some vague speculation. This intensified when, on 14 September, Parkinson suddenly and surprisingly resigned as Party Chairman. The unknown John Selwyn Gummer took over with the Party Conference only three weeks away. We may surmise that Parkinson and the Prime Minister felt that the publicity likely to surround the affair would make his Central Office job impossible. Those who seek an explanation of the origins of John Gummer as a national figure need look no further. God, it may seem, looks after his own.

On 5 October, while lawyers for both parties were trying to agree a joint statement, *Private Eye* delivered its own interpretation of a rapidly moving story. 'Why was Cecil Parkinson asked to step down as Tory Party Chairman? I can assure readers that it had nothing to do with his marital difficulties which have recently caused raised eyebrows in Tory circles.' The magazine went on to break the story that his secretary, Sara Keays, was pregnant.

Keays telephoned Parkinson and said: 'If you don't do something about it, I will. You've got until midday to decide whether or not you are going to issue a statement and if you won't then I will.' It was their last exchange. It was the most awkward moment imaginable for her threatened torpedo, which was to come nine days later in her statement in *The Times*.

Parkinson's own pre-emptory statement at 11.45 p.m. on 5 October, in time for the next morning's newspapers, was dramatic:

> To bring to an end rumour concerning Miss Sara Keays, and her family, I wish, with her consent, to make the following

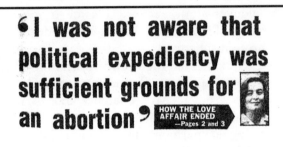

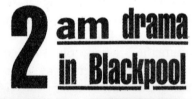

CECIL PARKINSON has gone from the Cabinet but the Parkinson affair has not gone away.

HUMILIATED: Parkinson, forced to quit by revelations of ex-mistress Sara Keays

HUMILIATED: Mrs Thatcher, gambled her party would stand by Mr Parkinson.

Daily Mirror, 15 October 1983

statement. I have had a relationship with Miss Keays over a number of years. She is expecting a child, due to be born in January, of whom I am the father. I am of course making financial provision for both mother and child.

During our relationship I told Miss Keays of my wish to marry her. Despite my having given Miss Keays that assurance, my wife, who has been a source of great strength, and I, decided to stay together and to keep our family together. I regret deeply the distress I have caused to Miss Keays, to her family and to my family.

The only other statement that night was from Downing Street, in which Mrs Thatcher said she regarded the issue as a 'private matter'. It was plain she saw no reason for her favourite Cabinet minister, tipped as a future leader, to stand down.

Within minutes, gangs of reporters were camped on Parkinson's doorstep, and on the doorstep of the Keays family home in Marksbury. Holed up inside, the pregnant Sara Keays read with increasing frustration each day's press coverage of the affair. Parkinson was enjoying a wave of sympathy for having 'come clean'. Keays was being portrayed as bitter, clinging and vindictive.

The much-read John Junor in the *Sunday Express* wrote a column which was decidedly sympathetic to Cecil Parkinson.

Even Mary Kenny in *The Times* was unforgiving towards Keays. 'Men who tell the truth and face their responsibilities are, in my view, far more worthy of public office than men who take the easy way out. I trust Cecil Parkinson more for having done the brave thing.' Parkinson, buoyed, he wrote, by 16,000 supportive letters against only forty-six demanding his resignation, seemed to have survived.

Sara Keays was enraged. She thought Mrs Thatcher's advisers were orchestrating a campaign of misinformation against her.

A week after his statement he was emerging as the unfortunate victim of a scheming woman who had tried to trap him into a marriage by 'deliberately' becoming pregnant . . . it seemed not to have occurred to a single commentator, certainly not to any of his colleagues, that he had acted selfishly. No one had commented on what was being done to me . . . I had to put a stop to these accusations for my child's sake as well as my own. I had to refute the rumours that I was promiscuous and had had a casual affair with Cecil.

Whatever their differences now, Keays had learned something from her former lover about the art of timing in politics. Her long, detailed statement to *The Times* was released to coincide with Mrs Thatcher's rousing end-of-conference speech. Parkinson was due to take his place at the PM's right hand side.

Keays wrote:

Press comments, Government pronouncements and the continued speculation about this matter have put me in an impossible position. I feel that I have both a public duty and a duty to my family to put the record straight.

She detailed Parkinson's alleged broken promises and pledge to divorce. The baby, she said, had been conceived in a relationship she felt was leading to marriage after he had proposed, in 1979, an offer she says he had repeated.

Her statement was immediately flashed to the Imperial Hotel in Blackpool, where Parkinson was staying only a few yards from the Prime Minister's suite. As he walked the short distance to her room he knew it was over. They spoke for fifteen minutes. No decision was made. But it was plain that Keays would not fade into the background. He knew he had to go. He had no choice. Mrs Thatcher spoke to a subdued conference that afternoon. One section of her triumphal Leader's speech had been rewritten. Instead of eulogizing Parkinson's achievements as mastermind of the election victory, she said: 'We do not forget today the man who so brilliantly organized the campaign.' But she did forget to mention him by name. I remember a warm and sympathetic cheer from the hall. The underlying feeling among representatives and MPs – of whom I was one – was of bafflement.

Parkinson had already left Blackpool for Hertfordshire. When he surfaced the next day, the mobile multitude of journalists and photographers was camped outside. 'Just before I left for the office,' he says, 'I received a telephone call from a friend who was the editor of a popular daily newspaper. He advised me not to say a word, not even "good morning", to his jackals or to anyone else's. I suggested if he felt like that, perhaps he could take his away. He replied that as long as other people's were there he could not move his!'

Two days later Parkinson escaped to Portugal with Ann. There was little respite. They were discovered on a golf course by the press. A slim Mrs Parkinson took a full swing at the ball and was congratulated by photographers. She replied sweetly: 'Perhaps I am stronger than I look.' She had supplied the next day's headlines: '"I am a very strong lady" says Ann Parkinson.'

On New Year's Eve 1983, Sara Keays gave birth to Flora – 8lb 3oz. Parkinson was informed of this by two *Daily Mirror* reporters. He did not visit, but in a statement wished his daughter, for whom he was providing financially, 'peace, privacy and a happy life'.

Since then something has been made of Parkinson's separation from the child. Few commentators seem to have asked themselves whether an absent parent might not be concerned mainly for the child's privacy and peace. Visits to the child would (whenever the press found out) be given prominent coverage in the newspapers. Parkinson may feel that, with the relationship broken down and with constant media interest, the child could easily become a battleground. He has suggested as much when talking to Anthony Clare in the radio programme 'In the Psychiatrist's Chair'. The little girl is handicapped and the publicity would be cruel and confusing for her. There is something disgusting about the way the media can make a normalization of human relations impossible, then scream its outrage that relations are not normal.

Parkinson retired to the backbenches. He never faced any serious threat from his constituency association. For years newspaper rumours would circulate claiming he was on his way back into government. But Mrs Thatcher, under pressure from the whips, decided there could be no return until the voters in his constituency had delivered a verdict. On the eve of a Cabinet reshuffle in August 1985 she rang him to explain that she did not feel able to appoint him until a General Election. She was giving new jobs to Douglas Hurd and Leon Brittan.

'I was expecting nothing, Margaret,' Parkinson replied, 'but may I offer one word of advice? Brief the press that I stay out of the Cabinet *now*, to get that story out of the way in tomorrow's papers. Then the following day's story will be Douglas's and Leon's.'

'Oh Cecil,' she replied, 'I'd never have thought of that. *That's* why I want you back.'

And she undoubtedly did. Despite gossip at the time about his continuing ambitions, the evidence is that it was Mrs Thatcher who believed he could recover. Parkinson lost confidence that he could. This was not just realism on his part (though it was realistic). It was also, I believe, emotional. Though a self-made man who had always worked doggedly for his success, it is fair to say that until then Cecil Parkinson had been used to winning. He had that air about him. He never gave me the impression of someone who knew what it was to hit the kerb. Unlike (for instance) Jeffrey Archer, he had no experience of being broken, crushed, or knocked down, and crawling back from the wreckage. I do not think Parkinson was or is emotionally well adapted to large reverses. I think he would accept this observation.

Still, Mrs Thatcher kept trying on his behalf. When Parkinson was returned in 1987 with an 18,000 majority, an increase of over 3,000 – he was judged to have served his penance. He took the relatively junior Cabinet post of Energy Secretary and two years later became Transport Secretary. Mrs Thatcher was pushing.

He managed both jobs with his customary fluency and ease, but Cecil Parkinson never recovered the electric touch. He was never again seen as a contender for the leadership. He resigned from the Cabinet on the same day as Mrs Thatcher. He stood down at the 1992 election and was elevated to the House of Lords.

He says little about the affair. Keays, who was given a significant financial settlement but remains unreconciled to her former lover's behaviour, has spoken often since. Last year she addressed a conference on single motherhood. The sight of Sara Keays lambasting Tory wives for turning a blind eye to their cheating husbands' infidelities raised an eyebrow or two.

Parkinson does briefly break his silence on his relationship with Keays in his memoirs, *Right at the Centre*. Whereas she devoted an entire book to the subject, he devoted seven pages – to what he called 'The Keays Affair'. It shed little new light on one of the most widely talked about scandals at Westminster for a decade.

It is perhaps worth observing that one curious moral does seem to emerge from the affair: that in media eyes the greatest modern sin is not to get divorced. Men who divorce to marry their secretaries, mistresses or constituents (and more than one successful modern Tory has done so) seem to provoke less moralizing than men who, after being unfaithful, return to their wives. Nor, for instance, was there ever much media interest in the original Mrs Thatcher, Denis Thatcher's first wife.

It is an open secret that Parkinson would have been Mrs Thatcher's choice for Foreign Secretary if he had been divorced from his wife. After all, our last Foreign Secretary is twice-married, though in vastly different circumstances. When Parkinson left the Cabinet, he was replaced by Nicholas Ridley, who had left his wife and later married his secretary. The ratio of divorced to undivorced Cabinet ministers altered from 10:11 to 11:10. An intriguing victory for modern morals.

Cecil Parkinson did not, it seemed, want to marry Sara Keays. But the media hardly appear to have noticed that this choice was probably not open to him anyway. He could not have divorced Ann, who was blameless. She (those of us who have met the impressive Lady Parkinson may surmise) would not have divorced him.

Flora Keays, now eleven years old, has never met her father. Keays has never married. Parkinson is still with his wife. Those who like to believe that even supermen have feet of clay, those who like to believe that pride comes before a fall, and those who like to believe that Hell hath no fury like a woman scorned, have all enjoyed the confirmation of the proverbial wisdoms which the tale of Cecil Parkinson and Sara Keays provides.

KEITH HAMPSON – 1984

An Accidental Brush with Scandal

As the naked male go-go dancer strutted his stuff on the stage of a Soho nightclub, Keith Hampson enjoyed a late-night drink before meeting his wife at a party. But unknown to the Tory MP for Leeds North-West, the man standing beside him on the night of 3 May 1984 was an undercover police officer on 'routine surveillance'.

Earlier, Hampson, the Parliamentary Private Secretary to the then Defence Secretary Michael Heseltine, had been drinking with colleagues in a pub near Conservative Central Office on the fifth anniversary of the Tories' 1979 election victory. He downed five pints of his favourite brew, then went back to his office to work on a speech for Michael Heseltine. He nicknamed the beer 'brain damage'. This may explain the tone and content of Mr Heseltine's speeches, whatever it may do to account for Mr Hampson's subsequent behaviour. He was due to meet his wife later on.

After completing the speech he decided to kill a few hours in Soho. By chance he went into the Gay Theatre in Berwick Street which features non-stop male strip shows. Inside, smoke filled the club, the music was throbbing, and a male stripper, Luscious Leon, was dancing naked on the stage.

Hampson's attention was captured by a woman – or was it a man in drag? – standing nearby. Hampson couldn't tell. He bent forward for a closer inspection. In the process he accidentally brushed the thigh of the man standing next to him. The man was an undercover policeman acting as an *agent provocateur*. The woman was a police colleague.

The phrase 'accidentally brushed' was Hampson's. The policeman claimed a left hand was placed on his buttock, while his groin was grasped by the right. The subsequent court case turned partly upon whether the PC's evidence was believed, but others asked what – were this evidence true – the constable

246

thought he was up to, getting himself into these situations. Hampson was arrested for indecent assault and led from the club. The club manager, Russell McCleod, had seen it all before. He would have been well advised to warn his clients that the club was a regular haunt of plainclothes police.

Forty-year-old Hampson kept quiet about the arrest. He did not tell Heseltine – in his case rather like keeping a secret from God. But when a crime reporter on the *Sunday Telegraph* started asking questions, Hampson consulted his boss, then resigned as Heseltine's PPS. His wife supported him, testifying that her husband was perfectly heterosexual.

Marcus Fox, a senior Tory and fellow Yorkshire MP and steady, as ever, in everything but a crisis, proclaimed that he was 'staggered that he (Hampson) was in a place like that'.

Hampson blamed the incident on personal stress and alcohol but the manager of the club made Hampson's plight worse when he claimed that he was a regular client as were three or four other MPs.

A few days later, Hampson was charged with indecent assault. With the party split over whether or not he should resign as an MP (so causing a by-election), he decided to tough it out. He opted for trial by jury.

In October he appeared before Southwark Crown Court, the prosecution basing their case on the disputed police evidence. For the defence, character witnesses such as Lord Tonypandy, former Speaker of the Commons, impressed the jury. The judge told jurors that to suggest Hampson was a homosexual was 'absurd and unthinkable'. He urged the jury to remember that the 'history of mankind is littered with debris of men who have acted more stupidly than anyone else would have thought possible at the time'. After five hours the jury had failed to reach a verdict.

A week later the Attorney-General, Sir Michael Havers, announced that because of the widespread publicity and exceptional circumstances there could be no retrial. A verdict of not guilty was recorded.

Many had assumed at first that all was lost. But for every case cited as evidence that it is best to go quietly because to struggle only makes it worse, there is another suggesting that one should fight every inch of the way. Hampson was adamant throughout that the charge was false; so those of us who questioned whether

TORY MP Keith Hampson told a court yesterday how he "brushed the thigh" of a plainclothes policeman in a gay club.

I BRUSHED PC's THIGH

Sun, 19 October 1984

the behaviour alleged – in the place where it was alleged – should anyway have led to a prosecution, were denied the opportunity to support Keith by such an argument, probably to his considerable relief.

Keith Hampson came perilously close to going under, survived, and his reputation has largely recovered. Bristol University and Harvard educated, a former personal assistant to Edward Heath and a clever, clubbable and liberal Tory, Hampson remains the MP for Leeds North-West. He co-ordinated Michael Heseltine's bid for the Tory leadership in 1990.

HARVEY PROCTOR – 1986

'You haven't murdered anyone, have you?'

Harvey Proctor MP never did anything more shocking than spank people – and willing victims at that, for he paid them for their pains. Today his behaviour would not come to court. In 1987, however, the affair was a celebrated scandal. Though taken with as much amusement as shock, it wrecked his political career.

Harvey Proctor, a Conservative MP since 1979, was popular in his Basildon (later Billericay) constituency for his hard-line views on 'new' Commonwealth immigration. In fact his opinions, sometimes Right-wing, sometimes libertarian, could not be as crudely pigeon-holed as the media suggested – he voted consistently for such liberal causes as reform of the mental health act, homosexual rights, penal reform and freedom of information – but he was described as being 'one of the Thatcher praetorian guard'. Such over-simplifications served to shield him from censure in Billericay, where palms are hairy and Proust is hardly read. But they also deprived him of support or sympathy in the liberal press and among fellow MPs on the ideological Left, when his own colourful lifestyle hit the news. As the whispers about Proctor's sexual behaviour grew at Westminster and in Fleet Street, so did the support he always maintained from his Essex constituency association.

Proctor would not see it like this, but my impression was that Right-wingers among his Tory officers persuaded themselves that their MP was the victim of a liberal conspiracy to discredit him, and believed in him all the more fiercely. Gradually, an unbridgeable gap yawned between the two sides – political and private – of his life. It was a chasm into which he eventually tumbled.

In September 1981 Proctor, educated at state schools and a graduate from the University of York, had his first brush with scandal. He had always enjoyed a tempestuous relationship with Terry Woods, his long-standing boyfriend. Woods became furious when, after he had walked out of Proctor's small Fulham flat, the MP refused to let him return. Woods spoke to journalists in Dublin, prompting a *News of the World* story.

Private Eye's exposure of Proctor's homosexuality was followed by the national press. They pursued him on a parliamentary visit to Finland, *News of the World* journalists checking in, incognito, to his hotel there and telephoning him in the middle of the night to see whether he was alone. Although a conscientious MP, he had only a modest majority (5,180) and could not afford a scandal. He dismissed the stories Woods had prompted as a 'campaign of political character assassination'. His constituency party, inclined to believe their independent-minded MP, backed him.

The problem seemed to be that though Proctor and Woods were genuinely fond of each other, Woods would often drink too much and lose control of his tongue. Proctor, however, who had known Woods since 1973, was unwilling to lose his friendship or turn him away. Woods was married with two children, though he separated from his wife. He did not return to live with Proctor until much later (1988) but saw him often. He was to feature in this story again.

Five years later, in 1986, a series of lurid allegations in the *People* proved harder for the bachelor MP to shake off. The newspaper and Proctor had been snarling at one another over the

MP's successful libel action against them after they had (wrongly) alleged Mrs Thatcher was refusing to call Proctor 'my hon. friend'.

That summer the *People* printed a huge story, over three pages, about Proctor's proclivities. A male prostitute said that Proctor would play the headmaster. 'I would have to pretend to be a pupil who had done something wrong. He said I must call him Sir at all times and must not answer back. He took me into the bedroom and told me to put on a pair of white shorts.' Then the spanking sessions took place. The MP was gentler in bed, according to the newspaper. The young man in question had moved in with Proctor for a while, the paper alleged. Proctor denied this but said the man had stayed in his flat for a few days, at his mother's request, to study for his exams.

The MP, who had moved to the safer Tory seat of Billericay after boundary changes, was accused by the *People*, the following Sunday, of using a rent-boy network. A gay massage parlour boss was procuring youths for the MP at £35 a time, according to the newspaper, which alleged that youths would take part in sex games at Proctor's flat and that the politician would spank them 'while he watched by-election results on television'. Given the direction of subsequent Tory fortunes at by-elections, it is surprising the practice did not become more generalized.

At this time, Proctor refused to comment on sexual allegations, saying that his private life was his own business and did not interfere with his parliamentary or constituency work. He later told friends that what was published was usually a mixture of truth, half-truth, and falsehood. He lacked the funds to gamble on libel actions, which he feared would degenerate into confused disputation over half-truths, damaging him regardless of whether he won the individual arguments.

But of course failure to sue only whetted the newspapers' appetite for new stories. Friends would telephone Proctor after encountering men in gay bars or clubs showing photographs of the MP and asking whether anyone knew him. The *People*'s next scoop was sensational. They ran it as a 'splash' story for six weeks running.

One of the *People*'s informants was a young man whom Proctor says journalists had been hunting for some time. He was an eighteen-year-old rent boy, who had told Proctor he was twenty-one. He was allegedly called Max, though nobody was ever sure of this, and he cannot now be traced. Armed with the *People*'s hidden tape recorder, he had visited Proctor and, under the pretence of chatting about the MP's life and desires, gathered the evidence the paper wanted. 'Max' was paid by the *People*.

Wired for sound, 'Max' assured the MP that he was over twenty-one (this could be heard on tape.)

These stories were proving a serious embarrassment to some Billericay Tories, who were facing a General Election within eighteen months. Their chairman, Frank Tomlin, was no fan of the MP. Proctor has claimed that, unlike most of the Billericay Conservative Association, Tomlin was embarrassed by his MP's views on immigration, which he did not share. He now demanded an explanation. His wife, Proctor's agent, agreed.

The *People* sent six reporters to Billericay in the run-up to the Executive Committee meeting which had been called, in October 1986. The journalists repeatedly contacted members of the Executive Committee, and managed to secrete a tape recorder into the meeting, with one of Proctor's opponents who sat at the front. After a stormy meeting Proctor won the day by thirty votes to ten. The Tomlins resigned, as did the deputy chairman and the treasurer.

Proctor announced he would not be suing the *People* because of the prohibitive costs involved. The newspaper, regarding this as an admission of guilt, turned over their dossier to the vice squad. Reading the early edition of the paper late on a Saturday night, the MP immediately telephoned Scotland Yard to offer to give evidence. For the time being, however, the police made no effort to talk to him. But Proctor discovered they were making inquiries of a number of other people.

The next story – which appeared in the *Daily Mirror* – concerned Proctor's recent jaunt to Morocco. The headline read: 'Naked Arab under MP's bed'. At the Ali Baba hotel in Agadir it was alleged that a naked young Moroccan man had been forced, with Proctor's help, to escape discovery by hiding under the bed in Proctor's room. A journalist seems to have extracted this story from a friend of Proctor's. Proctor protests that the 'youth' was in fact twenty-five, and not naked at the time.

With a General Election only months away, the MP again attracted the attention of the press. Or rather, Terry Woods did.

Woods, an art dealer, once again found himself on the wrong side of Proctor's front door in the early hours of the morning. He was wearing only underpants.

By now the interest of the Metropolitan Police was aroused. In April 1987, several months after receiving the *People* dossier, detectives swooped on Proctor's flat in a dawn raid. The raid was led by Chief Superintendent Marvin of the Serious [*sic!*] Crimes Squad. Interestingly, whenever the police went to Proctor's flat there was always a media circus in attendance, and this was no exception. The press had been tipped off and were waiting to watch a grim-faced Proctor leaving his flat at 10 a.m. to accompany detectives to Fulham, then Cannon Row, police stations. At this point Proctor's solicitor resigned his case.

That Saturday night, Proctor went to a Tory cheese and wine party in Billericay. He was cheered by most of those present, but the loyalty of the MP's local party was now being strained to the limit as indications grew that a third General Election might not be far off. Feelings in Billericay were divided. One member said: 'The papers say Harvey's a racist one minute, then the next minute they say he's slept with an Arab boy in Morocco. They can't have it both ways, can they?' Others suggested that have it both ways was exactly what he had done.

Another homespun Billericay expert commented: 'I was in the navy during the war and I can spot a homosexual at 50 feet; Harvey Proctor is not one of them.' Throughout, Proctor commanded intense loyalty among many. In March 1987 his local association had given him an overwhelming vote of confidence by 220 votes to 62.

The police raided his flat again, early in the morning. He was not there (the police apparently thought he had 'escaped') but with his brother, where he watched, on Breakfast TV, the police and press surrounding his flat.

Proctor once told me he understood that 'Max' had until then always refused to give the police a statement. But after the April raid they had told him that Proctor was to be prosecuted regardless, and that 'Max' must not 'pervert the course of justice'. Max now agreed to make a statement.

On 11 May, the same day the Prime Minister announced a 9 June election, the police decided to prosecute on four charges of gross indecency. Proctor was due in court on 20 May – during the

PROCTOR IS GUILTY: RENT BOY TELLS OF SPANKING

New sex scandal rocks the Tories

Star, with additional headlines *Daily Mirror*, 5 March 1987

election campaign. On Saturday, 16 May he finally bowed to the pressures and announced his intention not to stand again. That morning, when he forewarned his association officers of his decision, many, even the men, were in tears. Perhaps they had reason. Billericay Conservatives chose Teresa Gorman to replace him.

Until now Proctor's response to allegations had been a refusal to talk about his sexuality to the press, insisting he had not committed any criminal act. He had believed throughout, he told me, that those with whom he slept had been twenty-one or over, and had always checked. His legal advice, however, was that some of his contacts had been under-aged, and (unlike the law on heterosexual sex) a belief that they were not under-aged was no defence. Proctor had been under a misapprehension.

Shorn of what he had always supposed would be a defence, Proctor had no alternative but to plead guilty. He admitted to four counts of gross indecency (in private, in his own flat) with two under-aged rent boys (it was said that they were seventeen and nineteen) whom he had believed to be twenty-one. He listened impassively at Bow Street Magistrate's Court as allegations were recounted, with no detail, however embarrassing, spared. The age of consent for homosexuals was then twenty-one. None of this behaviour would be likely to be prosecuted today.

Until the court case, the MP had consistently denied the allegations, famously issuing a statement in which he described them as a 'tissue of lies'. When he pleaded guilty to the charges Billericay Tories were dismayed. One association office-holder remarked: 'All Proctor's denials were a tissue of lies.' Proctor told me later that he pleaded guilty because the police threatened to go on digging for more allegations, and, after nearly two years of continuous harassment, he had had enough.

Proctor's solicitor, the late Sir David Napley, said the youths were willing partners. He attacked the press for paying people to give evidence in the pursuit not of justice but of higher newspaper sales. Sir David said: 'He has not only brought this terrible shame and despair on himself, but on his colleagues and constituents.' Proctor was convicted and fined £1,450 with £250 costs.

Later, Chief Superintendent Marvin retired from the Metropolitan Police and retailed his story to the *Sun*. One of his 'revelations' was that Proctor was involved in a call-boy network at the House of Commons. Proctor said this was simply not true. Another was that when he raided Proctor's flat he found a blackmailing message on Proctor's telephone answering machine. It was implied that this was a justification for prosecution – because as an MP Proctor had opened himself to blackmail.

Proctor has given me his own version of this story. Months earlier, he said, one of the police witnesses had tried to blackmail him, offering to withdraw his evidence in return for cash. Proctor had tape-recorded this threat and handed it to his solicitor, keeping a copy in his own flat. It was this that the police raid 'found' among his legal files, through which they delved.

Over three issues of the *Sun* Marvin wrote about three cases, including his investigations into Russell Harty. I split a bottle of champagne with Harty not long before he fell ill and died and discussed with him his reaction towards media and public interest in his sexuality. I remember leaving Harty's flat convinced that his attitude verged on the paranoid. Now one begins to see why.

I shared a kitchen supper with Harvey Proctor the night before his trial began. He appeared calm, even cool, anxious only at the possibility of a prison sentence. His main concern seemed to be for his elderly mother, who was stuck in their home in his ex-constituency. I had the impression that they did not have much money. Harvey displayed remarkably little outward fury towards the newspapers. He seemed to feel that, though what they had done was disgraceful, he should have expected it, and half had.

After the trial was over, the police, who had systematically leaked details of Proctor's life to journalists, continued their briefings. An unnamed police source arranged an impromptu meeting with the press at which he gave further details and opinions concerning the case – which had already been decided – calling the MP a 'Jekyll and Hyde' character. All this was duly printed.

Proctor ended his relationship with his constituency where he had built up a 14,615 majority, where he and his mother lived, and to which he seemed devoted. There were few tears for him in the newspapers, even in the more sober titles, and criticism of the methods of the tabloids was muted in this case by widespread disapproval of Proctor's politics.

At Westminster, however, Proctor gained a measure of support within the Parliamentary Conservative Party. A number of MPs, disturbed by the nature of his entrapment, rallied round. After all, they said, Proctor's telephones had been tapped; he had covered the first three pages of the *Sunday People* six Sundays running; at least one rent-boy had been hired by journalists, and wired up with hidden tape-recorders before entering Proctor's flat; two trespassing reporters had barged into his Billericay house, which he shared with his mother, then in her late seventies, demanding to know where he was; every detail of his bedroom games had been broadcast; and the onslaught had continued for more than eighteen months.

This constant coverage had become unbearable to a backbencher with no ministerial ambitions. None of the leading players in the spate of more recent scandals, even David Mellor (see p.285) or Tim Yeo (see p.311), was to endure such sustained, hostile coverage.

So colleagues' sympathy towards him was understandable, but two questions sprang to mind. One was: if Proctor had been so traduced, why had he not taken up his grievances in the press or through the courts? Proctor's reply (and I am wholly convinced by it) is that litigation can be ruinous and he had no capital. The experience he had gone through had given him an unreasoning horror of journalists, a fear that he would be misrepresented again, and a suspicion (in which he was right) that newspapers are restrained in attacking each other's methods. There was also an overwhelming sense of wanting to turn his back on a period of sustained terror, anger and humiliation. Harvey retains all these feelings to this day.

The second question is: why was he not more open about his sexuality from the start, or at least once it became clear that the press were on to something in which there was a large element of truth? Harvey's insistence that his private life is no business of the press is very deeply felt and has been consistent. He would sometimes go further than 'no comment', however, and describe allegations as lies. His justification to friends has always been that newspapers said many things about him, some true, some half-true and many false. It was not for him to disentangle these. It was better to advise that the picture as a whole was wrong.

I think this is disingenuous. In hindsight Harvey would have been better to start with 'no comment' and stick rigidly to it. I suspect he would like to review a period of his life in which he was often close to panic, and see it as though he had acted with more consistency than he did. But it is hard not to sympathise with his plight. Proctor told London's *Evening Standard* last year that he had contemplated suicide after the court case. 'I equipped myself with pills, but I did not even try to swallow them.'

Mrs Proctor, under great emotional stress, turned once to her son and asked: 'I just don't know what's going on, can you just answer me one question – you haven't murdered anyone, have you?' 'They could not have been more invasive of my privacy and hers if I had murdered somebody,' Harvey said last year.

One of the reasons Proctor kept the respect of the Tory Party hierarchy at Westminster was that, despite his sometimes eccentric politics, he never played fast or loose with the whips, who always knew where they stood with him, and were able to rely on his vote. Privately, the whips defended him fervently. A group of sixteen Tory MPs and ministers, notably from the Left as well as the Right and including Michael Heseltine, Tim Yeo, Neil Hamilton and Tristan Garel Jones, then the Deputy Chief Whip, invested a total of £80,000 in the new business venture to which Proctor turned, with what capital he had (£20,000) on leaving the Commons: a high-class men's shirt shop, *Proctor's Shirts and Ties*.

A second followed. *The Spectator* printed a cartoon in which Proctor's shop bore the sign 'Shirtlifters will not be prosecuted'. Gritting his teeth, Proctor bought the original, and displays it in his shop in Brewer's Lane, Richmond. The first shop has since folded, a victim of the recession. Proctor keeps in touch with figures on the Tory Right. Neil Hamilton (see p.327), the Thatcherite former Trade minister, came to the rescue last year when Proctor was attacked in the shop by queer-bashers. Hamilton, a regular customer, exchanged blows with one assailant who was eventually chased down the street by the minister's even more formidable wife, Christine. Hamilton's nose was broken in the fracas. The two assailants were jailed.

To this day Proctor remains close to his friend Terry Woods. I believe their friendship is still deep, but that press intrusion into their lives – it is occasionally resumed, even today – has been traumatic for both, and for their relationship. 'One must plod on. After a while you can put up a front to people who are being beastly. You get accustomed to feeling everybody is against you, so when you come across someone who isn't, well, you are so baffled you are not sure how to react.'

I recall Proctor telling me, after this chapter in his life was over, that since the age of fourteen he had always wanted to be a backbench MP, and a good constituency member; and that he believed he had achieved that. He was still receiving letters of support and good wishes from former constituents.

Proctor was adamant that he could never be accused of hypocrisy, and that this charge, at least, had never been levelled against him in the press. He said that he had never been asked publicly whether he was a homosexual, and nobody could accuse him – and nobody did – of letting private life interfere with professional duties. It never involved constituency or constituents. He would never confirm what went on in his flat, he said, or with whom. He would simply not discuss his private life with the press. 'Nor will I today.'

His mother, Mrs Hilda Proctor, died just before this book went to print. I make no apology for showing sympathy to Proctor, who remains a friend. Readers who share it might care to buy their next tie at his shop.

KEITH BEST – 1987

'By the skin of his teeth'

One of the claimed successes of 1980s Thatcherism was the £4 billion sell-off of British Telecom in 1984. So enthusiastic for the plan was the thirty-four-year-old backbench Tory MP Keith Best that he bought six times more shares than the 800 he was entitled to. After their value doubled he sold them. Best might claim to have uttered for Fleet Street the cock-crow to the dawning era of 'Tory sleaze'. It was only a cheep. His shares sold for £6,240.

At first, nobody noticed. Keith Best had narrowly overturned a

Labour majority on the Isle of Anglesey, promising his bemused constituents that he would learn Welsh. He worked hard and was popular with his Tory association. By the run-up to the 1987 General Election he may have forgotten his little flutter with Telecom. Having served as PPS to Welsh Secretary Nicholas Edwards, the energetic young MP's dream of ministerial office looked close to fulfilment, for Tories from Wales are in short supply. His appointment to the Welsh Office would have been a popular move: Best was a bright, likeable and articulate government member.

It was now, however, that the *Labour Research* magazine started to sift through the 51,000 pages of BT share applications to check whether any MPs had broken the rules. Keith Best's application was there. So was Lander Best's. And Keith Lander Best's. K.L. Best MP had used three variations of his name, together with four addresses, including his widowed mother's. He had used four bank accounts across the six different applications.

Labour called for his resignation and arrest when the story broke on 1 April 1987. His Welsh constituency party stood by him. John Biffen, the Leader of the Commons, berated Labour's 'sanctimonious and distasteful' demands.

Best had not used false names, merely variations, and the wording in the prospectus was unclear. Best's explanation was that he had made multiple small BT applications (individuals were limited to only one) because, with the offer likely to be heavily over-subscribed, he wished to ensure that he did not miss out if, as expected, the bids were scaled down. Colleagues, I remember, were sceptical, but the Director of Public Prosecutions was reluctant to prosecute.

Though Best had assured his constituents this was a single indiscretion in an otherwise blameless career, the press had been busy. The *Observer* soon revealed that he had made four applications in the Jaguar cars sell-off. These were legal.

Days later, after consultations with the whips' office, the normally bouncy MP, for once crestfallen, announced that he would not stand again at the imminent General Election. In the belligerent mood of the hour, his climbdown brought no respite. Labour's Brian Sedgemore, an enthusiast for investigative work in the financial world, called the resignation 'political expediency at the expense of the integrity of Parliament'. Neil Kinnock, the

Labour leader, said he was 'waiting to see if we get a sermon on moral values from Mr Norman Tebbitt in the next few days. He has fallen strangely silent.' The media then focused on Best's eager, but legitimate, purchase of shares in TSB, British Aerospace, British Gas, Cable and Wireless, Britoil and Enterprise Oil.

Labour Research had discovered another MP with more BT and British Gas shares than was normal. Eric Cockeram, the Tory member for Ludlow, claimed his grand allocation was for his grandchildren. He admitted to 'the right motive but the wrong method. . . I may have committed a technical breach about which I am of course very concerned.' Under pressure, Cockeram announced on 10 April that he would not be standing in the forthcoming election. On 29 April the CPS confirmed they would not be prosecuting.

Keith Best was not so lucky. His public pledge that the profits from the BT venture would go to charity cut little ice. Four months after his party was returned to government he went on trial in October 1987 at Southwark Crown Court, pleading not guilty to 'dishonestly attempting to obtain more shares than his entitlement'. Once, he wept in the witness box. He was found guilty on three charges of attempting to obtain BT shares by deception, and fined £3,000 with £1,500 costs. A four-month prison sentence was quashed and the fine increased to £4,500. But not before Best had spent an uncomfortable weekend in the hospital wing of Brixton prison.

At the Monday morning appeal, the judge, announcing his decision to release Best, said that it was 'only by the skin of his teeth that this appellant escapes gaol'. Richard Caborn, a Labour Trade spokesman, called the decision 'appalling'. Best's mother, Peggy, said at the time: 'This will completely finish him.' It finished the Conservatives in his Anglesey constituency, now renamed Ynys Mon. Plaid Cymru captured the seat in 1987 and held on in 1992.

But Keith Best, whom I like, seemed irrepressible. Promising to donate his winnings to charity proved more than public relations. Best began working for the National Children's Home and Prisoners Abroad, campaigning for the release of gaoled Britons abroad. His rehabilitation seems to go from strength to strength. Best is now the head of the Immigration Advisory Service with an annual salary of £35,000. He has stood unsuccessfully as a Tory candidate in local government elections, but laughs at rumours that he is seeking a second parliamentary career. At the last election, his wife, Elizabeth Gibson, stood as the Conservative candidate in Birmingham Hodge Hill, a safe Labour seat. Her agent was Keith Best.

He had few enemies in the Commons. Most regretted his downfall, but few imagined he could have expected otherwise. Still, his £3,120 profit proved rather modest by comparison with the (perfectly legal) windfalls which were later to come the way of senior management in the utilities then being privatized.

At the time, almost nobody would have supposed he had any future in government, the Conservative Party, or public administration. We would have advised him to seek new fields. But walking away – or keeping your head down – is not always the answer: a certain shameless buoyancy can work miracles in public life.

GEORGE GALLOWAY – 1987

'I bonked for Britain'

When I accused George Galloway of being a 'medallion man', he responded, 'That is the unkindest cut of all. I have never worn a medallion! I've never even worn a *vest*, for God's sake. I'm a Scotsman!'

So let's put it like this. Few MPs could pass unnoticed in a provincial disco or a Club 18–30 package holiday, and the sub-playboy image is not thought to sit well with any MP's role, let alone a socialist's. But it has to be said that 'Gorgeous George' Galloway seems to have carried it off. The Scots Labour MP for Hillhead, and flamboyant champion of what the tabloid papers called Labour's 'loony Left', could not present a more striking contrast with the man he ousted for his Glasgow seat, Roy Jenkins. One imagines that each man's personal vision of Hell would probably feature a small cell and the permanent company of the other.

In fairness, Galloway is not a member of the 'loony Left'. He never joined Labour's Campaign Group. He has never been part of any group. He has made fun of the old Labour-led Greater London Council, calling them a 'greenhouse of exotic pot-plants'. However, he is basically a Left-winger and in some ways an extremist. But he is his own man. In Fleet Street, a usefully libel-resistant catch-all term to imply (variously) a louche, pleasure-seeking or startling quality is 'colourful'. The name George Galloway has seldom appeared in a newspaper without it. Yet Galloway is no fool. Few modern politicians have survived more bad publicity, and even prospered from it. A combination of cunning, charm and chutzpah has landed Galloway in more hot water, and delivered him from it, than a less brazen character could dare expect. He is sharp, astute and consistent in debate.

Fixed, perhaps, in many minds is the day in 1987 when – as though one alleged scandal were not bad enough – the MP and General Secretary of War on Want had called a press conference to try to clear his name over allegations of fiddling the charity's expenses. Galloway was insistent that his energies and activities were devoted to the public good. But, straight in to the television cameras, Galloway, married with a five-year-old daughter, was forced to admit instead to a string of sexual infidelities on an expenses-paid charity trip to Greece.

The following day the *Star* was merciless: 'I bonked for Britain.'

Thirty-three-year-old Galloway had become General Secretary of War on Want, one of Glenys Kinnock's favourite charities, at the age of twenty-nine, before becoming an MP. His flair for publicity and fundraising matched his ability at self-promotion, and brought a record 26 per cent increase in donations. Within four years his autocratic style of management landed him in difficulty with some of the charity's officers. However, in March 1987 an auditors' inquiry at War on Want cleared him of any impropriety, dishonesty or bad faith over his expenses.

Selected as candidate for Hillhead, Galloway went on to record a famous victory at the General Election over Roy Jenkins, ending the latter's Commons career and sealing the fate of his SDP. Fêted on all wings of the Party for the humiliation of Jenkins, Galloway, now a hero of the Labour movement, may have thought his troubles were behind him.

But all was not well at War on Want. Executive members, concerned about his allegedly extravagant expense claims, called in the Charity Commissioners in the summer. They cleared the MP of any wrongdoing but demanded that the charity tighten up its procedures.

Galloway agreed to repay £1,720, including £525 for a *World Marxist Review* seminar, in Athens, on the Ethiopia–Eritrea war. A further £850 was for minicab trips to and from his house. The repayment was, some said, small beer for Galloway. The following month the *Sun* alleged his total expenses were £20,000 in eighteen months. In fact they were for a longer period, and included travel for War on Want to many countries and throughout the UK, and all associated costs. As a bald headline, however, the figure looked dreadful.

In September 1987, BBC Scotland ran a critical programme on the 'colourful' MP's stewardship of the charity. He immediately hit back, issuing a libel writ seeking six-figure damages and called what would prove to be an ill-fated press conference.

Galloway was horrified when a reporter fired a question about alleged sexual infidelities while on the sunny Greek island of Mykonos, after the Athens conference. He may not have been entirely surprised, however, as photographs of him with his girlfriend Lillian had been stolen from her London flat. They had now reached the possession of the press.

The MP hardly hesitated. 'I spent lots of time with women . . . I actually had sexual intercourse with some of them.' He has never, he points out to me, slept with more than one at the same time, or claimed to have, but such subtleties are too deep for Fleet Street where one is a love-nest and two is an orgy. 'Gorgeous George', as he was fast nicknamed the next day, encountered headlines such as: 'My Sex Orgy – By MP'. Sketchwriters made what they could of the fact that the conference had been grappling with the Horn of Africa. By now Galloway's wife, Elaine, was slamming down the phone on reporters.

Declaring himself an 'extremely sad man' after the 'explosion of lurid headlines', Galloway explained the reason for his out-

Gorgeous George: I bonked for Britain

MY SEX ORGY BY MP

Star, 15 September 1987

burst: 'I had said I would answer any questions. I could not lie.'

Matters went from bad to worse when it was disclosed two days later that while his wife stayed in Scotland, Galloway was spending time in a one-bedroom flat with a partner, Lillian Grewar, in the East End of London. The 'disclosure', Galloway points out, was of something he and Lillian had never hidden. They were lovers for nine years, and had started living together (which they did for five years, until 1992) after he and his wife separated in 1987. There was never any secret, he says.

Galloway brazened it out. He is an intelligent and quick-witted man, an excellent Commons speaker, and politically original and brave. He is also, by common account, likeable company. He received a loyal vote of confidence from his local party the following month.

A month later his future was in jeopardy again. A Channel 4 documentary, 'In the Red', alleged that Galloway and three other MPs – former leading figures in the Dundee Labour Party – were involved in the transfer of funds from three Labour social clubs in the city. The money had gone to the Dundee Labour Party. The clubs were so heavily in debt at the time that they could not pay their rents, said the programme. Channel 4 claimed that £100,000 in the clubs' accounts was not accounted for. Senior Labour Party figures had cashed personal cheques of up to £600 at the clubs. Some had subsequently bounced. Galloway called the programme 'despicable', and again threatened a libel action. He also demanded a police inquiry which, after two years, charged nobody with wrongdoing except the manager of one club, who had made the allegations on the programme.

In early February 1988 his local party executive passed a vote of no confidence which was ratified later the same month by the party's General Management Committee. In Labour's re-selection round the following year he was once again re-selected. Where more timid fellows might have gone to ground, Galloway had raised his profile and won new popularity through his support (to the fury of the Labour leadership) for poll-tax non-payers. At the 1992 General Election he was re-elected with an increased majority.

Asked what he would do with huge damages awarded to him after a successful libel action against the *Daily Mirror*, he is said to have replied that he hoped to invest the money in a restaurant in Havana, Cuba – an investment made, he said, 'from the ashes of Robert Maxwell's empire'. Apparently, however, he has run into difficulties with Cuban socialist bureaucracy – poetic justice some would say. Hopefully these could be sorted out. Fidel Castro might then attend the opening. Like Castro himself, having tested almost to destruction his ability to get into and out of scrapes, 'Gorgeous' George must now doubt whether there is anything which can dislodge him.

To those who know Hillhead – prim, well-to-do territory where a crèche is a motor accident, sex is what the coal comes in, and there are no rates, only a few wee mace – the irony of its being represented by George Galloway is delicious. There are things, he told me, that he regrets, and things he would prefer to forget, 'but it is, and must remain, a free country'.

RON BROWN – 1988, 1990

'A bit daft but at least he's daft on behalf of us'

Ron Brown presents a problem for any directory of parliamentary scandal. The problem is how to file him and where to start. A fervent admirer of the reviled Colonel Gadaffi and the Soviet regime in Afghanistan, he outraged the Commons by swinging the mace and, unlike Michael Heseltine, dropping it.

Then there were the hotly denied reports of sex in the Commons shower, but not with his long-suffering wife and secretary, May. An appearance in court followed his highly publicized break-in at his former mistress's home when he was caught brandishing his swag: two pairs of ladies' knickers. Sam Galbraith, the Labour MP and brain surgeon, is reputed to have said, 'There is nothing I can do for him professionally.'

Brown's pedigree at his election as Labour MP for Edinburgh Leith in 1979 gave some hint that his parliamentary career might prove stormy. In 1972 he was sacked as an electricity board fitter for leading an unofficial twenty-four-hour strike in sympathy with the striking miners. A prominent councillor, he was suspended for three months from the Labour group on Lothian Regional Council for defying the whips over spending cuts.

His maiden speech in the Commons signalled the style of things to come. Traditionally maiden speeches are non-controversial affairs, but Brown ranted about Margaret Thatcher declaring a 'class war'. In 1981, to the fury of the Labour leader, Michael Foot, he visited Afghanistan after the arrival of the Soviet tanks. Worse was to come. He appeared to endorse the new regime by posing for photographs next to a tank.

He was twice expelled from the Commons for calling Nicholas Fairbairn (see p.228) (then Solicitor-General for Scotland) a liar and for waving a 'Hands off Lothian' banner. By now the antics of the Honourable Member for Edinburgh Leith provided daily copy for newspapers keen to seize on Michael Foot's battles with his 'loony Left'.

When Brown was suspended from the Commons for the second time the Labour Chief Whip, Michael Cocks, was taking no chances. He locked Brown in a room until Black Rod arrived to escort him off the premises.

In 1982 Brown made his mark on Mrs Thatcher's visit to the Holiday Inn at Glasgow by lunging at her, yelling: 'You're not welcome here.' He was fined £50 for a breach of the peace. The tabloids had another field day.

In 1984 he flew to Libya for secret talks with Colonel Gadaffi. Public opinion was outraged. It was only months since the murder of WPC Yvonne Fletcher, shot outside the Libyan embassy.

The last leg of Brown's ignominious journey to expulsion from his party began on Monday, 18 April 1988, during a debate on the hated poll tax. The headlines the next day featured Brown picking up and promptly dropping the ceremonial mace. Brown denied he was drunk: 'I'd only had a pint of Younger's Tartan. The bloody thing was heavier than I'd expected.' His offer to have it repaired by the Amalgamated Engineering Union, which sponsored him, failed to assuage Labour MPs whose assault on the government had been hijacked once again by their maverick colleague. The union replied by withdrawing its sponsorship from Brown.

The following day Brown provoked uproar in the Commons when he ten times refused to read the apology he had agreed earlier with the Speaker, Bernard Weatherill. For six minutes the Commons descended into farce as Conservative MPs made unpleasant noises while the Labour leader, Neil Kinnock, sat white with fury. Don Dixon, Labour's Deputy Chief Whip, signalled furiously at Brown to read the statement. 'I didn't write this rubbish,' he yelled back. 'Mr Speaker, since you want a grovelling statement, I am not going to read it. I don't accept it, all right?' Three times the Speaker ordered him to leave the Chamber. Once again a whip took matters into his own hands. The burly Don Dixon bundled Brown out.

The following afternoon, Brown was suspended from the Commons for twenty days and ordered to pay for the repair of the mace. The Shadow Cabinet withdrew the party whip from him for three months. Neil Kinnock went on record with a denunciation of the 'louts and loudmouths' of the Party's Left wing.

On 19 May, the day Brown's suspension from the Commons came to an end, the Parliamentary Labour Party met to consider the Shadow Cabinet's decision to withdraw the whip. During the stormy meeting which followed, and to Brown's rage, the Labour MP Michael Martin questioned Brown's sobriety when he brandished the mace. The PLP backed Kinnock but his victory was spoiled when a popular Left-winger, Tony Banks, resigned as a whip in protest.

Brown's next appointment with scandal came the same night. Bill O'Brien, a Labour MP, told the press he had seen Brown dash out of a Commons shower 'with only his mace visible'. Brown's researcher, Nonna Longden, denied she had run after him screaming: 'I want your baby! I want your baby!' Brown said Longden had wandered in by mistake. Protesting innocence, he told reporters: 'I may be bonkers but I wasn't bonking. Because I drop the mace, I also drop my trousers?' He denied having an affair with Longden: 'I can assure you that at my age, forty-seven, I have sex weekly – very weakly according to my wife . . . My credentials certainly leave something to be desired – that's why I keep my

MYSTERY OF NAKED MP AND GIRL IN COMMONS

By SIMON WALTERS

A LABOUR MP claimed yesterday he saw mace-throwing Leftie Ron Brown walk naked from a men-only Commons bathroom—and heard a WOMAN'S voice inside.

Former miner Bill O'Brien said fiery "Red Ron" came out of a cubicle in the plush ground-floor MPs bathroom.

"The only thing that was visible was his mace," said Mr O'Brien.

He added: "I heard a female voice and a male voice, but whether they were coming from a radio or not I don't know.

"The voice said the word 'Ron', but I did not see a woman."

Other MPs who rushed to investigate said they also heard "voices" coming from Mr Brown's cubicle.

The story sparked a Tory demand yesterday for a full inquiry by Commons authorities into "an abuse of the facilities."

LAUGH

But last night Mr Brown shrugged off the story, saying: "It's a great laugh—but it is totally untrue.

"I can assure you that at my age, 47, I have sex weekly—very weakly according to my wife.

"I'm guilty of many things, but not dropping my trousers.

"I'm sure most women would run a mile if they saw me like that—I have not much to show.

"My credentials certainly leave something to be desired—that's why I keep my trousers up."

Mr O'Brien, MP for

MP Brown .. "sex weekly"

Normanton, Yorkshire, said he was bathing in the bathroom at 9.45pm on Thursday night.

Only hours earlier, Mr Brown had been kicked out of the Parliamentary Labour Party for damaging the ceremonial Commons mace.

Mr O'Brien, 59, said he was getting dressed when Mr Brown came out of a cubicle and asked for a towel.

He added: "What startled me was hearing voices in there.

"I could identify a female voice or voices. Whether or not he had a radio in there I don't

Continued on Page Two

Sun, 21 May 1988

trousers up.' A few weeks later he denied reports that Longden was pregnant by him: 'It would be physically impossible . . . A doctor can examine me if he wishes. These operations do work, don't they?' But Nonna Longden would return to haunt him.

In June of the same year Telford magistrates issued a warrant for his arrest. The warrant had been requested by a solicitor, John McMillan, who thought Parliament had been too soft on Brown after the mace incident. The MP, facing a private prosecution under the 1971 Criminal Damage Act, made the front pages again when the Edinburgh Sheriff's Officer claimed Brown hit him when he served him with the summons. Brown denied it. The Director of Public Prosecutions halted McMillan's case.

The following week, Brown's constituency party passed a vote of censure on him for the affair with the mace. A similar motion on his voting record as an MP was narrowly defeated.

In January 1990 he was back in the dock. At Lewes Crown Court he denied charges of theft and causing £800 of criminal damage at Nonna Longden's flat in Charles Road, St Leonards, on his way back from the TUC Conference at Eastbourne.

Brown admitted that a three-year affair with his researcher Longden had ended the previous March. Longden claimed that after she had rejected Brown's pleas for a reunion he had turned up blind drunk at her flat. She beat a hasty retreat with her new boyfriend. Brown promptly went berserk in her flat. When the police arrived, he had fled, leaving behind a trail of destruction. The spurned lover had left a testament to his undying devotion: the word 'love' scrawled in lipstick on a smashed mirror.

Brown, under police interrogation, denied having returned to resurrect the love affair, but insisted he had gone back to retrieve politically sensitive documents and tapes. The mirror had been broken, he claimed, as he ducked to avoid objects being hurled at him by the man who had replaced him in Nonna Longden's affections. When the police searched him they found hidden under his raincoat two pairs of ladies' knickers and some jewellery.

After a six-day trial he was acquitted of theft, but found guilty of criminal damage and fined £1,000 with £2,500 costs and £628 compensation. Brown interpreted this as a 'moral victory' and celebrated with his wife, May, at his side, showering reporters with champagne on the courtroom steps. Up in Edinburgh, watching the spectacle on television, his local party secretary and friend, Bill Axon, said: 'People here think he's a bit daft but at least he's a bit daft on behalf of us and they are prepared to forgive him.'

He spoke too soon. Brown's constituency party turned against him for the last time and asked the Labour leadership to re-open the selection process. A delighted Neil Kinnock was quick to grant the request. Ignoring Brown's protestations of a 'shamocracy', the party passed a formal vote of de-selection on 5 April 1990. A typically defiant Brown hit back. 'Ron Brown is a fighter. Ron Brown believes in the Leith motto and that is to persevere. What have I done except be a thorn in the flesh of some people? When I get a chance I will sock it to them.'

He got that chance on 24 July 1991. Along with three Labour MPs, the fiery Scot visited Terry Fields MP, serving sixty days in jail for non-payment of poll tax. Against prison rules, Brown smuggled in a tape recorder, interviewed the prisoner-MP, and played the tape to journalists waiting outside. On tape, Fields embarrassed Neil Kinnock by claiming many long-serving Labour MPs were so disillusioned with him they could resign.

Typically, Brown appealed against de-selection, fighting all the way to the Court of Sessions, Scotland's supreme civil court, and losing. At the 1992 General Election, he was forced to stand as an independent. He trailed home, second from last, with only 4,142 votes. The official Labour candidate won comfortably, with 13,790 votes. Uncharacteristically, Mr Brown accepted defeat.

In December 1994 *The Times* revealed that Brown had a long association with Oleg Gordievsky, the former KGB controller in London. Brown passed on information about his Labour colleagues which he claims the Soviet spymaster could have read in 'the *Beano*'. But unfortunately Brown never realized that Gordievsky was, in fact, a double agent. Brown now fears that his insights on the Labour Party were more useful to Margaret Thatcher as Gordievsky was probably passing on most of the information to MI5!

Brown still lives in Edinburgh with his wife. When last encountered he was doing the Edinburgh 'knowledge' to become a black-cab driver. Hopefully, this venture will be more successful than his last foray into the world of work. Brown applied to become the steward at an upmarket Hong Kong golf club. The scruffy working-class former MP was deemed inappropriate for the task of pouring gin and tonics for English expatriates. Perhaps he should re-apply on 1 July 1997.

JOHN BROWNE – 1990

'Public schoolboy, Guards officer, banker, MP, and whinger'

With his Guardsman's bearing, his chiselled features and his brilliantined hair, John Browne MP was a baffling figure to us, his parliamentary colleagues. He gave every appearance of being a fine upright man, an officer and a gentleman. He also seems to have behaved in ways which were not only disgraceful but, in the end, ludicrous. And to all the world he acted throughout as though utterly convinced of his own innocence. He genuinely seemed to believe he was the victim of a cruel and baseless persecution. None of us could work it out.

Embarrassing the Prime Minister, Mrs Thatcher, in a 'cash for questions' scandal was bad enough, but John Browne also tossed in a messy public divorce. Dubbed a 'cad' and the 'love-cheat MP', he was accused of walking away with his former wife's fortune and leaving her homeless and on the brink of imprisonment. It was no wonder Mrs Thatcher nodded in approval as this former Guards officer was dismembered by his critics.

John Ernest Douglas Delavalette Browne was elected Conservative MP for Winchester in 1979. During the 1970s he was a director of Middle East operations for the European Banking Company. So it seemed perfectly natural when he stood up on 25 November 1982, to ask the Prime Minister a seemingly innocuous question about the freezing of assets. But what he failed to disclose was that he was at the time compiling a study on the subject for the Saudi Arabian Monetary Agency for which he would receive $88,000 – more than an MP's annual salary. Browne also failed to disclose a £2,400 yearly retainer from a firm of Lebanese consultants who had a keen interest in his supposed access to Downing Street.

It was almost eight years before these allegations emerged – by which time Browne had found notoriety in another field. In 1983 he divorced his wife Elizabeth, the daughter of a wealthy shipping magnate, after eighteen years of marriage. It was not the divorce, but the terms, which raised eyebrows. Browne walked off with a £175,000 settlement, then dismayed his colleagues and constituents when he returned to court in November 1986, for enforcement of the outstanding £65,000 of the settlement. Critics said he hardly needed the money, having by this time married another wealthy heiress.

The former Mrs Browne showed a flair for publicity. Throwing herself on the mercy of the court and claiming she would be financially ruined (she had already paid him £110,000 plus £90,000 court costs), she attracted huge public sympathy when she posed for the cameras, Paddington Bear-like, clutching what she said were her only possessions: a suitcase full of clothes. Forty-eight-year-old Browne was unmoved. His former wife only narrowly avoided a spell behind bars for her failure to pay. Friends of both, and neither, said that the whole affair was a great deal more complicated than ever emerged from the rival stories of each.

'I have been painted as a cad, and it's bound to colour the judgement even of well-meaning people,' protested Browne, defending himself against a hostile press. The well-meaning voters of Winchester halved his majority at the ensuing General Election. Re-elected, Browne tried to regain the offensive by introducing a private member's bill to outlaw media invasions of privacy. This only attracted more derision. Colleagues were unimpressed and the bill was thrown out.

Behind the headlines, the *Observer* and the TV documentary series 'World in Action' were now delving into Browne's financial past. They uncovered the $88,000 payment and the Lebanese retainer. The allegations led to an investigation by the Select Committee on Members' Interests. Its report was grave. Early action by Parliament was recommended. Labour MPs demanded Browne's resignation. Tories were at best lukewarm in their support for him, but the last thing they wanted was a by-election. Many, however, suggested he declare his intention not to stand again. Browne ignored all advice. A hundred members of his Winchester constituency party signed a motion calling on their committee to adopt a new candidate.

I remember Mrs Thatcher's chilling failure to support him the following day. Asked to comment from the Dispatch Box, she said: 'The report of the Select Committee is serious and must be considered carefully. My honourable friend will want to consider what it says very carefully . . . I would think that it would be courteous to leave it at that.' In print this looks restrained. In the circumstances it sounded fatal.

Sir Geoffrey Howe, Leader of the House, proposed a humiliating punishment: suspension without pay from the Commons for twenty days. In a highly charged debate on 7 March 1990, Browne, whose new wife was watching from the public gallery, declared he was 'truly sorry'. MPs voted overwhelmingly to suspend him. As Sir Geoffrey said that Browne's 'acts and omissions' did not measure up to his responsibilities, the Prime Minister was seen nodding furiously. Winchester Conservative Association agreed, voting to begin the process of choosing a successor candidate.

Calling the debate a 'five-and-a-half-hour internationally televised show trial', Browne fought on – to the surprise of his colleagues. He published an open letter to his constituents, urging them to resist 'a clique who would rather have a minister than a grassroots MP like me'.

Finally, even Mr Browne realized that all was lost. But even as he announced his decision to stand down at the next election, Winchester was subjected to another tirade: 'My decision is not the result of any democratic process but de-selection by the media.' He was the victim of a 'venomous witch-hunt' and blamed the press's 'unrelenting coverage of my divorce, my Privacy Bill and the recent Select Committee report.'

Occasional rants continued right up until the end. In the summer of 1991 he tabled a Commons motion, which nobody signed, condemning Sir Geoffrey Howe and others, and accusing them of dirty tricks. They had offered him, he alleged, a less critical suspension motion if he promised to go quietly at the next election. The allegation may well be true: these things happen all the time, and such an offer would not be thought by most MPs as anything other than merciful if Machiavellian, but (as one minister commented) 'he seems to be dwelling in a sort of twilight zone where he sees conspiracies at every turn'.

The twilight zone stretched into November, when Browne sought advice from the Attorney-General about his chances of appeal under the UN Convention on Human Rights 'especially where a quite deliberate injustice has been perpetrated by senior ministers intent on injustice to a Member of a sovereign Parliament by misleading that Parliament'. The Attorney-General was unable to help. By this stage Browne's Commons colleagues were finding him a source more of embarrassment than indignation.

But he was not finished yet. In the next parliamentary session, after a Commons ballot, Browne won the opportunity to speak on a subject of his choice on the morning of Friday, 28 November 1992. I remember the groan. He chose a subject close to his heart: himself. He was 'the victim', he said, 'of a grand and deliberate injustice, a show trial, and a conspiracy'. He repeated his accusations, including complaints against the ex-Chief Whip, Timothy Renton, possibly the mildest and most humane Chief Whip in modern history. After his speech, Labour's John Fraser suggested an epitaph: 'public schoolboy, Guards officer, banker, MP, and whinger'.

Next, Browne confounded the impression which had grown that he would not stand again. Winchester Tories had already chosen Gerry Malone, a former MP, as their candidate. In an emotional appeal, Browne begged them to dump Malone. They refused. He announced his intention to stand as an independent candidate. Even his loyal Commons secretary now resigned.

Renton's successor Richard Ryder wrote what was for a Chief Whip an unusually colourful letter to Browne, withdrawing the party whip (effectively expelling him from the Parliamentary Party) and commenting that in the 'unimaginable' event of his winning he would never get it back. The letter was leaked to the press. It was available in Winchester during the next General Election.

Browne was incensed. Having given up all hope of

rehabilitation with his own party, his behaviour in the chamber became bizarre. In July 1991 he appeared in an enormous black top hat which he refused to take off, except to speak. Apparently this was part of a campaign of protest against the Ministry of Defence's refusal to award compensation to certain legless ex-Guardsmen. Mr Speaker Weatherill did his best to take no notice. Once, the MP beside Browne sat on his hat, by mistake, to general hilarity. Then Browne sat on it himself.

At the ensuing election Browne campaigned furiously under the slogan 'Vote Browne and Blue', with rosettes to match. Every national newspaper received a copy of his election address. But despite three weeks of exhausting self-promotion he finished last, polling only 3,095 votes. The Official Conservative, Gerry Malone, won.

Browne has never succeeded in re-entering politics. A prolific letter-writer to national newspapers, he stood in the Newbury by-election in 1993 as an independent Conservative, but to no avail.

PADDY ASHDOWN – 1992

Paddy Spoilsport: Top MP
Refuses to Deny All

The Paddy Ashdown scandal was a five-minute wonder and a model for students of damage limitation, but it earned the Leader of the Liberal Democrat Party a sobriquet which he will never live down: 'Paddy Pantsdown.'

The former Royal Marines Captain, only days before the 1992 General Election, activated his ejector seat in the nick of time. Rather than give Fleet Street the opportunity of breaking the story of his short-lived affair with his former secretary, he went public at a dramatic press conference at Westminster. It was a classic spoiler operation which took the wind from the newspapers' sails.

Tricia Howard had been separated, but not yet divorced, from her husband. In 1987 she fell for the Yeovil MP who was destined to become leader of the Liberal Democrats. He was supposedly happily married to Jane. They had two children. Had rumours spread at this time, it is questionable whether Ashdown's bid to assume the leadership of his party would have succeeded.

But it did succeed, the following year. In 1990, with the affair long since over, Mrs Howard was in the throes of divorce. Fearing his own name might come up, Ashdown consulted his solicitor, Andrew Phillips, about the affair. The lawyer wrote an *aide mémoire* and locked it in his safe.

Two years later, in late January 1992, reporters from the *News of the World* were camped outside Tricia Howard's Wiltshire home. After refusing their lucrative offer for her story of the affair, a distressed Tricia Howard called her former lover. Fifty-year-old Ashdown in turn rang Andrew Phillips. The solicitor checked his safe – and discovered the worst. The document he had written two years earlier was missing. His London firm, Bates, Wells and Braithwaite, had been burgled two weeks earlier, but the solicitor had not noticed at the time the disappearance of such a sensitive document.

That document was held at the time by Simon Berkowitz, a forty-five-year-old painter and decorator. A few days earlier Berkowitz had arranged a secret assignation with a *News of the World* reporter in the booking hall of Victoria Station. For £5,000 he had offered him documentary proof that Ashdown had enjoyed an affair with his former secretary. His price eventually rose to £20,000. The *News of the World* refused to pay but went straight to Tricia Howard.

Deeply embarrassed, Ashdown's solicitor gained an instant injunction against the newspaper, the rest of Fleet Street, and the other news media, preventing publication of the document. Because its circulation arose from a criminal act, Phillips assured his client, it would be protected by the full force of English law, and would give at least a breathing space.

It was correct legal advice, but Ashdown, a veteran observer of many encounters with the press, knew better than to rely on it. He called a late-night conference with a handful of his closest advisers. Having broken the news of the affair to his wife, he had her support in making a complete revelation at a press conference.

In the event he was rushed into it – before, even, he could warn Liberal Democrat colleagues. The *Scotsman* was not covered – and could not be – by the English injunction and ran the story on Wednesday, 8 February. National newspapers were still silenced by the injunction.

Ashdown was forced to hold a hastily convened press conference at Westminster, and an impromptu one outside the front door of his home with his wife Jane 'standing loyally by his side'. 'Paddy Pantsdown' was the *Sun* headline. It is still in common use by hecklers and even – occasionally and affectionately – among supporters.

There was instant and unreserved support from John Major and Neil Kinnock. The Liberal Democrats were riding high in the polls and many observers expected them to hold the balance of power after the election which had to be called within six months. John Major and Neil Kinnock would be the only beneficiaries of a scandal involving the Liberal Democrat leader. Both the Tory and the Labour Party were anxious to avoid any suggestion they were involved in dirty tricks.

Tricia Howard, knowing media interest in her would not disappear immediately, decided to pre-empt it. She read a carefully prepared statement outside the London solicitor's office where the break-in had taken place. It was a calm, dignified performance which engendered widespread sympathy for her and her former lover. Porters working at the nearby Smithfield meat market demonstrated their support by hurling rotten eggs at the press pack, perhaps the decade's most heart-warming spontaneous public demonstration.

The following day, Berkowitz was charged with stealing and handling the document. He was joined in the dock by his former wife, Maria Watson, who was charged with handling. Berkowitz, a former member of the Conservative Party, denied that his crime was politically motivated. His ex-wife agreed, memorably: 'Sure Simon was a Tory. But first and foremost he looked after himself – that's why he admired Maggie Thatcher so much.' Berkowitz was sentenced to two and a half years for handling but was

Sun, 6 February 1992

acquitted on the theft charge. He asked for scores of other offences, including other burglaries of solicitors, to be taken into account.

Ashdown's personal popularity increased in the aftermath of the scandal. 'It says more about the British people than it does about me,' he commented. Toy manufacturers cashed in on this new twist to his 'action man' image by producing a range of best-selling Paddy Ashdown dolls in full army fatigues. Tricia Howard declined a complimentary model from the manufacturers.

Never overlook the virtue of those who have saleable stories to sell, but refuse to sell them. Tricia Howard could (I reckon) have sold her story to the press for £30,000–60,000. She has foregone that sum in the cause of one small but notable decency.

Max Clifford, the publicist who acted for (among others) Antonia de Sancha (see pp.287–94) told me he would recommend the Ashdown case as required reading for any politician keen to learn how scandal is best handled. I agree. I do not, though, share the widespread opinion that Mr Ashdown was unharmed. I believe he was deeply, perhaps fatally, damaged.

ALAN AMOS – 1992

Schadenfreude

When the police went down to the woods on the afternoon of Saturday, 7 March 1992 they had a bigger surprise than they expected. One of the two men they arrested on Hampstead Heath, a well-known homosexual cruising area, was a Tory MP. Only days earlier John Major had launched the General Election campaign.

The thirty-nine-year-old Alan Amos, MP for Hexham, was

unlucky. Only ten men had been arrested on the Heath in the previous twelve months, though scores of gay encounters take place there daily. Nothing about Amos's behaviour, for which he was never charged and of which detailed reports were never published, sounds – in the circumstances of the Heath – anything other than routine. Admitting only to 'a childish and stupid act', Amos denied he was gay, but was forced to resign his seat.

Alcohol, so often the excuse to which men accused of apparently uncharacteristic behaviour retreat, was not available as an explanation for poor Amos, a convinced teetotaller, a campaigner against smoking and abortion and a proponent of birching for criminals. He had been described by *Private Eye* as a 'horribly enthusiastic goody two-shoes'. There were suggestions that, horrified as his Hexham constituents were to discover their MP had been misbehaving in the bushes, it was the publicity given to his teetotalism which really finished Mr Amos off in the North-East.

The episode, though unremarkable, is worth mentioning for the light it casts on three elements of many modern scandals, and for one amusing footnote. First: how did the story reach the press? There was never a court case. It is probable that the police, realizing they had an MP on their hands, leaked what they knew would be a good story. As journalists know well, individual police officers, contrary to their professional rules, sometimes leak stories of interest to the press for money. We also know that this can be organized on an institutional basis: at a busy police station there may be a particular officer, known to Fleet Street, acting as unofficial press link. In Amos's case the police denied wrongdoing; the press took a robust view: 'Mr Amos,' said the *Telegraph* loftily, 'cannot blame his tragedy on the messengers who reported what befell him. He merely made an error of judgement, for which he has now been obliged to pay the price.'

The outcome was that a man who was never charged, or tried for any crime, or afforded the opportunity to defend himself at any neutral or unexcited hearing, saw his career wrecked within days. To accept a caution is to admit some kind of guilt; but the procedure was never intended to lead to public pillorying of the kind Amos received (for instance) in the *Daily Star*:

Amos is a teetotaller, opposes abortion, and brands smoking a 'dirty, dangerous, and anti-social habit'. Hopefully he is now questioning his judgement in wandering at dusk, at a place which has been turned into a no-go area for decent families by perverts practising what many people – even smokers – would call another dirty, dangerous and anti-social habit. His downfall must be sad for him. But he shouldn't try to tar us with his own muck.

Some might say the destruction of a career through corrupt briefing such as the press were accused of in this case, would in itself be a greater scandal than whatever Mr Amos did or didn't do at Hampstead. Should you wonder why the British press has never much interested itself in that question, a moment's thought may supply the answer.

Another instructive feature in this case is the potency for a British audience of what the Germans call *Schadenfreude*: pleasure taken in the misfortunes of others, particularly those who might have seemed in a position to wag their fingers at us, or set themselves above us morally or in wealth or power. The press regularly preface their exposure of an MP's indiscretions with an account of how this individual supposed himself to be qualified to lecture us, or organize our lives.

Part of the reason is that editors feel defensive about muck-raking and anxious to imply a 'public interest' defence of their story; but it is also because we know readers hug themselves with pleasure when the apparently pious fall. 'How are the mighty fallen!' MPs like Alan Clark or Steven Norris, who conspicuously refrain from moralizing about others, do not tempt us to attack in the way a 'goody two-shoes' does. *Schadenfreude* is a kind of suppressed aggression by the underdog towards his masters. A wise MP avoids triggering it. Underdogs hunt in packs.

A third lesson the episode teaches is that for a delinquent MP it still matters where your constituency is. Had Amos been the MP for a southern and inner-city constituency, his constituency officers would not have acted as decisively as Hexham's did. One weekend's headlines (typical was 'Tory MP quizzed in gay sex swoop' from the *Daily Star*) and Amos's association dumped him. Yet he was a respected constituency MP. The North-East of England is famously intolerant of homosexuality. I doubt whether, when I was an MP, my own Tory association in the East Midlands (upset though they would have been) would have acted as Hexham did. But I never got caught.

Amos, the chairman of the parliamentary anti-smoking group, to this day alleges he was the victim of a plot hatched by the pro-smoking lobby. An unnamed supporter of Forest, the pro-smoking group, told the *Sunday Times* some members, acting independently of the main group, 'put up money for private detectives because they got sick of Amos shooting his mouth off. He was followed for about three weeks up to his arrest.'

Having lost his association's backing, he resigned. What followed in Hexham provides a footnote. Before the Tories could select a new candidate for the General Election, which was only weeks away, Hexham voters were shaken by further gay revelations. Jonathan Wallace, the Liberal Democrat's winsome twenty-eight-year-old candidate, admitted he was 'gay and proud of it' – albeit with a little prompting from a Sunday newspaper. The hastily appointed and happily married Tory candidate romped home with a majority increased from the 1987 election. As I once remarked to the Chief Whip: 'It's always the amateurs who get caught.' He laughed merrily.

In September 1995, Amos announced in the *Independent* that he was quitting the Tories to join Labour. Still denying he was gay, he said that his experiences had nevertheless shown him that the Conservative Party was a 'foreigner-hating, minority-bashing Party.' Warming to his theme, he attacked the police, the House of Lords and the monarchy. He also blamed the Tories for litter and graffiti.

Thanks, Alan, but where were you when we needed you?

DAVID MELLOR – 1992

'If you can dish it out, you've got to be able to take it'

Few modern ministers have dished it out more brutally than David Mellor. Few have taken it with more chutzpah.

In political ethics, this affair presents a dilemma of gripping intensity. David Mellor's behaviour was at the same time wholly reproachable, yet irrelevant to the ministerial post he held. Such was his talent and expertise that when he left office a whole area of national life lost a formidable ally. Such were his antics that even his friends despaired of recommending any other course.

Not least among this Cabinet minister's contributions to cultural life, during his brief but colourful stint as Heritage Secretary, was to acquaint the English with a new word: shrimping. Not least among the disappointments which have arisen since is the discovery that Mr Mellor and his friend may never have shrimped. She now says the story, along with the story that he made love in a Chelsea strip (the apparel of the football team Mellor follows), was invented.

'To shrimp' is a term imported from the United States. It describes the Putney MP's alleged penchant for having his toes sucked by his partner: a passion also indulged, it was alleged, upon the Duchess of York, though not by Mr Mellor. Thanks probably to both, it was included for the first time in the latest edition of *Chambers's Encylopaedic English Dictionary* after becoming probably the best remembered allegation concerning Mellor's unlucky affair with actress Antonia de Sancha. When Mellor was finally forced out of office and on to the backbenches the *Sun* summed up his fall from grace with one of its punchier headlines: 'From Toe Job to No Job.' The nation remains in some confusion as to whether Mr Mellor was alleged to have sucked his friend's toes, or *vice-versa*.

David Mellor, elected (as I was) in 1979, was a colleague I often drove home to South London (where we both lived) after late-night sittings at the Commons. In career terms he quickly outstripped me, and was soon a minister. Some indication of his skills is provided by the way he persuaded me, for two years, that his Putney home was on the way from Westminster to Clapham where I lived.

We often agreed, and often crossed swords: once or twice quite unpleasantly. Arrogant, rude, capable, ambitious, entertaining, quick-minded, sharp-tongued, liberal in his thinking and brutal in debate, Mellor was a man of steady and humane judgement in public affairs, yet often unbelievable insensitivity and self-defeating impatience in personal and political relationships. He both impressed and infuriated, often at the same time.

He also became a friend and ally of the man who was to become Prime Minister: John Major, a fellow Chelsea Football Club supporter. There was no surprise when Major created a tailor-made job for him after the April 1992 election: the first Secretary of State at a new Department of National Heritage. Responsibilities included the press, broadcasting, heritage and the arts. There were high hopes for Mellor: probably the

Sun, 25 September 1992

Cabinet's only genuine aesthete, one of whose boasts was the possession of the largest classical music collection on CD in South London. But Mellor was also Parliament's most articulate authority on football. In his new job he was quickly dubbed Minister for Fun.

And Mr Mellor was having much more fun than many of us realized.

A key part of the Heritage portfolio was the media. In July Mellor, educated at Swanage Grammar School and Christ's College, Cambridge, commissioned Sir David Calcutt, the eminent lawyer, to produce a report into press freedom. Mellor, whose own doubts about state interference with the press had never been a secret, and never changed, was under political pressure to reduce unwarranted intrusion by the press into individual privacy. He warned the press barons they were 'drinking in the last chance saloon'. Unbeknown to all of us, least of all himself, he was about to provide trebles all round.

David Mellor was forty-three and married with two children. On Saturday, 18 July 1992, he received a tip-off that the *People* newspaper was to splash a story the next day about his affair with the thirty-one-year-old actress, Antonia de Sancha. Her telephone in the Finborough Road flat in West London where she lived and where he frequently visited her, had been bugged. Her landlord had co-operated in this with journalists, who had been tipped off about the story after Mellor had been recognized. Within weeks, the press were publishing photographs of the room, with a mattress on the floor.

Mellor immediately rang the Prime Minister to offer his resignation. The offer was refused. John Major reassured his old friend that he had his full support. He stood by Mellor the next day and publicly made clear that there was no question of any conflict of interest: Mellor would handle the Calcutt Report.

It is worth making clear that Miss de Sancha was not accused of having tipped off the press, or assisted in any way in the first 'scoop'. She too was – at least at first – a victim. And now she was under siege. The press uncovered her single most memorable film role: her portrayal of a one-legged prostitute who has sex with the pizza delivery man in the soft porn film, *The Pieman*. Photographs of bottoms, and of Miss de Sancha, taken from the film, graced many tabloid front pages.

Antonia de Sancha's story of the media circus in which she became involved makes extraordinary reading. Cast into the wilderness by the man she claimed had declared his love for her, she chose to enlist the services of the near-legendary freelance publicist, Max Clifford, who presumably stood to gain a cut of her earnings from the affair. She made a shrewd appointment. She later told Julia Langdon in a *Guardian* profile that the Chelsea strip story had been made up during a conversation with Clifford (she says he suggested it; he says she did; he 'laughs uproariously' at the suggestion that he knew the story was untrue, and denies it). Clifford told me the coincidence of Derek Hatton's claim some years ago that he made love in an Everton strip is no more than that: a coincidence.

In Antigua, taking a respite from the affair, de Sancha says she rang Clifford to try to break off the deal whereby he was to represent her. He said, 'Calm down, It's all right. I've just had a call from Los Angeles and Jack Nicholson wants you to play Catwoman.' He had suggested to her, she says, ('to keep the story hot') that she pretend to be pregnant and resting in Antigua while deciding whether or not to keep the child. Julia Langdon adds, 'Max Clifford laughed when this was put to him. "Really," he said, "I don't remember saying that!"'

On her return from Antigua, de Sancha says, she found her 'Chelsea strip' story had been sold to the *Sun*. 'I thought, I just don't think I can do this. It was like it wasn't me doing it.' . . . 'Max stormed into the room and said: "Antonia, tell her [a woman reporter from the *Sun*] about the Chelsea strip" . . . It was just awful, awful, awful. I'd have to look them in the eye and say "Yes, it's true."'

The toe-sucking story, de Sancha told Langdon, 'was complete and utter garbage'. Although she admitted her mistake in going along with these stories, 'she did manage to stop some others. She did not, for example, allow her PR adviser to promote the story that she was pregnant with Mellor's child – to be followed later by a miscarriage. And she refused to make a video on how to suck toes. "I hate feet."' Clifford has not recognized any such account of events.

At this point the minister was forced to admit the difficulties this was causing his marriage of almost twenty years to his obviously devoted wife, Judith. On the steps of the National

Heritage Department the following day he appealed for privacy for his family, especially his two young boys.

There were also difficulties in his relationship with his father-in-law, Professor Edward Hall. Two days after the *People*'s story, Hall attacked Mellor in the media. 'If he'll cheat on our girl he'll cheat on the country.' The next day there were allegations that Mellor had responded with a threat that Hall would never see his grandchildren again. Judith Mellor stepped in to deny it.

Two days later came a small but critical mistake in the Mellor campaign for survival. Having appealed for privacy, he arranged a photo-call at the home of his parents-in-law. A smiling Mellor posed with Judith, the boys and the in-laws. They stood at the gate of Professor Hall's property before disappearing inside for a cosy family lunch. Those who live by Saatchi & Saatchi die by Saatchi & Saatchi. Britain cringed.

Yet still he seemed likely to survive. The scandal had broken in the summer when Parliament was not sitting. He did not have to appear at the Dispatch Box. And it was universally agreed that he was doing a good job as Heritage Secretary. The Prime Minister and most Conservative MPs backed him, resentful of the media furore. There was also widespread anger at the way the *People* had netted the story, aided by the bugging devices secretly installed at de Sancha's flat.

By an unlucky coincidence, the following Friday the BBC broadcast Mellor's 'Desert Island Discs' on Radio 4 – recorded five days before the controversy erupted. The programme had an unusually high audience in Fleet Street. Nor were journalists disappointed. Mellor told his interviewer, Sue Lawley: 'I think one of the great things about politics, you know, is that if you can dish it out, you've got to be able to take it. It never does you any harm.' Mellor also revealed a gift for unwitting irony: 'The sad thing about politicians is that they often give the impression that they want to stay for ever. They have to be dragged kicking and screaming off the stage.'

This storm, too, he weathered. The worst he had to endure through the summer was the revelation from North Petherton, Somerset, that a bespectacled potato called 'David Mellor' had won a vegetable look-alike competition.

On Monday, 7 September, the *Sun* began the serialization of de Sancha's story. No details, or alleged details, were spared. There

were photographs of the mattress o..n the floor where the couple
first made love – a replica of the bottle of cheap white wine which
he always brought to woo her, in the foreground. There were the
cheap red silk bedclothes. And there were, of course, the famous
disputed accounts of how Mellor was said (by de Sancha) to enjoy
being given a 'toe-job'.

Mellor was reduced to a laughing stock as readers of the *Sun*
feasted on de Sancha's story about Mellor's penchant for dressing
up in his beloved Chelsea soccer strip – centre-forward – for his
'sex romps with the leggy de Sancha' (who loathed football). The
Sun even mocked up a photograph of the tubby MP in his
favourite number nine shirt. It guaranteed Mellor a permanent
spot in soccer terrace folklore. His name was sung out for months
by rival football fans.

Herself the object of ridicule, anxious to be taken seriously, and
by now a hot, not to say exotic, media property, Miss de Sancha
was seldom off the television or radio. But still the Prime Minister
stood by Mellor who, he insisted, would oversee the Calcutt
Report. 'I am not one of these people,' Mellor said, 'who will
change my views merely because I have been getting a bit of stick
myself.' The Tory Chairman, Sir Norman Fowler, assured Mellor
there was no pressure from the backbenches for him to quit.

Three days after the *Sun* started its serialization, the *Daily Mail*
printed allegations about Mellor's friendship with an investment
businessman called Elliot Bernerd. He had loaned the politician a
chauffeur-driven Mercedes during and after the recent General
Election.

Still David Mellor survived. Then fate struck another blow, this
one fatal. The Mellors' family holiday at the Marbella home of
Mona Bauwens, daughter of one of Yasser Arafat's main funders
in the Palestine Liberation Organization, became front-page
news. Bauwens had started a libel action against the *People* over its
stories. Unluckily for Mellor it reached the High Court on 14
September, just when his fight for ministerial survival was at a
critical stage. The four-week holiday at the six-bedroom villa had
begun the day before Iraq invaded Kuwait. Internationally
isolated, the PLO were almost alone in supporting the invasion.

The press tore into what they saw as the minister's lack of
judgement with headlines such as 'I had Mellor – for tea' and 'Mr
Mellor's Mona Tea-ser.' Bauwens, who was suing the *People*

because it had cast her in the role of 'social outcast and leper', was mortified. The first day's reports made her want to 'throw up'.

The *People* had hired the formidable libel lawyer, George Carman, who described the Mellors' holiday as 'politically insensitive and possibly insulting to the families of British citizens. . . Marbella has sand, sea and sunshine and if a politician goes there and, in the honest view of some, behaves like an ostrich and puts his head in the sand and thereby exposes his thinking parts, it may be a newspaper is entitled to say so.'

After a week-long trial the jury was split 6–6. The *People*'s editor hailed it as a 'terrific victory'. He demanded Mellor's resignation. Bauwens never went for a re-trial, despite her immediate statement that she wished to.

Mellor was not giving up without a fight, though. Bolstered by advice from Sir Tim Bell, Margaret Thatcher's favourite advertising man, he toured the television studios on the night of 23 September 1992, the night after the trial ended, hoping to salvage his reputation. 'Undoubtedly I behaved foolishly,' he told the world, 'and I have never made any secret of that – but I think that to a lot of people in this day and age that was not a resigning matter.' He repeated his defence that he still had the backing of the Prime Minister, who had told him the Bauwens holiday was within ministerial guidelines. 'Who,' asked Mellor, 'decides who is to be a member of the British Cabinet – the Prime Minister or the editor of the *Daily Mail*?' It did not take long to find out the answer.

Earlier in the evening the minister had insisted on going ahead with a long-standing engagement to address the Newspaper Press Fund's annual reception, attended by many of the editors who were baying for his blood. It was a brave and stylish performance. Mellor thanked the press for asking him along: 'I was going through a quiet patch so it was good of you to invite me tonight.'

With the morning came unhelpful tidings from Sir Marcus Fox, Chairman of the backbench Conservative 1922 committee. Fox was not hopeful about the outcome of the 1922 meeting scheduled for that afternoon. For those anxious to discover how backbench opinion is moving in the Tory Party, Marcus Fox has always been a useful weather-vane. Mellor called the Prime Minister and told him he was quitting. Initially reluctant, Major finally agreed. David Mellor's Cabinet career was over.

I reported his Commons resignation speech the following day thus:

> The fun – *Mr Mellor: A Personal Statement* – was scheduled for 11 a.m.: a civilised time for a lynching . . . Just before 11, Mr Mellor arrived for his ritual humiliation. Tory numbers had doubled. They had come for the usual show: pale figure of minister – head bowed – old school tie – restrained regrets concerning own folly – delicate references to nature of folly – heartfelt thanks to colleagues for support during difficult time – sit down – 'hear hear' from all sides – shoulder-patting from pals – dignified exit, to kindly buzz of 'poor David', 'there but for the grace of God . . .' etc from outwardly mourning, inwardly sniggering colleagues.
>
> By 11, the Tory benches were full: a charcoal waste of Tories, one of whom has a new wig. From backbenches, where he was a stranger, Mellor rose. Something within him said 'stuff the lot of you'. The speech was not an outburst: more of a shrug of the shoulders, a brave grin, and two fingers fidgeting to make a rude sign.
>
> 'Having become heartily sick of my private life myself,' he said, 'I cannot expect others to take a more charitable view.' It was an eccentric statement, by degrees chatty, defiant, funny, menacing and bitter: but devoid of self-pity. His colleagues had come to reward a show of regret. But of regret there was little, so sympathy was tinged with bemusement.
>
> A fortnight of total cock-up ended yesterday with just one resignation: a man agreed on all sides to be good at his job.

The behaviour of 'certain tabloids', Mellor had said, had made him wonder whether 'one was living in Ceaucescu's Romania or John Major's Britain'.

Mellor's father-in-law could not conceal his glee. 'It was inevitable. We all get our just desserts, don't we?'

The next day a short letter appeared in *The Times*:

> Sir,
>
> In David Mellor we had a secretary of state committed to and with a deep understanding of the arts. Could we not have allowed him to get on with his job?

It was signed by many of the leading lights of British music, opera, theatre and television. A (then) little known minister, John Redwood, commented that a man who could betray his wife could betray his country. Mercifully, we do not imagine that a man who could betray his Leader could betray his wife. Mrs Redwood is secure.

Any chance of an early return to government vanished in November 1994 when the *News of the World* uncovered a very different affair. David Mellor had fallen for an attractive and talented viscountess, Lady Penelope Cobham, a past adviser at the Heritage Department, and an energetic member of many public bodies. 'I know this sounds a bit Mills and Boon,' he told a hostile press, going on to insist that this was a romance, whereas the affair with de Sancha had been a fling. Developments since seem to bear Mellor out, but it was a distinction the beleaguered couple never had much chance of persuading the press to feature. 'Mellor: new mistress' was about the limit of it.

The press wolves now circled David and Judith Mellor's Putney home, waiting to be fed. Mellor, who had said he would seek a divorce, agreed to step outside for the cameras. It was a disaster. In a friendly exchange with reporters on his way to post some letters he quipped: 'It's no big deal.' He had written the next morning's headlines.

The Mellors were under immense pressure. The MP railed against the media, in the media. Judith Mellor even rang a breakfast-time TV studio to insist she was not the distraught abandoned wife she was being painted as. Even this backfired. With Mr Mellor standing behind her, she asked the TV presenter if he wanted her husband back on the phone. 'Do *you* want him back?' the presenter asked. 'I'll have him back,' she laughed. It was virtually all the media reported. It was in any case too late: Mellor's and Lady Cobham's plans to marry were soon on public record.

The ex-minister's constituency remain loyal. And he has had a last laugh. Having long before told 'Desert Island Discs' there was 'life after politics', Mr Mellor seems to be proving it. Far from 'toe job to no job' he has a broadening career in writing and broadcasting. The world continues to hate him, envy him and seek him out.

My own view is that David Mellor is a brilliant communicator but a lousy self-publicist. Wittingly or unwittingly he has encouraged the world to see him as a sex-cheat and a rat. Certainly he has provided the evidence for both charges. But an uncensorious study of his political and media career provides evidence of another side to his character: Mellor's work in home affairs, heritage and the media adds up to a focused, sustained and principled effort in the public interest, conducted with energy and intelligence. This has been widely overlooked in the desire to criticize his adultery. Well, the adultery has been punished. And we have lost one of the few politicians able properly to champion the arts.

David Mellor is now earning vastly more than he did as a minister; more than most of the newspaper editors who helped to bring him down. It is also possible that he is having more fun than when he was Minister of Fun. And within a few years his former post was occupied by an Arts minister with no known interest in the arts, or sport. Perhaps that was safer.

NORMAN LAMONT – 1993

'Je ne regrette rien'

No single incident in Norman Lamont's long career qualifies him for a place in a book of great parliamentary scandals. The clever, but not always wise, former Chancellor is notable, rather, for a spectacular series of small parliamentary blunders. His story is worth recounting in some detail here for the light it sheds on the media's power to turn caricature into virtual reality.

'Accident-prone' is a wonderful media cliché. It tends to prove self-reinforcing since, as minor accidents are occurring in most people's lives for most of the time, the evidence is seldom hard to gather – *if* you try to gather it. Once the impression settles around the person of any politician that he is 'accident-prone', endless small stories confirming it can be found, and become newsworthy as evidence of a famous characteristic in this man. The caricature takes shape and sharpens, and the virtual reality grows. Just ask former Tory Chairman Jeremy Hanley.

Not that Mr Lamont did not from time to time assist his caricaturists. The often and widely predicted downfall of one of history's most 'accident-prone' Chancellors of the Exchequer was attended by no more than an hilarious succession of minor misfortunes. First impinging on the popular consciousness as the only politician ever to conceal a black eye by wearing sunglasses on 'Any Questions', he seldom disappointed the newshounds. And yet he is a capable and often prescient man, so why the mutterings and whence the caricature? Mr Lamont would recognize the word 'louche'. The murmur was never far from bar and Smoking Room assessments by fellow Tories of our colleague. It well encapsulates both the criticism, and what his friends would see as the unfairness of the criticism, for it is pointedly unspecific.

When you examine the record, nothing disgraceful emerges. There has never been any hint of real dishonour in the conduct of his career. I suspect Lamont is more honourable a politician than some of his less beleaguered contemporaries. But . . . that puffiness under the eyes, that morning-after look. The *Sun* put it best, the day after his fall: 'For years, bad publicity . . . has dogged Norm like a bad smell.'

There were embarrassing allegations over an unpaid credit card and hotel bills. There was what was (inaccurately) reported as the use of taxpayers' money to evict a self-styled sex therapist, 'Miss Whiplash', from the basement of his London home. Perhaps less forgivable to the underlying public sentiment which hardened against him, there was a series of unhappily timed remarks, often reported quite out of context, during a long and (for many) hideous recession.

In October 1991 he declared: 'The green shoots of economic spring are appearing once again.' In fact they were. But they did not appear to most ordinary people at the time. Lamont was 'singing in the bath,' he said, shortly after Britain had been forced out of the European Exchange Rate Mechanism in circumstances

which appeared to most a humiliating fiasco in which billions had
been staked unsuccessfully to prop up the pound sterling. That it
was made in an ambiguous context is quite forgotten. Lamont put
it like this to me: 'The remark about singing in the bath was made
the week after Black Wednesday, in Washington DC. I was there
for the IMF Conference and gave a press conference about the
G7 meeting and the Russian economy. It was a very nice day and
I had just been for a walk in the sunshine in the Embassy garden.
A reporter asked me, "Why are you looking so well today?" I
replied that I didn't know but that it must be the case because my
wife had complained that I had been singing in the bath. The
remark was at the end of the formal proceedings and was nothing
to do with economics.'

The 'singing in the bath' remark was never (he has insisted)
meant as a comment on exit from the ERM; even if it had been,
subsequent economic news was to vindicate any bathroom song.
But this did not make the report welcome at the time.

Millions, including hard-pressed Tory voters, already
remembered – and would not forgive – an earlier remark: 'rising
unemployment and the recession . . . has been a price well worth
paying' for getting inflation down. This was no more than a frank,
if brutal, statement of an arguably successful policy. Those who
call for more candour from our politicians should look at what the
press and public do to politicians who offer it.

Lamont, elected MP for Kingston-on-Thames at a by-election
in May 1972, became Chancellor after organizing John Major's
leadership campaign in 1990. Born in Shetland during the war he
was part of the Cabinet's 'Cambridge mafia', his university
contemporaries including John Gummer, Michael Howard,
Kenneth Clarke and Norman Fowler. After a stint at
Conservative Central Office he joined the merchant bank N. M.
Rothschild (he is on the bank's board today). When Mrs
Thatcher won the 1979 General Election he was brought into the
government for the first time.

In July 1985 Lamont, forty-three, married to a strong-willed
woman, Rosemary, and with two children, hit the headlines for
the first time. He surprised a Radio 4 studio audience by
appearing in a pair of dark glasses. They barely concealed the
Trade minister's shiner. Lamont told friends he had walked into
a door. The other story was that he had been thumped when he

made a late-night call at the Bayswater home of Olga Polizzi, the eldest daughter of Lord Forte.

Richard Connolly, also forty-three, a wealthy art dealer, was already at the £350,000 home of the glamorous Mrs Polizzi, who had separated from her Italian husband in 1980. Connolly, alleged Nigel Dempster in the *Daily Mail*, laid into Lamont. 'I was very angry with this man, who is a member of the Government. I was so angry that I chased him down the street and caught up with him in the next street. I won't tell you exactly what I did to him but he would have difficulty passing it off as an accident with the filing cabinet.' By the time he returned to the Commons, a plaster was insufficient to cover his embarrassment. The affair was 'innocent but complicated,' Lamont remarked. It did not seem to bother the oddly worldly Prime Minister, Margaret Thatcher.

Lamont wisely kept a low profile after that until April 1991 when a *News of the World* reporter called at the basement flat of his Notting Hill home. By now Lamont was Chancellor. His estate agents had let the flat five weeks earlier to Miss Sara Dale. Unknown to the Chancellor she was running a thriving 'sex therapy' business in the basement. Miss Whiplash, as she became known, offered to dress up in a school teacher's mortar board and gown to fulfil her clients' domination fantasies. Whiplash, who also dressed in rubber, denied being a £90-an-hour prostitute, but admitted the newspaper revelations would be 'good for business'. They were not so good for her hapless (and until then unwitting) landlord, the Chancellor, who promised to remove her if the allegations were true.

The following day the *Sun* gave him all the evidence he needed. 'Lamont tart says: "I'm not budging from this house."' She admitted she stripped naked while massaging clients. The paper featured a two-page spread under the heading: 'Welcome to my vice den. The tart in Mr Lamont's house shows it all to the *Sun*.' The story then faded . . . Until September when it emerged that the Treasury had authorized a £4,700 payment towards Lamont's £23,000 legal costs – 'to evict Miss Whiplash', said the papers. Tory Party benefactors paid the rest.

Or so the newspapers suggested. In fact the Treasury payment was made to Lamont's solicitors not for the cost of eviction but for handling press inquiries. Normally media or public inquiries would have been handled by the Treasury Press Office, at the taxpayers' expense. In this case Lamont's personal solicitors took responsibility for inquiries about the Chancellor's affairs and the Treasury recognized this by contributing, for work they would otherwise have handled. As to the 'Tory Party benefactors', Lamont comments: 'The bill was paid by Conservative Central Office. Whether there was an individual or a group of individuals, or no one, I do not know.'

Outcry ensued. According to the media, Lamont was accused of breaching Cabinet Office guidelines that ministers should not accept gifts worth more than £125. He was criticized for not disclosing the financial assistance from Conservative Central Office. Mr Lamont comments: 'I did not do so because it never occurred to me a Conservative MP could register as an interest help from his own Party. There have been many examples over the years where Members in financial difficulties have been helped by their Party.'

Lamont raises an interesting point here, which I am not aware of seeing discussed. Indeed one could go further: it was not, until

"WHAT DO YOU THINK...SEX THERAPIST OR GOVERNMENT CHIEF WHIP?"

Cartoon by Cookson, 15 April 1991 (courtesy of *Sun*)

recently, uncommon for a Tory parliamentary candidate to pay for or contribute towards his own election expenses. Overwhelmingly, his or her local association now funds these. Members who are not financially reliant on their own local officers have an important independence – and the remainder an important dependence – which is of potential interest to press and public. But nobody has ever suggested that this is a declarable interest.

As to the Treasury money, Lamont explains: 'the decision . . . was made by the Permanent Secretary of the Treasury, the Head of the Civil Service and the Prime Minister. It was not made at my request . . . They came to the conclusion that those costs arose out of my public position. For the same reason the Prime Minister decided . . . that it was reasonable for the Conservative Party to help me with the total legal costs I had in evicting my tenant. These costs were way above those that would normally arise in a situation like this . . . [because of the Chancellor's public position] it was necessary to accelerate legal procedures in order to end the ridiculous publicity. I would point out that I also incurred large legal costs because of allegations made over 'Threshergate'. These were completely without foundation. But I had to pay a large bill.'

Given that there was never the hint of a suspicion that Lamont himself was involved in or had even known about Miss Whiplash's business, he was unlucky to attract the publicity he did. But it was hardly damaging, and caused only giggles. A parliamentary aide well placed to know told me at the time that all Norman's friends were urging him to relax and treat the matter lightly. 'But he was in a great state about it,' and determined to act. When I put this to the former Chancellor, he remarked that there may have been no 'printed hint' linking him to Miss Whiplash, but 'there were plenty of threats to make such allegations, which is why I had to engage libel lawyers'.

I still believe the Chancellor over-reacted. The scent of potential writs excites as well as frightens editors. But it would not be surprising, in light of his experiences so far, if the Chancellor were becoming increasingly defensive. He adds: 'All the photos of this woman in my family's house were immensely distressing to my wife and to my children. As a matter of politics as well, the view in Government was that it was essential to end the publicity as soon as possible.'

And what was the *private* view among media folk? The reader may find this immoral, even shocking, but I have to report that journalists' reaction was one of hilarity that a non-story which some of our tabloid cousins were doing their tongue-in-cheek best to present as an issue of national importance (but which we all knew readers would take with a large pinch of salt) should be causing such a flutter in the Chancellor's dovecote. The media often remind me of a boisterous and undisciplined infant, gazing with amused bafflement at what it has broken in its romps. Most of the press does not believe that its readers really believe what it writes. Most politicians believe they do. This can cause a mismatch between the two groups' attitudes to media behaviour.

After the débâcle of the ERM withdrawal in October 1992, Lamont found himself in a scrape with the press which was really not his doing. The *Sun* reported that the Chancellor had walked out of the Grand Hotel after the Conservative Party Conference in Brighton without paying his bill.

The story was a travesty. It is, after all, hardly credible that a man as easy to find as the Chancellor of the Exchequer would try to do a runner from a Brighton hotel. In fact Lamont had arranged with the hotel that his bill should be sent to him at Conservative Central Office. The same arrangement was made for many of the guests at the time. The *Sun* (says Lamont) obtained the information that Lamont's bill had not been paid by telephoning the hotel and pretending to be Conservative Central Office, asking for a list of all those whose bills were to be forwarded. 'The list included several ministers but the paper chose to write the story only about myself. At the time the *Sun* ran the story I had not even received the bill. The management of the hotel said the story was completely untrue.'

The *Sun* seemed to have it in for Lamont. The following month the paper announced that he had exceeded his credit card limit twenty-two times in the last eight years. He was £470 over his £2,000 limit. He had received five warning letters from Access. 'This,' Lamont told me, 'is about the only allegation in the newspapers that was broadly true. For some years I simply paid my credit card bills every two or three months in order to save myself the bother of writing endless small cheques. Some people may or may not approve of this. But it seems to me an entirely private matter . . . A much more important question was why newspapers felt it right to obtain access to my own financial records and to publish them.'

Of course by now a familiar dynamic was in play. Once a public figure has attracted a reputation for some supposed defect, any news which remotely embellishes it becomes a good story. An impression grows of 'mounting evidence'. There must be dozens of other MPs who are late in paying Access bills, or who enjoy socializing until the small hours, but with Lamont it had become a story. A Tory Chancellor's unpopularity at a time of economic recession had much to do with the delight the tabloid press and its readers took in Lamont's discomfiture.

The *Sun* now said Lamont had last used his card at an unidentified Thresher's off-licence. It was the cue for the Chancellor to become embroiled in 'Threshergate'. The assistant manager of Thresher's in Paddington, one of the seedier parts of town, claimed to reveal what Lamont had used his credit card for: a bottle of Bricout champagne at a 'recession-busting' price of £15.49 and twenty Raffles cigarettes, at £1.98. Neither Lamont nor his wife smokes Raffles.

The Chancellor disputed the date, and this purchase, at this branch of Thresher's. The Treasury went to the extraordinary and undignified lengths of producing a credit card slip, signed by Lamont, which did show he had spent £17.47 – but on three bottles of wine in the more upmarket Connaught Street branch of Thresher's, near Marble Arch. On 30 November the Thresher's assistant at Paddington admitted inventing the story. It must have been the first time in history that normally staid senior Treasury officials found themselves in the position of showing their Chancellor's credit card slips to journalists.

Tory MPs said that it was proof Lamont was the victim of a smear campaign. 'Maybe the man in the off-licence is a Left-winger,' said John Townend, a senior Tory Right-winger and chairman of his party's backbench Finance Committee. In fact the conspiracy may not have approached such exotic proportions, but Lamont points out that 'the management of Thresher's told the economic adviser Sir Terence Burns that Thresher employees were offered money to make up this story, when it was completely untrue'. One newspaper, he adds, 'offered a woman, whom I did not know, £100,000 to embellish the story in a further, predictable, way.'

Lamont limped on until May 1993. More serious policy troubles than these dogged him, but the damage done by the note of farce from which no profile of the Chancellor was now free, should not be ignored in any assessment of his final downfall.

Unleashed on voters during the Newbury by-election campaign, and pressed on whether he was proud of his achievements in office, Norman Lamont was reported as delivering his final flippant quip: 'Je ne regrette rien.' It was reported on television that night. What quickly disappeared from the record (and has now been entirely forgotten) was that the remark came in response to the question 'Which do you regret more: singing in the bath, or seeing green shoots?' Treating the question as frivolous, Lamont replied, 'As Edith Piaf said, "*je ne regrette rien*".'

It was only after the by-election was lost that the media played up the remark, ignoring its original context. Nobody really supposes it damaged the Tory candidate's chances. However, it was turned into a hallmark of the Chancellor's supposedly insouciant attitude to political life and party managers warned John Major that his Chancellor had become a serious political liability. Bitterly – and only hours before he was due to be sacked – Lamont mused: 'I am sure I seem responsible for the sinking of the *Titanic*.' On 27 May, offered the post of Environment Secretary as a consolation, Lamont walked out of the government.

The news was relayed to the world not by Downing Street but by eighty-three-year-old Irene Lamont, Mr Lamont's splendidly doughty mother. She had told the *Grimsby Evening Telegraph*. The *Grimsby Evening Telegraph* told the world.

The tabloids celebrated his departure with a series of biting, but none-too-subtle, obituaries. The *Daily Mirror* ran a front page with a cartoon of a gravestone. Etched on it was 'RIP Norman Lamont 1990–1993.' 'Hooray, Hooray, We're Norm Free Today,' trumpeted the *Daily Star* in one of the decade's least clever headlines.

Chris Moncrieff, the political editor of the Press Association, tried to put Lamont's achievements in perspective in the London *Evening Standard*. He had brought inflation down to a twenty-five-year low of 1.3 per cent, said Moncrieff, but all anyone remembered was that his credit card was overdrawn. He had run

John Major's campaign for the Tory leadership but talk of a bizarre sex therapist hogged the headlines. Interest rates were at a fifteen-year low but memories lingered on of an episode which had never happened: the Chancellor being chased out of a Brighton hotel for not paying the bill. 'Where others glide gracefully into the water, Norman Lamont does a bellyflop.' Moncrieff put it well, but as a veteran newspaperman loyal to his trade he did not add what we might: that once the press has decided to present you as a bellyflopper, photographs of your better dives will never get past the picture editor's desk.

The final insult was delivered by the Boundary Commission later that year. It abolished his Kingston constituency. He is still looking for a seat to fight at the next election. Whether his increasingly public dislike of the government his party is running is assisting him in this search is open to debate. Questioning the Tory leadership, Lamont has described John Major as 'in office but not in power'.

In March 1995 he amazed colleagues and commentators by voting with the Labour Party on a motion criticizing the government's European policies. In June, after appearing ready to stand himself against the Prime Minister in the 4 July leadership contest, he openly backed John Redwood's challenge. It failed.

But it may be that it is not ambition which drives Lamont now, but anger. He would say – and honestly believes – that it is principled objection to some of the government's central policies. He sits at the back, arms folded, often pale with fury – in George Eliot's phrase – 'like a malign prophecy'. Emerging from Room 12 on 4 July after having presumably voted against Major, he smiled thinly at waiting reporters and remarked, 'I enjoyed that.' His bitterness on the backbenches is palpable.

He has some reason to be bitter. I wonder what a snap poll of British voters would show, for instance, about recollections of 'Threshergate'? I believe that with many people a hazy memory of the Raffles and Bricot episode remains, while the fact that the story was finally found to be wholly untrue has never sunk in. And still the image dogs him. On 24 July 1995, the *Sun* reported that, after filling his tank with petrol, he found he had left his wallet behind. To which of us has this not happened? But Lamont made the front page. Of the songs Norman Lamont might choose to sing in his bath, *Je ne regrette rien* is not one.

MICHAEL MATES – 1993

'Don't let the buggers get you down'

But they did. Although not in the way Michael Mates, a junior Northern Ireland minister, had expected. The words were engraved on a £20 watch which Mates had given to Asil Nadir at a dinner to celebrate the Turkish Cypriot businessman's fifty-second birthday. Nadir's new watch became the most talked-about item of jewellery since Gerald Ratner, the High Street jeweller, labelled his own products 'crap'. Mates became the only minister ever to believe he was the victim of a Serious Fraud Office plot. Media interest in the affair has evaporated, yet that allegation has never really been cleared up.

Nadir, the founder of Polly Peck, was the subject of a Serious Fraud Office investigation into thirteen charges of fraud and false accounting worth £30 million. Mates had bought the watch to cheer up the millionaire businessman, whose own £3,500 Blancpain watch had been confiscated in one of the SFO's raids; and it was out of indignation against these, says Mates, that he first became involved. Nadir's adviser was his constituent.

Three days later, on 4 May, Nadir jumped bail of £3.5 million and escaped to his sumptuous home at Lapta in his native Northern Cyprus, which has no extradition treaty with Britain. In the rush to flee he left behind many treasured possessions, but he made very sure to take the watch.

For the next three weeks Nadir's business reputation was torn to shreds in his absence by MPs from both sides of the House. Nadir hit back from exile in the orange groves of Lapta and threat ed to reveal corruption at the highest level of government.

The corruption revelations never materialized, but on 30 May the watch did. The following day Mates faced the first blow. Nadir praised the Minister's 'unflinching help' in the fight for justice. It is not clear that it was Nadir who first broke the story to the press, or that he had intended to embarrass the minister, but that was the effect. Mates was taken aback. Of the watch he declared: 'it was a light-hearted gesture'. And, admitting he had helped put Nadir's case within government, he insisted he had been within his rights to do so while a minister.

Sleaze was already on the agenda. Now Labour MPs demanded to know why a minister of the Crown had been fraternizing with a businessman accused of one of the biggest frauds in history. They soon found out more. The first in a steady series of leaks revealed that Mates, advised by Anthony Scrivener, defence counsel to Nadir, had written three letters to two attorneys-general, questioning the conduct of the SFO.

There was uproar. Labour bayed. Tory MPs were dismayed. The wounds from David Mellor's and Norman Lamont's bitter departures from office were still fresh. Colleagues were puzzled at this choice of friend by a former lieutenant-colonel in the Queen's Dragoon Guards.

Mates, the fifty-seven-year-old MP for Hampshire East, had led Michael Heseltine's leadership campaign against Margaret Thatcher. Perhaps surprisingly for an apparently genial ex-military man, a good communicator and a persuasive politician, Colonel Mates was not without enemies on the Tory backbenches. He looks every inch an army officer with his black bushy eyebrows and brusque intimidating manner. But he was in deep trouble.

On 6 June, Michael Heseltine, always a close ally of Mates, admitted he had briefly interceded on Nadir's behalf – after a lunch with Christopher Morgan, Nadir's public relations adviser. But the following day John Major let it be known that Mates's resignation was neither sought nor offered. The following day Major told the Commons that his minister was guilty of a 'misjudgement' but it was not a 'hanging offence'.

Richard Ryder, the Chief Whip, was drawn into the fray when he admitted he had been approached by the Nadir camp. But he had summarily dismissed them and told Nadir's advisers to raise their client's case with their constituency MP, Peter Brooke, the Heritage Secretary.

Mates seemed safer. But a week later the affair erupted again when it emerged that the Tories had accepted a £440,000 gift from Nadir, who owed creditors millions of pounds. On 16 June Sir Norman Fowler, the Tory Party Chairman, was forced to concede that any money 'which had been stolen' would be repaid. On 17 June Nadir renewed the pressure by claiming that he had evidence of a Watergate-type scandal.

The allegations, so remarkable that the press tended to treat the affair as bizarre, involved the charge that someone (who, it was never revealed) had tried to involve the judge in the case against Nadir in some kind of conspiracy. MPs, however, and to some extent the media, never entirely came to grips with all this. Easier to handle was the known fact of Nadir's help for the Conservative Party and friendship towards Mates, and the unusual intervention on Nadir's behalf by a Tory minister – Mates.

Tory funding – always a favourite Labour topic – was back on the front pages. Sleaze and corruption dominated the headlines. Colonel Mates was watching the lift from the bottom of the lift-shaft. Elected in 1974, he had spent the Thatcher years in the political wilderness. A minister since 1990, he was determined not to return to it. He fought with tenacity, but on 20 June the steady flow of leaks designed to undermine him became a torrent. Newspapers disclosed that the minister had borrowed a car for his estranged wife from Nadir's public relations adviser. And this was after Nadir had jumped bail.

Support, never warm, was ebbing. But still the Prime Minister, unwilling to be bounced by the press, backed Mates.

On 24 June the *Daily Mail* published the text of the minister's letter to the Attorney-General. Mates was accused in one newspaper of basing this on a draft he had been given by Nadir – an accusation which has since been withdrawn.

The Prime Minister, now conspicuously failing to give public backing to Mates, found his own leadership criticized for failing to rid the government of another lame duck minister. Mates arrived at the Northern Ireland Office declaring it was business as usual. But the lunchtime ITN news revealed that he had dined at the Reform Club the previous evening with Nadir's PR adviser. Mates declared: 'It proves you cannot trust the Reform Club. It would never have happened at the Garrick.'

It was an error of judgement and a dinner too far for John Major. A meeting was hastily arranged at Downing Street. At 2 p.m. Mates offered his resignation 'with regret' not, he said, because he had done anything wrong, but to spare the Prime Minister embarrassment. At Question Time Mr Major announced that Mates had finally gone: twenty-five days too late for most Tory MPs.

The galloping Colonel, however, had not finished. On 29 June, in one of the most remarkable resignation speeches heard in the Commons, he accused the SFO of improper conduct and exerting pressure on the judge who was to have tried the case. A packed Chamber listened in numb amazement as Madam Speaker, in a series of weird clashes with the MP on his feet – Mates – warned him nine times to quit the subject because of the *sub judice* rule. But Mates, cheered by Labour MPs revelling in the government's discomfort, bulldozed on and completed his speech. He has the distinction of being the only MP, so far, to have successfully brushed the assertive Miss Boothroyd aside.

I remember watching from my seat almost above her chair as her Assistant Clerk, Donald Limon, scowling under his wig, kept turning to her to hiss that Mates must be stopped. At one point (said Simon Hoggart in the *Observer)* 'the Attorney-General, Sir Nicholas Lyell, could be seen signalling' the clerk to get Mates silenced. He never was.

A few days after his resignation speech, at a prize-giving at his old school, Blundells, in Tiverton, the former minister said: 'Can I say what a relief it is to be on my feet without Madam Speaker present.'

As for Asil Nadir, he no longer wears the watch. Mates confessed afterwards: 'I very nearly never had it engraved. It cost £32, which was even more than the watch. I wish I had sent it to the Prime Minister instead.'

Colonel Mates was throughout – and continues to be – doggedly loyal to John Major. He believes the Prime Minister did his best for him. He tells friends that Major's government was more important than his own woes and that, to take the heat off the Prime Minister, it was best for him to pipe down, and go. They remain friends.

There appeared a curious footnote to the affair, when what had been intended as a private conversation between the Prime Minister and the TV interviewer Michael Brunson was published in the *Daily Mirror* after hints emerged that Major had called some of his Cabinet colleagues 'bastards'. As Hoggart writes, that was the issue absorbing the nation, and few noticed Major's reply to Brunson's criticism that he had held on to Mates too long, and should have 'swatted' him. People would have said that Mates had been 'set up', protested the Prime Minister. 'As the Cabinet Secretary [Sir Robin Butler] told me, "It was an act of gross injustice to have got rid of him." Nobody knew what I knew at the time.'

And still nobody does. Mates has enemies in the Parliamentary Conservative Party and too few colleagues were prepared to stick out their necks for him when he got himself into a mess. Even friends agreed he conducted his defence imprudently. But in some minds (including mine) the suspicion remains that important elements to this story never emerged.

STEVEN NORRIS, TIM YEO, UNCLE TOM COBLEY and ALL – 1993–5

Back to Basics

John Major's call to go 'back to basics' at the Tory Party Conference in October 1993 met with a rapturous reception. It came two days after Peter Lilley had been cheered to the rafters for his attack on single mothers on state benefits who leapfrogged to the top of housing waiting lists.

At last the party faithful, demoralized by months of bickering over Europe and Britain's humiliating withdrawal from the ERM, had something to applaud. Major's carefully crafted slogan underlined the party's traditional values by attacking the progressive doctrines of the dreaded 1960s. A Conservative government stood, said Mr Major, 'for a country united around those old common-sense British values that should never have been pushed aside.' The message was easily understood in the constituencies. The Conference, I recall, warmed to it instantly. I wrote at the time that, whatever the media thought of the speech, ordinary Tory workers had cheered.

But I remember, too, the pre-speech press conference at Blackpool, minutes before the Prime Minister took the floor, given by Tim Collins, one of Major's chief spin-doctors. Journalists had seen an outline of the speech. They asked Collins how important the 'back to basics' theme was to the overall message and he confirmed that Downing Street intended it to be a dominant one. Within seconds, journalists were asking sceptical, cheeky, or downright lewd questions about divorce, adultery and waywardness among Major's own colleagues.

John Major is not personally or politically a morally censorious man. At no point did he mention sexual morality. He had probably hoped to centre the 'basics' theme more around basics in education, school discipline, respect for the law, civic-mindedness, cricket, warm beer, ginger snaps and cocoa. But the press saw it differently. If the Prime Minister had needed an early indication of just how differently, Mr Collins could have warned him before he even made the fateful speech. And at Westminster, too, some MPs saw the danger signs of a party, with a long and glorious history of scandal of its own, leading what could so easily be represented as a moral crusade.

They were right. The media, anxious to expose any whiff of hypocrisy, lost no time in exploiting what they somewhat fancifully declared to be the new mood of moral self-righteousness at Conservative Central Office. Thus began what was really a kind of undeclared open season on the private lives of Tory MPs. Over Christmas and the New Year the public was fed an almost daily diet of ministerial misdemeanours. Resignations followed, some faster than others.

The first minister to have reason to regret the campaign dreamed up (apparently) by the Downing Street Policy Unit, was Steven Norris, the forty-eight-year-old Transport minister. Norris, married with two children, was revealed as having not one but *five* mistresses.

This bombshell first hit the news-stands during the Party Conference, almost before the Prime Minister's standing ovation had died. Steven Norris had been supposed by most of us to be living with his wife of twenty-four years, Vicky, in their cottage in his Epping Forest constituency. But Mrs Norris knew differently. A niece of Cardinal Basil Hume, the head of the Roman Catholic Church in England and Wales, she was by then (says Norris) living in her own house in Berkshire. She knew her husband was a weekday Romeo. He says she knew about all his mistresses.

They did not, apparently, all know about each other. But they soon found out, once the press got the story. Five mistresses were located: a lady surgeon who dated Norris for eight years until 1986; a forty-six-year-old sales executive who took over from the

Photograph by Mike Poultney, 10 October 1993 (courtesy of the *Sunday Times*)

surgeon but dumped Norris in January 1991 when he told her about mistress number four; a forty-five-year-old colleague of my own on *The Times* – a divorcée with two children who had actually rented a home to share with the philandering MP; a forty-year-old director of *Harpers & Queen*; and a twenty-nine-year-old secretary to another Tory MP, who left Norris on discovering the existence of an earlier mistress, but was, at the time of writing, reunited with the minister.

The tabloids called him 'a serial adulterer', and for some weeks the discovery of new Norris mistresses brought on a chuckle at many British breakfast tables.

Mrs Norris formally separated from her husband. She has wisely and with dignity refused consistently to utter a word to the press. Her husband's constituency party had plenty to say. But the congenial and persuasive former car-salesman, who has never moralized about others and who is popular with colleagues, comfortably saw off threats to de-select him in January 1994. Norris kept his ministerial job. Nobody really knows how, but few wish him ill.

Steven Norris has commented that 'what appeared in the tabloids was considerably at variance with the facts, but there is no mileage for me in going into it'. On 4 July 1995, emerging from Room 12 at the Commons after voting (for the Prime Minister) in the Tory leadership contest, Mr Norris remarked: 'I owe him one.' Aware perhaps that the Prime Minister does *not* owe him one, he later announced that he would retire at the next election to pursue businesss interests

Tim Yeo had a rougher time of it. As families in his Suffolk South constituency were eating their leftover turkey on 26 December 1993, they discovered in the press that the married Environment minister had a six-month-old 'love child' (the word 'bastard' was now effectively cornered by the Prime Minister for use in describing his own Cabinet colleagues). It was Yeo's misfortune that the *News of the World* decided to break the story of Julia Stent's baby on Boxing Day at the beginning of a traditionally quiet news period. This served the paper well. They ran the story almost without distraction, and for nearly a fortnight other papers picked up on this too, featuring it prominently.

There was an instant fuss. Yeo's mistress was a single mother. Journalists were not slow to dig up a quote the minister had once

made to a local newspaper after visiting a constituency branch of
the marriage guidance group Relate. 'It is in everyone's interests to
reduce broken families and the number of single parents; I have
seen from my constituency the consequences of marital
breakdown.'

This was unfortunate and uncharacteristic. In fact Yeo was not
one of those MPs who habitually preached about moral issues.
Like Steven Norris he is a liberal and uncensorious man.

Much good it did him. Worse still for party managers, the new
woman in the minister's life was a Tory councillor – one of the
handful who clung on in Hackney. He had met her at a party
conference, but not the 'back to basics' one.

Yeo's wife, Diane, performed the traditional role of a Tory wife
and appeared for photographs 'standing by' her man. Yeo had
told her in February that the girlfriend, Julia Stent, was pregnant.

John Major immediately pledged loyalty to Yeo, declaring that
it was 'a private matter'. Yeo took his wife and two grown-up
children for a holiday in the Seychelles. It was unlucky, the
holiday having been booked long before, partly as a treat for his
son Jonathan, a talented painter who was recovering from
Hodgkin's disease. A decision to go ahead with the trip – made
for kindly reasons with family interests in mind and when the last
thing Yeo wanted to do was have a holiday – was represented as
betraying an arrogant disregard for the gravity of his situation.

While he was away, David Evans, a voluble Tory backbencher,
demanded Yeo's resignation. Evans was at least consistent. He
had also called for Norris to go. In fact both the Foreign
Secretary, Douglas Hurd, and Virginia Bottomley, the Health
Secretary, spoke up strongly for Yeo, but it was Evans who got the
attention.

When Yeo returned, the press were waiting. The Environment
minister made the mistake of hiding from the cameras on the floor
of the family car.

On 2 January, elements of his constituency party, which had
warmly embraced 'back to basics', were in a state of revolt. A local
Tory mayor, Mrs Aldine Horrigan, had written to the Prime
Minister expressing her disgust with Yeo. She repeated her
demand to the press the next day: Yeo should resign as a minister.

On 4 January, Yeo was summoned to a meeting with the eight
officers of his constituency association. He echoed the fateful

words of David Mellor: 'The Prime Minister decides who is in his government and not the tabloid newspapers.' He was wrong. The constituency party was about to have an unusual say in the matter.

He was dismissed from the meeting, which lasted six hours. The next morning the officers issued a statement which pledged less than wholehearted support. Yeo, who wanted to fight on, was called before Sir Norman Fowler, the Party Chairman, and Richard Ryder, the Chief Whip. The ministers, faced with this apparent revolt in the constituency, told Yeo he had lost his Prime Minister's support. He resigned the same day.

On 14 January the much larger and arguably more representative Executive Council of the association, comprising some 100 members, voted overwhelmingly in Yeo's favour, many expressing dismay at the statement of the officers' meeting. But it was too late for the ex-minister.

Though a local association has often been instrumental in forcing an MP to resign his seat or not to stand again, this had been different. Officers of the Suffolk Conservative Association nudged their MP not out of Westminster, but out of Whitehall. Rarely if ever has a constituency party taken the decisive role in removing a minister from government.

On 7 January, days after his resignation, Yeo criticized, in the *Daily Express*, the local mayor who had led the campaign against him. 'When I think of what I have done for her. I have campaigned for her in local government elections. And I rescued her husband's business when it was in receivership.'

On Sunday, 9 January, with the 'back to basics' campaign in tatters, the *Mail on Sunday* disclosed that in 1967 the ex-minister had fathered another child while he was at Emmanuel College, Cambridge. He was twenty-two years old at the time. This daughter, who will be twenty-eight this year, was adopted. She did not know that Yeo was her father. Mrs Yeo had known about the child before they married.

Doubts continued about his future as an MP when he refused to say whether that future would lie with his wife or his Hackney mistress. Some local activists said that losing the seat at a by-election was a price worth paying for getting rid of Yeo. But after spending a week telephoning his local party members one by one, Yeo survived a vote of confidence.

On 19 January Julia Stent resigned as a Hackney councillor – over non-attendance in the previous six months. She can be forgiven for her distraction. On 21 January, Diane Yeo, widely regarded among the press as 'a good thing', told *The Times* she had actually received hate mail for standing by her husband, whom she still loved.

The same day Yeo was pictured entering one of London's more fashionable restaurants, Langan's Brasserie in Mayfair, with his mistress. They stayed for three hours. Again, the tabloids' implication was clear – but unfair. Yeo was trying to act decently towards Stent.

Nobody close to Yeo ever criticized him in the newspapers at the time, and none has since. This had been a 'story' which had resulted entirely from an investigative campaign by a newspaper. It did not result – as so many other stories in this book did – from the actions of an aggrieved party stirring up the media as an act of revenge. We may surmise that Yeo dealt straightforwardly both with his family and with Julia Stent, and never lost the trust of any of them. As I remarked of the Parkinson affair, not getting divorced seems to be the modern sin. I think Yeo was rather unlucky.

He was not, however, bitter. Some time later, writing in the *Independent*, Yeo attacked the notion that the press could by legislation be made less prurient. 'Newspapers print stories they believe their readers want to read,' he said.

By now the alleged scandals were coming thick and fast. Alan Duncan, the newly-elected millionaire MP for the safe seat of Rutland and Melton, had resigned as a parliamentary private secretary on 8 January.

The young Mr Duncan, known as 'Hunky Dunky' at Westminster for his bonsai good looks, had taken advantage of the Tories' right-to-buy policy by arranging for the purchase of a council house adjoining his own in Westminster. It involved a private deal with his neighbour Harry Ball-Wilson, who benefited from a £50,000 tenant's discount. The deal, about which Duncan had always been completely open, is common in Britain, and there was no suggestion of illegality. Other MPs have availed themselves of it and a comparable arrangement is now offered to council tenants by the commercial banks.

Embarrassingly to journalists labouring to present Mr Ball-Wilson as the impoverished victim of Tory greed, the old boy was on holiday in Hawaii at the time of the fuss. He appears to have been the winner, as Duncan has paid handsomely for, and repaired, a dilapidated freehold with a sitting lifetime tenant (in rude health) in a falling property market: an outcome the MP had always contemplated (I remember him telling me so when he embarked on the deal).

But that would have been too subtle for the newspapers. In a different atmosphere the story would not have warranted mention. It is a telling indication of the hysteria gripping the nation over 'basics' that this was given front-page treatment by the *Daily Mirror*. The newspaper went on to point out that Duncan's own tiny house (which it was his plan to expand sideways) had been the headquarters of John Major's leadership campaign. Duncan's comments, when tracked down on a skiing holiday in Switzerland, were unprintable but may be summarized as a robust expression of the thought that if he were to be indicted for immorality, he could think of immorality which would have been more fun.

The following day, along with the exposure of Tim Yeo's second love child, reports about the previously obscure backbench MP David Ashby provided an irresistible sideshow to the 'back to basics' fiasco.

Ashby's credentials were impeccable. His 1992 election address stated: 'Married with a family, and therefore understands the needs of families. He is a man of integrity who believes in traditional moral values, discipline, and effective law and order.' It was claimed on 9 January 1994 that the MP for Leicester North-West had left his wife because of a 'friendship with another man'. The *Sunday Times* had been talking to Silvana, the MP's Italian-born wife. The Ashbys say that Silvana was asked leading questions.

Mrs Ashby, fifty-one and married for twenty-eight years, had spoken to the newspaper's journalist on the Friday before, at the family's home in Putney. Ashby, fifty-three, turned up and rang the doorbell. Entering, he silently pointed the *Sunday Times* man out of the door. He spent eighty minutes with his wife before driving off. He refused to comment.

The following day, Monday, 10 January, Mrs Ashby insisted on issuing a statement of her own, setting the record straight. She and her husband were not separating. But Ashby admitted he had shared a bed with a man in a French hotel on a holiday over the New Year. Newspapers tittered that it was a 'queen-sized bed'. His reported reaction was: 'I've been all over the bloody place and shared bloody beds.'

Ashby said he had 'spent a holiday with a close friend. We went to two hotels. In the first one we managed to find twin beds, and at the second one we didn't. It doesn't make any difference. It was much cheaper; it halved the price.' It appeared that the problem may have arisen, he has explained, through his friend's use of the words *'chambre double'*, which does not, as it might seem to, imply two beds in French.

David Ashby survived the gossip. Though he is one of many Tory MPs to have supported the lowering of the age of homosexual consent to sixteen, suggestions that this was relevant to the bed-sharing incident were illogical and insulting. Most of those who went into the 'sixteen' lobby were heterosexual. To my knowledge, a number of those who voted for eighteen or even twenty-one were homosexual. There is simply no correlation. I was always very grateful for Ashby's open help and support when I was campaigning myself on this issue, in the 1980s, before the cause became fashionable. Later he made great efforts to persuade the Home Affairs Select Committee to investigate the 'age of consent' issue before the Commons debate in 1994. Friends admire him for his courage in unfashionable causes: Ashby openly despises the far Right in the Conservative Party and speaks up for a more liberal Conservatism.

The *chambre double* affair has left Ashby bitter about what he calls 'the intrusion'. The allegations, he told me, he could handle, but the personal intrusion he found wounding in a way he cannot put out of his mind. Ashby is suing the *Sunday Times*. He says that another newspaper 'used a pink filter in photographing a bedroom where we stayed'. 'I kept thinking of the McCarthyite question: "Are you now or have you ever been . . .?" It's the worst experience I've ever faced. It had a profound and devastating effect on me. I can't forget it. It gnaws at you.'

I was surprised at the depth and intensity of the MP's feelings. Most journalists, including me, regarded his spot of bother in 1994 as hilarious rather than serious. What to most of the world is simply a giggle, can be little short of crushing to the individual concerned.

Much the same was true of the next story, which broke two weeks later. In an atmosphere of heightened media interest in 'love-children', the investigative zeal of the tabloids 'uncovered' even poor Gary Waller, the harmless and little known backbench Tory MP for Keighley, celebrated (until then) only for his tubby appearance and his dogged four-hour-plus London Marathons. He escaped with his life, his seat, and most of his reputation.

On 23 January 1994, the *News of the World* revealed that the long-time 'church-going' bachelor Waller was the father of a child by a mistress. 'Another Tory Shaker' said the headline, across a graphic of the top of the tower of Big Ben flying into the air. The paper said he had been 'booted off the books of a posh dating agency' for claiming he was single and fancy-free. He had also described himself, said the paper, as 'intelligent, humorous, career-oriented and youthful in approach'.

Had he belonged to the agency? 'Waller: "I did, but I was very, very reluctant. I only took it on on a trial basis."' In fact, far from being fancy-free, 'Waller (forty-eight) has a long-term girlfriend *and* a love-child by a Commons secretary.'

The phrase 'So what?' occurred even to hardened journalists at the discovery of this shocker. Waller did not resign. Nobody called on him to. The top of Big Ben did not fly off. And the affair dropped fast from the news. It was only ever a giggle.

Utterly unfunny – but tinged with a dreadful element of black comedy – was the bizarre death a few weeks later of the high-flying young Tory MP, Stephen Milligan. It was sensational.

By lunchtime on Monday, 7 February, Vera Taggart, Milligan's secretary, who had followed him from the *Sunday Times* to the Commons when he was elected in 1992, was worried. He had not returned her telephone calls. Forty-five-year-old Milligan had failed to show for appointments in the Commons that morning, which was totally out of character. The energy and intelligence of the new MP for Eastleigh in Hampshire had already been noticed by the Prime Minister and the whips. He had been made PPS to the Chief Secretary to the Treasury, Jonathan Aitken.

Vera Taggart had set off for Milligan's Chiswick home. On arriving there she was alarmed to find milk still on the doorstep. She let herself in with a spare set of keys. She found her boss slumped over the kitchen table. He was naked apart from a pair of stockings, a cord round his neck, a black stocking over his head, and a plastic carrier bag over that. There was also, it was widely reported, a segment of satsuma in his mouth.

Vera Taggart called the police at 4.20 p.m. The Tory Whips Office knew most of the details within thirty minutes. They suspected foul play. The press knew thirty minutes after that. Nobody has ever quite established how. The police blamed Milligan's political colleagues; MPs blamed the police. The story made the BBC evening news, although the details were still sketchy, and the BBC's initial phraseology was 'in unusual sexual circumstances'. Milligan's father heard about his son's death from the media.

The BBC later circulated an internal memo which said: 'We can now say that he was wearing women's clothing, we can say he had a plastic bag on his head, and we can mention that he was bound with flex. But on no account mention fruit.'

It emerged that Milligan, a bachelor, had used the £700-a-year dating agency, Drawing Down the Moon. An inquest later recorded a verdict of accidental death. The Tories were crushed in the subsequent by-election. Milligan's sexual habits were not an issue.

The tabloids struck again on 8 May. Michael Brown, the Conservative MP for Brigg and Cleethorpes, was revealed by the *News of the World* to have enjoyed an exotic Caribbean holiday with his twenty-year-old boyfriend. He resigned immediately, having technically broken the law, in which the minimum age was later (that autumn) to be reduced. The *Sun* reported that John Major had said it was not necessarily a bar to ministerial office to be gay. One source said: 'Michael had to go because the age of consent has not yet been reduced . . . Apart from that he did nothing to be ashamed of. The day when a minister could lose his job simply for being gay has passed. There is no more reason why a single male MP should not have boyfriends than girlfriends.'

Brown never commented or sued. His sexuality had been an open secret for years at Westminster and many in his constituency were aware of it too. A hard-working constituency MP, he was given support by his party organization in Brigg and Cleethorpes.

At the Tories' next conference, in Bournemouth, he made it clear (in an interview with BBC Radio 5-Live's 'Out this Week' programme) that he was gay. In doing so he joined Labour's Shadow Cabinet member Chris Smith, becoming the Commons' second, and the Conservative Party's first, openly gay MP. The Sunday tabloids hardly bothered to report the news.

The next victim of the newspaper feeding frenzy was also trained in the Conservative Whips' Office and seems to have taken Brown's example to heart. Elected for Harrow West in 1987, Robert Hughes resigned as a junior minister for the civil service and returned to the backbenches in March 1995. Unbeknown to his second wife, he had been having an affair with a Commons secretary. To our disappointment, she was a woman. In 1983 Hughes had stood for Bermondsey against Peter Tatchell. Both failed to be elected, and Tatchell was spectacularly 'outed' by the press. In Hughes's case the Curse of Bermondsey was longer in coming and took a different form.

'Minister Got His Oates Morning Noon and Night,' declared the front page of the *News of the World* ('full story pages 2, 3, 4 & 5') – the paper to which, after Hughes's resignation, Janet Oates had been persuaded to talk. 'Love-cheat Tory Robert Hughes was ready for sex any time of day or night, his mistress has revealed.' Details followed. It seems that Hughes had first met Oates when she went to him as her local MP for help. She had sought his advice after being assaulted by an ex-boyfriend. Their friendship blossomed. He gave her lunch at the Commons. She gave him a cuddly bear, and more.

The press dug up a photograph of Hughes embracing another lady friend at a Young Conservatives ball in 1993. Perhaps wisely, he had already resigned as a minister at the weekend on 4 March, days before all this hit the news-stands. His sparsely worded announcement gave no details.

The following Monday, a rapidly appointed successor boned up on the questions Hughes was to have fielded. The following weekend Oates went into further details in the *News of the World*. She had threatened to take Hughes to an industrial tribunal after he had dismissed her, she said; he had begged her not to. (Hughes denies this.) The newspaper did its best to keep interest in the affair alive; but it quickly died.

. . . To be replaced, a few weeks later, by perhaps the most indefensible in a line of increasingly indefensible press intrusions into MPs' private peccadilloes. 'Tory MP, The Tycoon and the Sunday School Teacher,' said the front page of the *News of the World* on 9 April: 'We expose three-in-a-bed sex session. Exclusive'. It seems that a hitherto unheard-of MP, Richard Spring (Bury St Edmunds), had invited 'a financial whizzkid and a Sunday school teacher' (in fact an executive in a pension company and his girlfriend, who worked for him) to dinner. None of the three was married.

It seems to have been one of those parties which got out of hand. The woman (felicitously named Odette Nightingale) seemed able to recount events and conversation with quite remarkable recall ('allowing the laughter to die down, he added . . .') and to have reported it all to the *News of the World* ('still shuddering at the memory, Odette recalled . . .') with great promptitude. The unlucky Mr Spring was quoted as having told the dinner party that he found the Prime Minister's wife, Norma, attractive (who doesn't?) and considered the Employment Secretary, Michael Portillo, to be equally so. In this opinion he is probably joined by much of Britain, and certainly by Mr Portillo.

The bedroom scene was described in every detail, across many pages of the newspaper. 'All I could think of,' she trembled, 'was "How can I get out of here?"' The door does not seem to have occurred to Miss Nightingale as a possible means of exit.

Mr Spring's exit was swift. He was not pushed: he immediately quit as the Northern Ireland Secretary's Parliamentary Private Secretary. ('As Ulster peace talks near a critical phase, he would have been privy to sensitive information,' squeaked the newspaper.) By now, the press were regularly describing PPSs as holding 'government posts'. This is untrue. A PPS does voluntary, unpaid, political work as a sort of parliamentary bag-carrier for a minister. He is privy to almost nothing.

The Times complained it was an outrage for junior back-benchers to be expected to resign in these cases, and blamed both the tabloid press and the Prime Minister – who had (reputedly) made it the rule that any MP working for or as a minister was to resign at the first whiff of a sexual scandal. The paper said such resignations added credibility to the ludicrous claim that exotic private behaviour disqualified an MP from office and that media investigations into such behaviour were therefore in the public interest. They were not, said *The Times*. Ministers should take no notice of them.

As for 'back to basics', nothing has been heard of it since.

DENNIS SKINNER – 1994

'The Beast of Legover'

The headline in the *News of the World* of 20 February said it all. For Tory MPs the discomfiture of Bolsover's Labour MP, the famous socialist ranter, puritanical class-warrior, coal-mining hammer of wealth, decadence and privilege whom the sketchwriters had long dubbed 'The Beast of Bolsover', was delicious, a brief respite from the unrelenting tide of bad publicity washing over the government benches.

Dennis Skinner, scourge of the Tory fat cats and Liberal Lotharios, had been hoist with his own petard. Married to a no-nonsense Northern woman and living in a no-nonsense council house in his no-nonsense coal-mining constituency (and boasting that he would not travel abroad, did not own a passport, and relied upon public transport), Skinner had been having a secret affair with his forty-seven-year-old Commons researcher, in her Chelsea pad. And she was American! And she was teaching him to drive!

For the press there followed a short-lived field-day. Skinner was 'romancing his glamorous Sloane Ranger mistress Lois Blasenheim in her upmarket Chelsea flat'. Her neighbours in Carlyle Square included the Duchess of Portland, Felicity Kendall and Sir David Frost. It was a big leap for the former Glapwell colliery miner who describes his parentage in his *Who's Who* entry as: 'Good working-class mining stock.' The sixty-two-year-old MP had been educated at Tupton Hall Grammar School where he made the grades to go on to Ruskin College, Oxford, which was founded in 1899 for the sons of the toiling masses.

According to breathless tabloid reports, Skinner, who had never himself shied from publicity, would turn up at his lover's home even on hot summer evenings wearing a hat, scarf, and upturned collars on his jacket and shirt – to avoid recognition. He would never (they said) knock at the door, but lurk in the bushes until she let him in at a pre-arranged time.

Newsagents in Skinner's home village of Clay Cross, deep in

the heart of his Derbyshire constituency, reported a roaring trade in sales of the *News of the World*. But no one would say whether a copy had been taken by Skinner's sixty-one-year-old wife, Mary, who lived in the couple's three-bedroom semi.

Tory MPs, who had been the butt of Skinner gibes for years, hit back with a vengeance. Philip Oppenheim, a fellow Derbyshire MP, led the charge, saying: 'It is comforting to know that Dennis is human after all, but this does not reflect at all well on his researcher's tastes.' For some time the very sight of Mr Skinner rising to intervene in the Chamber would trigger calls of 'Where's your balaclava?' from the redoubtable Dame Elaine Kellett-Bowman (then seventy years of age), the Tory MP for Lancaster.

All good fun, and it must be said that Skinner asked for it. He gave no quarter and, when his turn came, received none. But the story of a working-class hero and son of the Derbyshire soil was never the whole man – of whom I came to know a little, as a neighbouring MP. Skinner (in my view) has always been a rather sensitive chap. He is known by friends in Derbyshire not as a political thug at all, but as the 'bookish' one of the family. The

News of the World, 20 February 1994

'Beast' image, which he undeniably enjoys, is something of an alias. And he has been effectively separated from his wife for some years, though they shared an address. Really, he has (in some ways) grown away from his boyhood Derbyshire, though his parliamentary career depends upon his association with it.

And Lois Blasenheim, whom I also know slightly, hardly fits the image (insinuated by the press) of a pleasure-seeking American heiress. She is a rather shy, middle-aged, single woman, living modestly in a tiny flat in Chelsea, who genuinely is Skinner's researcher and secretary, has been for years, works full-time for him and his constituency, and is completely devoted to his beliefs and causes – though latterly, no doubt, to the man too.

Ah well . . . such is the mythology of Fleet Street. I suppose a demagogue, who has lived and prospered by a mythology of his own, should not complain when he falls victim to a rival fairytale. One cannot help feeling that the real victim of all this was neither Skinner nor his foes, but Ms Blasenheim.

GRAHAM RIDDICK, DAVID TREDDINICK, TIM SMITH, NEIL HAMILTON and MANY MORE – 1994

Cash for Questions?

After 'back to basics' came 'cash for questions'. The premiership of John Major, though his personal integrity remained unquestioned, was again nearly swamped beneath a fresh wave of scandals. It began with two Tory MPs accused of selling questions in the Commons at £1,000 a go. For years Fleet Street had suspected MPs of abusing Question Time to line their pockets. The *Sunday Times* 'Insight' team set about proving it.

A reporter, posing as a businessman, offered ten Tory and ten Labour MPs £1,000 each to ask a parliamentary question. The Labour MPs rejected the inducement. Two of the Tories, Graham Riddick and David Tredinnick, fell for the bait, in slightly differing ways and circumstances. At the fake businessman's request, Riddick asked a question about a company called Githins Business Resources, Tredinnick about a drug called Sigthin. Crossword addicts may spot what the MPs failed to – both names are anagrams of Insight.

Newspapers were quick to point out that Riddick, MP for Colne Valley and PPS to a junior minister, and Tredinnick, MP for Bosworth and PPS to the Transport Secretary, had both suffered losses in Lloyd's – though this hardly distinguished them from dozens of their colleagues.

On Sunday, 10 July, the newspaper broke its 'cash for questions' story. The paper claimed a good old-fashioned scoop. Tory MPs cried foul – journalists had used 'entrapment' methods. But that was before the newspaper released a crucial tape recording.

Tredinnick, an Old Etonian, had angrily denied the allegations and claimed he had refused to accept any money. But on the

Monday the *Sunday Times* released the tape of a telephone conversation. Millions of people heard the forty-three-year-old MP ask for the cheque to be sent to his home. Thirty-eight-year-old Riddick initially accepted the cheque, had second thoughts, and sent it back. Tredinnick has pointed out that he at first refused to see the journalist (Jonathan Calvert) but Calvert told him a fellow MP had specifically suggested he approach Tredinnick – something which (I accept) would prompt most MPs to give the petitioner a hearing.

Neither MP had ever offended in this way before, and nobody suggested that either was in the habit of asking questions for money. The *Sunday Times* had prompted delinquency rather than discovered it. Nevertheless Richard Ryder, the Tory Chief Whip, acted decisively, determined to avoid further stories about MPs 'clinging to office'. He suspended them as PPSs the same day.

Betty Boothroyd, the Speaker, much alarmed that the honour of Parliament was apparently being sullied in the press, swiftly agreed to an emergency debate on Wednesday, 13 July. Riddick threw himself upon the mercy of the Commons. 'Beyond the challenge to my own integrity which I deeply regret, the thing that has mortified me the most is that my judgement may have undermined the general standing of MPs and even perhaps have damaged the reputation of this Parliament,' he said. Tredinnick stayed silent.

MPs voted overwhelmingly to refer the matter to the Committee of Privileges. The Committee, on the direction of Tony Newton, the Leader of the Commons, decided to hold its inquiry – to howls of protest from Labour – behind closed doors.

The All-Party Committee reached an agreed report on 3 April 1995. It concluded that both MPs' behaviour 'fell below the standards which the House is entitled to expect from its Members'. It recommended that Riddick be suspended for two weeks and have his salary docked by £900. For Tredinnick they recommended double that penalty. The House later endorsed these recommendations, after both MPs had apologized to Parliament.

I was in the Gallery for the debate. It was an unsatisfactory affair. No sustained defence of the two miscreants was mounted – their friends recognized that silence served them best – but one sensed a groundswell of anger and irritation from many on the

Tory backbenches at what they saw as a kangaroo court. Riddick had argued to the Committee that he had returned the money *before* there was any intimation that he had been set up; he had done so, he said, because he felt unhappy about the arrangement. The committee may have taken this into account, but its response was not outlined or explained to the House. This added to backbench unease.

MPs had been furious about the methods used by the *Sunday Times* to ensnare the two MPs: in the case of the Tory benches, angrier almost than they were with their two delinquent colleagues. The Committee concluded that the paper's 'conduct of its enquiries fell substantially below the standards to be expected of legitimate investigative journalism'.

I believe that this affair, which left the Prime Minister obliged to take what looked (crudely) like the media's side against members of his own party, kindled sparks of resentment among some of Mr Major's backbenchers. These were later to be fanned by backbench anger at what these MPs saw as Lord Nolan's intrusive and constitutionally unwelcome recommendations (see below).

The overall effect was subtly damaging to Major at a crucial time in 1995. Apart from being Prime Minister of the United Kingdom, a premier is also leader of his or her Parliamentary Party. The two roles are not the same. The leader of a party, like the leader of a gang, has a sort of duty (never quite articulated but deeply felt) to support members of the gang in trouble – even when they are in the wrong. Cases like Riddick's and Tredinnick's – victims of a below-the-belt attack by a rival gang, the media – caused Major's statesmanlike duty as Prime Minister to diverge from his tribal duty as Tory leader. Nolan was later to widen that breach. The importance of the warmth this lost him, among the gang, should not be overlooked.

On 29 July the previous year, just after the scandal had surfaced, the Press Complaints Commission had reached a very different conclusion. Their ruling that the entrapment of the MPs was justified in the public interest was a victory for the *Sunday Times*. After that, the long summer recess of 1994 came just in time for an embarrassed government. But within days of Parliament resuming in November 1994, long before the Privileges Committee's report, the 'cash for questions' controversy claimed two more prominent scalps, both ministers.

Tim Smith, who had been Northern Ireland minister, a post which Tim Yeo (see pp.311–14) had also held, quit when the *Guardian* claimed he had been paid by Mohammed Al-Fayed, and had tabled questions helpful to the businessman, during the Arab's bitter takeover battle for Harrods. Smith had not been a minister at the time. He conceded that he had been too late in declaring the payments he had received from Fayed.

Neil Hamilton, the Thatcherite Trade minister, denied similar allegations and issued a writ against the *Guardian*. Forced to accept a temporary, *sub judice*, silence on the issue of selling questions, the press found a welcome distraction. The minister responsible for business probity had once (in 1987, five years before becoming a minister) been Fayed's guest at his Ritz Hotel in Paris. The bill for the week-long stay by Mr and Mrs Hamilton had exceeded £3,000.

Hamilton says that as Fayed owns the hotel lock, stock and barrel, he viewed this personal invitation as if it had been to his country house. The figures quoted for the cost, he says, are notional – 'retail price equivalents' – and the room itself accounted for most of the cost. The hotel was not full at the time he stayed there, so the cost to Fayed was derisory. Hamilton paid his own travel expenses, and the focus of the invitation and the visit was to view the Duke of Windsor's villa.

Despite all this, and though the guidelines on MPs 'registering' such hospitality were not formulated until 1993, the story still represented trouble for the embattled Prime Minister. He dealt with it in an extraordinary way. Mr Major explained to a chamber agog, and a packed Press Gallery, that he had known about Al-Fayed's allegations for three weeks. But he told MPs he had refused to 'come to any arrangement' with Al-Fayed. There were audible gasps in the Press Gallery where I sat. What was the Prime Minister implying? Blackmail?

It emerged that Brian Hitchen, the editor of the *Sunday Express*, had acted as intermediary between Al-Fayed and the Prime Minister. But details of the one-hour conversation at Downing Street have never been published, though Major, having taken legal advice before Hitchen arrived, instructed his private secretary to take notes of the meeting. The stakes were raised when the Prime Minister told the Commons that the Director of

Public Prosecutions had been given the minutes of the meeting.

The Opposition was now on the rampage. 'Sleaze' knocked almost all else from the front pages. Labour seized the opportunity to attack a 'tarnished' government 'in power for too long'.

Pressure grew on Hamilton, MP for Tatton since 1983. The raffish MP, though in fact rather an intellectual and ideologically earnest politician, was famous for his acerbic wit, his penchant for horseplay, and his dreadful bow ties. He now tried to make light of his difficulties. Emerging from a visit to a factory with his wife, the formidable Christine, by his side, he brandished a biscuit he had been given by the management: 'I must remember to declare it in the Register of Interests.' Tories groaned. The Prime Minister was reportedly enraged.

Days later, on 25 October, the forty-four-year-old MP compounded the mistake by comparing his position to that of the Prime Minister embroiled, as Major once had been, in a legal battle with a satirical magazine over allegations of an affair with a caterer. The Prime Minister had been exonerated in the end, Hamilton pointed out, but had not felt it necessary to resign in the interim. Hamilton was sacked the same day.

The dismissal was bodged. In a tense encounter at 12 Downing Street, Richard Ryder, the Chief Whip, said further allegations had come to light, seeming to imply that it was in this new situation that Hamilton must now go. The minister was able to prove that these allegations were unfounded, as Michael Heseltine, his ministerial boss, looked on.

Hamilton's resignation letter made clear that he had been pushed. 'I think it is sad and deeply disturbing that I have been forced to leave office because of a foully motivated rumour and a media witch-hunt.' The editors who had led the calls for Hamilton to go had often been recipients of exactly the same hospitality at the Paris Ritz, he said.

Tory heavyweights such as Lord Howe, the former Foreign Secretary, and John Biffen, the former Leader of the House, were by now urging the Prime Minister to set up a committee to examine 'standards in public life'. The Nolan Committee was the result. Set wide terms of reference, including appointments to public bodies such as quangos and the assumption of business directorships by former ministers, Lord Justice Nolan headed a committee of the great and the good cross-examining witnesses, not – as the Prime Minister explained to the House – about their past conduct, but about rules for the future. Major was going down the same route as predecessors such as Harold Macmillan (over Vassall) and Lloyd George (over the honours scandal).

Meanwhile, Mohammed Al-Fayed was conducting a daily war of words in the newspapers over the conduct of government ministers. 'It was my public duty,' he declared when asked why he had made his allegations against Smith and Hamilton. Much remarked by critics, however, was the fact that Al-Fayed was still incandescent at a biting Department of Trade and Industry report into his financial affairs, in the aftermath of the Harrods takeover bid. Also suggested as adding to his outrage was the government's persistent refusal to grant him and his brother British citizenship.

Even as the DPP were considering whether to prosecute Al-Fayed for alleged blackmail over the clandestine meeting between Major and Al-Fayed's intermediary, the *Guardian* was about to play another card.

On Thursday, 27 October, Jonathan Aitken, Chief Secretary to the Treasury, and an independently wealthy man, joined the ranks of Tories alleged to have enjoyed Al-Fayed's hospitality at the now notorious Paris Ritz. Aitken's bill at the hotel was published. It was plain that Al-Fayed, the hotel's proprietor, was working with the *Guardian* in these exposures. Scores of men and women in public life in Britain inwardly resolved to steer clear of the Ritz for the foreseeable future, lest their requirements from room service become the talk of Britain's breakfast tables.

Mr Aitken's bill for a two-night stay in a single 'superior' class room was 8,010 francs, almost £1,000. A copy of the computerized bill, with Aitken's name on top, was spread across the front page of the *Guardian*. The bill had not been signed. There was no indication who paid it. The bill, said the paper, was debited to the account of Said Mohamed Ayas, a Saudi businessman staying in an 18,000-francs-a-night suite on the sixth floor. Settlement of the minister's bill by Mr Ayas might, it was said, have breached the 'Questions of Procedure for Ministers' guidelines, governing the acceptance of gifts.

Aitken stated that his wife had settled the bill with a cash payment to Ayas's Ritz account, after he had left France. Lolicia Aitken had been in Paris with their daughter Victoria – Ayas is her godfather – but staying elsewhere. Aitken told the *Guardian* the bill was settled with 'money given to her by me for this purpose, some hours after I had left Paris'.

The matter was referred to Sir Robin Butler, the Cabinet Secretary. Aitken had produced a letter from the manager of the hotel showing that a woman had indeed paid the bill. The letter said he had discussed it with the cashier who was on duty. 'I am pleased that he does in fact remember the transaction to which you refer. His recollection is that a brunette lady, of European aspect, paid the cash sum of 4,257 francs in favour of the account of Mr Ayas.' Critics questioned whether this description wholly fitted Mrs Aitken; and there followed a lively national debate as to her exact hair colouring. Mrs Aitken has maintained a dignified silence on this and other matters.

But the *Guardian* claimed the copy of the letter received by the Cabinet Secretary ended at the words 'cash sum' and never mentioned any figure. Sir Robin, while acknowledging there were discrepancies, was satisfied with Aitken's explanation. He was cleared of any impropriety. Aitken took the Dispatch Box at Treasury questions to defend his reputation. He called for 'an end to this hysterical atmosphere of sleaze journalism'.

Some hope! The same day Dame Angela Rumbold, a vice-chairman of the party, resigned as an executive director of a lobby firm, Decision Makers. Labour had reported her to the Members' Interests Committee. Their criticisms were based on the fact that Decision Makers had lobbied for the company which had won a lucrative government contract to build the Channel tunnel rail link station at Ebbsfleet, south of the Thames. Stratford, a Labour heartland in East London, with railway land to spare, was rejected. There was no suggestion that Dame Angela had acted dishonestly.

There followed a sudden rush of MPs, Labour and Tory, to declare junkets abroad and consultancies in the Register of Members' interests. One MP has declared the receipt of a gift of jars of honey. The Labour Leader, Tony Blair, declared a night out with his wife at a West End show.

Nor was the Ritz affair yet over. Peter Preston, the then editor of the *Guardian*, had made an error of judgement on which Tory critics were now delighted to seize. He had authorized the use of a fake (or 'cod') fax on Commons notepaper, purporting to come from Aitken's private office, to obtain a copy of the Ritz bill.

Abuse what else you will, but never abuse Commons procedure. Betty Boothroyd, the Speaker, was furious. She instructed the Serjeant-at-Arms to conduct an investigation. 'The House makes facilities available to the press so proceedings may be reported, not so the name of the House can be used to give false authority to a newspaper's own activities.'

Preston had thrown the government a life-raft. The Tories wasted no time in clambering aboard. Lord Tebbitt led the attack, accusing Preston of behaving in a 'scurrilous, scandalous, dishonest and wicked manner'.

The following day Preston was summoned before the Commons. Tory MPs had suffered months of media taunts about 'Tory sleaze'. Now, for a moment at least, came their revenge. This was media sleaze. Eyes bulging and blood pressure rising with righteous indignation, they vented their spleen at the hapless editor of the liberal broadsheet. Roger Gale, Tory MP for Thanet North (Aitken was MP for Thanet South) led the charge. The former television producer called Preston a 'whore from hell'.

Fleet Street editors, perhaps not untouched by envy at the *Guardian*'s scoops, laid into Preston with mournful glee. On 1 November he resigned from the Press Complaints Commission. A few months later the longest-serving editor in Fleet Street vacated the editor's chair and moved upstairs. He had been subjected to a further wave of criticism when it was revealed by a former member of the KGB, Oleg Gordievsky, that one of Preston's senior staff, Richard Gott, had been a long-standing KGB 'agent of influence'. Gott resigned, but Preston was criticized for paying tribute to him while accepting his resignation.

Some months later Gordievsky covered the front page of the *Sunday Times* with allegations that Michael Foot, Leader of the Labour Party before Neil Kinnock, had been an 'agent of influence' too. Nobody believed this. Foot sued. He settled for a substantial sum.

In April 1995, the national press renewed the attack on Jonathan Aitken. In a front page splash, the *Independent* claimed that an arms manufacturer, BMARC, on whose board Aitken had sat as a non-executive director for a fee of £10,000 a year from 1988 to 1990, had been exporting to Singapore weapons whose ultimate destination was Iran – a country covered by a British ban on arms sales. The former chairman of the company, Gerald James, has alleged that Aitken ought to have known of this project, 'Project Lisi'. Other directors say it was never known to the board that the destination of the arms was Iran. From the Dispatch Box Aitken made a biting attack on the newspaper allegations, blaming them on 'an unholy alliance between a failed chairman and a failing newspaper'.

Before the Westminster dust had settled on this affair, Granada Television's political documentary 'World in Action' screened a programme about the Chief Secretary, refusing his demand for a slot in which to frame his rebuttals personally, but including quotations from his answers to the allegations. The programme's allegations are currently the subject of a libel action brought by Aitken.

The episode had its lighter side. 'World in Action' hired a camel for a day (for £1,000) and filmed it trudging among dunes near Liverpool, in scenes intended to evoke Arabian imagery. Returning the media salvo from a studio in Conservative Central Office, and with the assistance of AutoCue (a first in the history of parliamentary scandal?) Aitken responded, angrily refuting such charges in some remarkable prose passages: 'If it falls to me to start a fight to cut out the cancer of bent and twisted journalism in our country with the simple sword of truth, and trusty shield of fair play' (and stout armour of AutoCue), 'so be it. I am ready for the fight.' Aitken attacked 'the worst press in the world'.

The libel cases grind on, exceedingly slowly. At the Cabinet reshuffle on 5 July, Mr Aitken resigned from the government – 'to spend more time with his solicitors', press wags suggested. He thought it best to fight his case from the backbenches. Within days of his resignation, Aitken faced yet further scandal as the *Sunday Mirror* reported an affair (fifteen years previously) with a prostitute. 'My wife long ago forgave me,' commented Aitken, 'I hope others will follow her example.'

Also continuing is the Scott Inquiry. Though somewhat outside this book's remit – which is scandals of the more personal sort – Lord Justice Scott's investigation into whether British arms sales to Iraq in the late 1980s were hustled past an unknowing legislature, has involved allegations that ministers have lied to Parliament (though not for personal gain).

Scott is still at work as I write. Leaks of his draft report have been critical of ministers. Mr Foot has settled his case against the *Sunday Times* out of court, for a reportedly substantial, but undisclosed, sum. Mr Hamilton was suing the *Guardian*, but the newspaper appears successfully to have claimed 'Parliamentary Privilege' as protection for the alleged libel – a nice irony, as Parliamentary Privilege is normally used to protect MPs themselves from lawsuits. Jonathan Aitken is suing practically everyone. Ron Brown is not suing the *News of the World*. Nobody, I hope, is suing me. Lord Lester of Herne Hill has alleged that peers, too, take cash for questions, and the Nolan Committee may investigate this.

...And the Committee's long-awaited recommendations on standards in public life are being pored over by an All-Party Parliamentary Committee. They include the establishment of a Parliamentary Commissioner for Standards to oversee and advise MPs; new checks and delays for ex-ministers desirous of employment outside politics; and a ban on MPs working directly for lobbying companies. Perhaps most controversially, MPs would have to declare the amount as well as the fact of consultancies to outside bodies.

Furthermore the Nolan Committee is to turn itself into a permanent body, with a rolling programme of inquiry and advice. After four centuries of sex, treachery and corruption – and an equal measure of ridiculous press hoopla too – it faces a Herculean task.

There is something delicious about an outcome in which a committee, staffed with government appointees, set up to investigate MPs' use of position to generate income, has deliberated long and hard, then proceeded to give themselves a job.

From
'Shadows'

...And if, in the changing phases of man's life
I fall in sickness and in misery
my wrists seem broken and my heart seems dead
and strength is gone, and my life
is only the leavings of a life:

and still, among it all, snatches of lovely oblivion, and snatches
    of renewal
odd, wintry flowers upon the withered stem, yet new strange
    flowers
such as my life has not brought forth before, new blossoms of
    me –

then I must know that still
I am in the hands of the unknown God,
he is breaking me down to his own oblivion
to send me forth on a new morning, a new man.

D. H. Lawrence

BIBLIOGRAPHY

Among the many books and works of reference we have found helpful (often acknowledged in the text) it is worth mentioning here just a handful of those upon which we have particularly relied:

ALLEN, Louis, *et al*: *Political Scandals and Causes Célèbres Since 1945*, Longman: Pearson Professional, 1991

BESSELL, Peter: *Cover-up: The Jeremy Thorpe Affair*, Simons Books, 1980

BOOTHBY, Robert: *Recollections of a Rebel*, Hutchinson, 1978

CLARKE, G. N.: *The Later Stuarts 1660–1714*, Oxford University Press, 1956

COLQUHOUN, Maureen: *A Woman in the House*, Scan, 1980

CULLEN, Tom: *Maundy Gregory, Purveyor of Honours*, Sidgwick and Jackson, 1974

DOIG, Alan: *Westminster Babylon*, Allison and Busby, 1990

DOIG, Alan: *Corruption and Misconduct in Contemporary British Politics*, Penguin Books, 1984

DONALDSON, Frances: *The Marconi Scandal*, Rupert Hart-Davis, 1962

HARVEY, Ian: *To Fall Like Lucifer*, Sidgwick and Jackson, 1971

HYDE, H. Montgomery: *A Tangled Web*, 1986

KEAYS, Sara: *A Question of Judgement*, Quintessential Press, 1985

KEELER, Christine: *Scandal!*, Xanadu, 1989

KNIGHTLEY, Philip, and KENNEDY, Caroline: *An Affair of State: the Profumo case and the naming of Stephen Ward*, Cape, 1987

LEWIS, Chester: *Jeremy Thorpe, A Secret Life*, Fontana, 1979

LYONS, F. S. L.: *Charles Stewart Parnell*, Collins, 1977

MARLOW, Joyce: *The Uncrowned Queen of Ireland: The Life of Kitty O'Shea*, Weidenfeld and Nicolson, 1975

PARKINSON, Cecil: *Right at the Centre, My Autobiography*, Weidenfeld and Nicolson, 1992

RHODES-JAMES, Robert: *Bob Boothby, A Portrait*, Hodder and Stoughton, 1991

RIDLEY, Jane, and THOMAS, Stephen: *The Young Disraeli 1804–1846*, Sinclair Stevenson, 1995

SEARLE, G. R.: *Corruption in British Politics, 1895–1930*, Oxford University Press, 1987

STONEHOUSE, John: *My Trial*, Wyndham Publications, 1976

VASSALL, John: *The Autobiography of a Spy*, Sidgwick and Jackson, 1975

FFAMILY-VALUES, Norman: *The McTory Book of Bonks*, McNaughty Books/BS Randle, 1994

INDEX